Group Care for Infants, Toddlers, and Twos

This volume extends the knowledge base supporting research-informed child care for infants and toddlers, while simultaneously highlighting areas of study ripe for future research. The authors demonstrate from a systems perspective, that the experiences and outcomes of very young children in child care are influenced by characteristics of and interactions between the children, adults, and settings. Varying methodological approaches as well as the utilization of newer data collection instruments inform the field's understanding of current practices and procedures while offering guidance for future programming and policy. In turn, the chapters highlight a plethora of open questions and a need for a new generation of research to support the field of infant/toddler care. Future challenges are evident in the recognition of the inadequate nature of our current measures of child outcomes and classroom processes, the field's unmet promise to incorporate interdisciplinary perspectives, and the need for newer methodological designs that blend the strengths of quantitative and qualitative approaches.

These issues are important given the growing demand for infant/toddler care and the increasing recognition of the unique role of this age period in serving as the foundation for all later development.

This book was originally published as a special issue of *Early Education and Development*.

Deborah J. Norris is an Associate Professor and Co-Director of the Research and Inquiry Network at Stone House with Kansas State University, USA. She examines the experiences of children and adults in play-based classrooms serving infants, toddlers, and preschoolers. In addition, she is the leader of the Early Childhood Leadership Link, a translational research entity that supports and strengthens pedagogical leadership in early childhood settings.

Diane M. Horm is the George Kaiser Family Foundation Endowed Chair and Founding Director of the Early Childhood Education Institute (ECEI) at the University of Oklahoma at Tulsa, USA. She is currently leading several applied research initiatives including program evaluation research in collaboration with Tulsa's Educare and Head Start programs. She is also leading the development of the Infants, Toddlers, Twos, and Threes Research Center, a designated University Strategic Organization, in which she is mentoring a diverse group of young researchers to partner with community agencies with the shared goal to improve services for young children and their families.

Group Care for Infants, Toddlers, and Twos

Edited by
Deborah J. Norris and
Diane M. Horm

LONDON AND NEW YORK

First published 2018
by Routledge
2 Park Square, Milton Park, Abingdon, Oxon, OX14 4RN, UK

and by Routledge
711 Third Avenue, New York, NY 10017, USA

Routledge is an imprint of the Taylor & Francis Group, an informa business

© 2018 Taylor & Francis

All rights reserved. No part of this book may be reprinted or reproduced or utilised in any form or by any electronic, mechanical, or other means, now known or hereafter invented, including photocopying and recording, or in any information storage or retrieval system, without permission in writing from the publishers.

Trademark notice: Product or corporate names may be trademarks or registered trademarks, and are used only for identification and explanation without intent to infringe.

British Library Cataloguing in Publication Data
A catalogue record for this book is available from the British Library

ISBN 13: 978-0-8153-7326-1

Typeset in Minion
by RefineCatch Limited, Bungay, Suffolk

Publisher's Note
The publisher accepts responsibility for any inconsistencies that may have arisen during the conversion of this book from journal articles to book chapters, namely the possible inclusion of journal terminology.

Disclaimer
Every effort has been made to contact copyright holders for their permission to reprint material in this book. The publishers would be grateful to hear from any copyright holder who is not here acknowledged and will undertake to rectify any errors or omissions in future editions of this book.

Contents

Citation Information   vii
Notes on Contributors   ix

Introduction: Group Care for Infants, Toddlers, and Twos   1
Deborah J. Norris and Diane M. Horm

1. Measuring the Multifaceted Nature of Infant and Toddler Care Quality   5
   Peter L. Mangione, Kerry Kriener-Althen, and Jennifer Marcella

2. A Mixed Methods Investigation of Maternal Perspectives on Transition Experiences in Early Care and Education   26
   Rebecca Anne Swartz, Katherine Elizabeth Speirs, Amy Johnson Encinger, and Nancy L. McElwain

3. Experiences of Parents and Professionals in Well-Established Continuity of Care Infant Toddler Programs   46
   Mary Benson McMullen, Na Ra Yun, Alina Mihai, and Hyojin Kim

4. Continuity of Care, Caregiver–Child Interactions, and Toddler Social Competence and Problem Behaviors   77
   Karen Ruprecht, James Elicker, and Ji Young Choi

5. The Four Roles of a Master Toddler Teacher   96
   Jill Uhlenberg

6. Teacher–Child Interactions in Early Head Start Classrooms: Associations With Teacher Characteristics   115
   Sherri Castle, Amy C. Williamson, Emisha Young, Jessica Stubblefield, Deborah Laurin, and Nicole Pearce

7. Attachment Predicts College Students' Knowledge, Attitudes, and Skills for Working With Infants, Toddlers, and Families   131
   Claire D. Vallotton, Julia Torquati, Jean Ispa, Rachel Chazan-Cohen, Jennifer Henk, Maria Fusaro, Carla A. Peterson, Lori A. Roggman, Ann M. Stacks, Gina Cook, and Holly Brophy-Herb

Index   159

Citation Information

The chapters in this book were originally published in *Early Education and Development*, volume 27, issue 2 (February–March 2016). When citing this material, please use the original page numbering for each article, as follows:

Introduction
Introduction to the Special Issue on Group Care for Infants, Toddlers, and Twos
Deborah J. Norris and Diane M. Horm
Early Education and Development, volume 27, issue 2 (February–March 2016), pp. 145–148

Chapter 1
Measuring the Multifaceted Nature of Infant and Toddler Care Quality
Peter L. Mangione, Kerry Kriener-Althen, and Jennifer Marcella
Early Education and Development, volume 27, issue 2 (February–March 2016), pp. 149–169

Chapter 2
A Mixed Methods Investigation of Maternal Perspectives on Transition Experiences in Early Care and Education
Rebecca Anne Swartz, Katherine Elizabeth Speirs, Amy Johnson Encinger, and Nancy L. McElwain
Early Education and Development, volume 27, issue 2 (February–March 2016), pp. 170–189

Chapter 3
Experiences of Parents and Professionals in Well-Established Continuity of Care Infant Toddler Programs
Mary Benson McMullen, Na Ra Yun, Alina Mihai, and Hyojin Kim
Early Education and Development, volume 27, issue 2 (February–March 2016), pp. 190–220

Chapter 4
Continuity of Care, Caregiver–Child Interactions, and Toddler Social Competence and Problem Behaviors
Karen Ruprecht, James Elicker, and Ji Young Choi
Early Education and Development, volume 27, issue 2 (February–March 2016), pp. 221–239

Chapter 5
The Four Roles of a Master Toddler Teacher
Jill Uhlenberg
Early Education and Development, volume 27, issue 2 (February–March 2016), pp. 240–258

CITATION INFORMATION

Chapter 6
Teacher–Child Interactions in Early Head Start Classrooms: Associations With Teacher Characteristics
Sherri Castle, Amy C. Williamson, Emisha Young, Jessica Stubblefield, Deborah Laurin, and Nicole Pearce
Early Education and Development, volume 27, issue 2 (February–March 2016), pp. 259–274

Chapter 7
Attachment Predicts College Students' Knowledge, Attitudes, and Skills for Working With Infants, Toddlers, and Families
Claire D. Vallotton, Julia Torquati, Jean Ispa, Rachel Chazan-Cohen, Jennifer Henk, Maria Fusaro, Carla A. Peterson, Lori A. Roggman, Ann M. Stacks, Gina Cook, and Holly Brophy-Herb
Early Education and Development, volume 27, issue 2 (February–March 2016), pp. 275–302

For any permission-related enquiries please visit:
http://www.tandfonline.com/page/help/permissions

Notes on Contributors

Holly Brophy-Herb is Professor of Human Development and Family Studies at Michigan State University, USA.

Sherri Castle is Senior Research and Policy Associate at the Early Childhood Education Institute, University of Oklahoma at Tulsa, USA.

Rachel Chazan-Cohen is Associate Professor of Early Education and Care Program Director at the Doctoral Program in Early Education and Care, Department of Curriculum and Instruction, University of Massachusetts, Boston, USA.

Ji Young Choi is Assistant Professor at the Department of Human Development and Family Studies, Iowa State University, USA.

Gina Cook is based at the Department of Psychology and Child Development, California State University, USA.

James Elicker is Professor at the Department of Human Development and Family Studies, Purdue University, USA.

Amy Johnson Encinger is a PhD student at the Department of Child, Youth, and Family Studies, University of Nebraska–Lincoln, USA.

Maria Fusaro is based at the Department of Child and Adolescent Development, San Jose State University, USA.

Jennifer Henk is based at the Department of Family and Consumer Sciences, University of Arkansas, USA.

Diane M. Horm is the George Kaiser Family Foundation Endowed Chair and Founding Director of the Early Childhood Education Institute (ECEI) at the University of Oklahoma at Tulsa, USA.

Jean Ispa is Professor at, and Co-Chair of, the Department of Human Development and Family Studies, University of Missouri–Columbia, USA.

Hyojin Kim is a member of staff at the School of Education, Indiana University–Bloomington, USA.

Kerry Kriener-Althen is Co-Director of the Center for Child and Family Studies, WestEd, USA.

Deborah Laurin is based at the Early Childhood Education Institute, University of Oklahoma at Tulsa, USA.

Peter L. Mangione is Co-Director of the Center for Child and Family Studies, WestEd, USA.

Jennifer Marcella is Research Associate at the Center for Child and Family Studies, WestEd, USA.

Nancy L. McElwain is Professor of Human Development and Family Studies, Department of Child, Youth, and Family Studies, University of Nebraska–Lincoln, USA.

NOTES ON CONTRIBUTORS

Mary Benson McMullen is Professor of Curriculum Studies in Early Childhood Education and Associate Chair of the Department of Curriculum and Instruction at Indiana University–Bloomington, USA.

Alina Mihai is Assistant Professor of Special Education at the School of Education, Indiana University–Kokomo, USA.

Deborah J. Norris is an Associate Professor and Co-Director of the Research and Inquiry Network at Stone House with Kansas State University, USA.

Nicole Pearce is Assistant Professor at Texas A&M University–Commerce, USA.

Carla A. Peterson is Professor at the Department of Human Development and Family Studies and Associate Dean for Research and Graduate Education in the College of Human Sciences at Iowa State University, USA.

Lori A. Roggman is Professor at the Department of Family, Consumer, and Human Development, Utah State University, USA.

Karen Ruprecht is based at the Department of Human Development and Family Studies, Purdue University, USA.

Katherine Elizabeth Speirs is based at the Department of Human Development and Family Studies, University of Illinois at Urbana–Champaign, USA.

Ann M. Stacks is based at Merrill Palmer Skillman Institute, Wayne State University, USA.

Jessica Stubblefield is based at the Early Childhood Education Institute, University of Oklahoma at Tulsa, USA.

Rebecca Anne Swartz is based at the Department of Special Education, University of Illinois at Urbana–Champaign, USA.

Julia Torquati is Professor of Child, Youth, and Family Studies at the University of Nebraska–Lincoln, USA.

Jill Uhlenberg is based at the Department of Curriculum and Instruction, University of Northern Iowa, USA.

Claire D. Vallotton is Associate Professor of Human Development and Family Studies, Michigan State University, USA.

Amy C. Williamson is Associate Professor at the Early Childhood Education Institute, University of Oklahoma at Tulsa, USA.

Emisha Young is based at the Early Childhood Education Institute, University of Oklahoma at Tulsa, USA.

Na Ra Yun is based at the School of Education, Indiana University–Bloomington, USA.

Introduction: Group Care for Infants, Toddlers, and Twos

Deborah J. Norris and Diane M. Horm

Infant/toddler care is currently the fastest growing and most sought-after form of child care in the United States (National Association of Child Care Resource and Referral Agencies, 2008). In 2010, 24% of children younger than 4 years of age with employed mothers attended child care centers, and 14% attended nonrelative home care settings (Federal Interagency Forum on Child and Family Statistics, 2011). A growing body of research documents the lasting impact of high-quality early care on later school achievement and life success (Institute of Medicine & National Research Council, 2012; Vandell et al., 2010). Research has also repeatedly demonstrated that high-quality infant/toddler center care serves to diminish the income-based achievement gap commonly reported (Duncan & Sojourner, 2012; Phillips & Lowenstein, 2011). These positive findings are tempered by a body of research documenting the inadequate quality of available infant/toddler care (Phillips & Lowenstein, 2011). Given its growth, prevalence, and documented long-term outcomes, little is known about the specific features or processes that optimize the group care experience for infants and toddlers, their families, as well as the caregivers. The primary aim of this *Early Education and Development* special issue is to fill some of these gaps.

The contribution of this special issue to our understanding of the experiences of young children, families, and staff within the group care setting may best be understood through the lens of the bioecological theoretical framework (Bronfenbrenner & Morris, 2006; National Institute of Child Health and Human Development Early Child Care Research Network, 2005). According to this framework, children's development is shaped by an interconnected network of settings, contexts, and systems. At the broadest macrosystem level, the scope and depth of the challenges facing children and families today call for systemic, collaborative, research-informed solutions such as the variety of quality improvement initiatives evident today. Examples include Early Head Start–child care partnerships and Quality Rating Improvement Systems (QRIS). Although these broad system-level solutions are not specifically addressed in the selected articles, findings from the articles in this special issue have implications for many of the issues and initiatives at the broadest system level.

For example, in their article Mangione, Kriener-Althen, and Marcella suggest that the proliferation of QRIS initiatives necessitates the development of tools for assessing the quality of settings, and they focus on those serving children younger than age 3. Their article summarizes the development of the Program for Infant and Toddler Care Program Assessment Rating Scale (PITC PARS) as a valid and reliable tool for assessing key features of quality infant/toddler settings. Through factor analysis they identify relationships among children, families, and staff; caregiver–child interactions; as well as policies and practices supporting development and learning as salient dimensions of quality. Their tool provides another perspective for investigating quality in infant/toddler settings. The next step within the field is for researchers to use this instrument while examining linkages among child care quality; caregiver and program characteristics; and outcomes for young children, families, and staff.

According to bioecological theory, development occurs within two primary settings or microsystems for many infants and toddlers: home and child care. The interactions, communications, and relationships between significant persons across these settings represent the mesosystem. Three articles within this special issue provide much-needed insight into this often neglected level of study in the child care literature. The contribution of a family–child care relationships subscale within a standardized measurement tool as proposed by Mangione et al. cannot be overstated because much research with the Infant/Toddler Environment Rating Scale excludes scores from the Parent–Staff subscale. Moving from this more global perspective of family–caregiver relationships, two articles use qualitative and mixed methods approaches to illuminate the intricacies of these interactions. Swartz, Speirs, Encinger, and McElwain specifically examine the power of interactions and communications among infants, mothers, and caregivers to facilitate the transition to the child care setting. McMullen, Yun, Mihai, and Kim highlight the importance of strong family–child care communication for successful implementation of continuity of care, an approach in which children and their families stay with the same teaching team for several years in infant/toddler group care.

Utilizing two different research methodologies, the McMullen et al. and Ruprecht, Elicker, and Choi articles provide much-needed research on the highly recommended practice of continuity of care. McMullen and her coauthors explore the benefits and challenges of implementing continuity of care within university-affiliated programs from the perspective of parents and caregivers. Ruprecht and colleagues examine caregiver–child interactions as well as child social competence outcomes in continuity of care and non–continuity of care community-based child care centers. It is interesting that both articles highlight the need for more exploration in the field around definitions and practices of continuity of care because the issues are more complicated than one might expect.

Within bioecological theory, proximal processes, or ongoing, engaging interactions with persons and materials, are the mechanisms of development (Bronfenbrenner & Morris, 2006). Two factors within the PITC PARS identify caregiver–child interactions as well as opportunities for engagement with materials that support learning and development. Castle and colleagues use another recently developed instrument for describing teacher–child interactions, the Classroom Assessment Scoring System (CLASS) Toddler, in Early Head Start classrooms with teachers with bachelor's degrees. The use of both the PITC PARS and CLASS Toddler provides helpful descriptive information about caregiver–child dynamics within classrooms. It should be noted, however, that classroom interactions that facilitate learning and language development as assessed by these instruments fall in the midrange and highlight the continued need for quality enhancement initiatives such as QRIS and Early Head Start–child care partnerships.

Enriching this more global look at proximal processes within the classroom offered by Mangione et al. and Castle et al. is Uhlenberg's qualitative study that captures the dynamic interplay among characteristics of toddlers, a master teacher, and the unfolding implementation of curriculum. This article illustrates the need for a variety of data collection strategies to inform our understanding of classroom experiences, as the qualitative approach highlights nuanced aspects of quality not captured by standardized assessment tools. This article also offers the possibility of hope for higher quality interactions when a highly skilled professional is in the classroom. Conclusions from this study suggest that professional development efforts should focus on helping classroom teachers develop effective observational skills along with a strong foundation in infant/toddler development and an understanding of emergent rather than packaged curriculum practices.

Characteristics of significant persons within settings, such as the children and teachers in a classroom, are expected to influence the proximal processes that emerge (Bronfenbrenner & Morris, 2006). Both Castle et al. and Vallotton et al. bring a fresh look at characteristics of adults with the potential to impact classroom experiences. Castle and her coauthors examine the direct and moderating effects of both resource characteristics of teachers, such as education and experience, as well as psychosocial, or force, characteristics, such as depressive symptoms, beliefs, and temperament. Their finding of the saliency of the early childhood education major over other degree options has direct implications for quality initiatives aimed at increasing the educational level of teachers in classrooms for children from birth to age 3. Current workforce estimates indicate that only 17% of these teachers currently have associate's degrees, whereas 19% have bachelor's degrees (National Survey of Early Care and Education Project Team, 2013). Vallotton and colleagues in turn raise many challenging questions for teacher preparation programs in their examination of associations among the adult attachment status of undergraduate students, their beliefs about children, and their projected classroom practices. Their work provokes consideration of the essential content and experiences required in bachelor's-level preparation programs for infant/toddler professional staff.

As described previously, the articles included in this special issue offer some important contributions to the field by filling some of the gaps in the infant/toddler research literature while also informing policy and practice. Early care and education settings explored in these studies include university programs, Early Head Start, and child care centers. Noticeably absent, however, is research conducted in family child care homes, a common child care arrangement for many working families with infants and toddlers. The breadth of research methodologies is a strength of the selected articles, and the richness of the mixed methods approach used by Swartz et al. can serve as a model to compel more researchers to pursue this methodological approach. In this age of accountability with a strong emphasis on the assessment of programs, practices, and child outcomes, the work of Mangione et al., Castle et al., and Ruprecht et al. offer new strategies for expanding the tools used in future research. However, given policy expectations for ongoing utilization of child assessment data, the dearth of submitted articles specifically exploring this area for infants and toddlers in group care was a surprise and highlights a continuing gap in the literature. In addition, the articles submitted for this special issue did not specifically address teaching strategies or systems for delivering optimal professional development for teachers in infant/toddler classrooms, a current void in the literature, as noted by Zaslow, Tout, Halle, Whitaker, and Lavelle (2010). Finally, our call for interdisciplinary research that can answer questions at the intersection of the various settings, contexts, and systems of development suggested by the bioecological theoretical framework went unfilled—again highlighting a continuing gap.

In sum, this special issue of *Early Education and Development* deepens the knowledge base that informs our understanding of early care and education settings for infants and toddlers. At the same time, it highlights the need for a new generation of research that will position the field to address future challenges.

ORCID

Deborah J. Norris http://orcid.org/0000-0002-5113-0791

References

Bronfenbrenner, U., & Morris, P. A. (2006). The bioecological model of human development. In W. Damon & R. M. Lerner (Eds.), *Handbook of child psychology: Vol. 1. Theoretical models of human development* (6th ed., pp. 793–828). New York, NY: Wiley.

Duncan, G. J., & Sojourner, A. J. (2012, December). *Can intensive early childhood intervention programs eliminate income-based cognitive and achievement gaps?* (Discussion Paper No. 7087). Bonn, Germany: Institute for the Study of Labor.

Federal Interagency Forum on Child and Family Statistics. (2011). *America's children: Key national indicators of well-being, 2011.* Retrieved from http://www.childstats.gov/pdf/ac2011/ac_11.pdf

Institute of Medicine & National Research Council. (2012). *From neurons to neighborhoods: An update: Workshop summary.* Washington, DC: National Academies Press.

National Association of Child Care Resource and Referral Agencies. (2008). *Covering the map: Child care resource and referral agencies providing vital services to parents throughout the United States.* Arlington, VA: Author.

National Institute of Child Health and Human Development Early Child Care Research Network. (2005). *Child care and child development: Results from the NICHD Study of Early Child Care and Youth Development.* New York, NY: Guilford Press.

National Survey of Early Care and Education Project Team. (2013). *Number and characteristics of early care and education (ECE) teachers and caregivers: Initial findings from the National Survey of Early Care and Education*

(NSECE) (OPRE Report No. 2013-38). Washington, DC: U.S. Department of Health and Human Services, Administration for Children and Families, Office of Planning, Research and Evaluation.

Phillips, D. A., & Lowenstein, A. E. (2011). Early care, education, and child development. *Annual Review of Psychology, 62*, 483–500. doi:10.1146/annurev.psych.031809.130707

Vandell, D. L., Belsky, J., Burchinal, M., Steinberg, L., Vandergrift, N., & NICHD Early Child Care Research Network. (2010). Do effects of early child care extend to age 15 years? Results from the NICHD Study of Early Child Care and Youth Development. *Child Development, 81*, 737–756.

Zaslow, M., Tout, K., Halle, T., Whitaker, J. V., & Lavelle, B. (2010). *Toward identification of effective professional development for early childhood educators: Literature review.* Washington, DC: U.S. Department of Education.

Measuring the Multifaceted Nature of Infant and Toddler Care Quality

Peter L. Mangione, Kerry Kriener-Althen, and Jennifer Marcella

ABSTRACT
Research Findings: The quality of group care infants and toddlers experience relates to their concurrent and later development. Recent quality improvement initiatives point to the need for ecologically valid measures that assess the multifaceted nature of child care quality. In this article, we present the psychometric properties of an infant and toddler quality assessment tool, the Program for Infant and Toddler Care Program Assessment Rating Scale (PITC PARS). Descriptive data on 222 center-based classrooms and family child care programs were used to examine concurrent validity, and a subsample of 101 center-based classrooms serving infants was used to examine the factor structure of this measure. Examination of the bivariate correlations with other commonly used measures of infant and toddler child care quality provided evidence of concurrent validity. Factor analysis suggested that the PITC PARS measures 3 distinct yet related dimensions of global child care quality. *Practice or Policy*: The results of this study suggest that the PITC PARS can continue to be used by practitioners for self-study. Furthermore, the PITC PARS may be an effective tool in the context of policy initiatives aimed at improving the quality of infant/toddler care programs.

Development that occurs during the infant and toddler period provides the foundation for later learning (Lally, 2010). Research indicates that the quality of group care infants and toddlers experience relates to their concurrent and later development (Loeb, Fuller, Kagan, & Carrol, 2004; National Institute of Child Health and Human Development [NICHD] Early Child Care Research Network, 2000; Vandell, Belsky, Burchinal, Steinberg, & Vandergrift, 2010). Yet quality of care has been shown to be quite variable and, on average, low in infant and toddler settings (Helburn et al., 1995; Kreader, Ferguson, & Lawrence, 2005; Phillips, Mekos, Scarr, McCartney, & Abbott-Shim, 2000; Phillips, Voran, Kisker, Howes, & Whitebook, 1994; Pungello & Kurtz-Costes, 1999; Schmit & Matthews, 2013). In response to widespread low-quality early care and education, policymakers have invested in quality improvement initiatives (Zaslow, Tout, & Martinez-Beck, 2010). The numerous initiatives to improve quality point to the need for ecologically valid measures that assess the multidimensional nature of child care quality (Bisceglia, Perlman, Schaak, & Jenkins, 2009; Child Trends, 2009; Paulsell, Tout, & Maxwell, 2013). In comparison to research on preschool quality, much less research has focused on the assessment of infant and toddler care quality (Sandstrom, Moodie, & Halle, 2011). In light of the need for additional investigation of measurement of infant and toddler care program quality, we present the psychometric properties of an infant and toddler quality assessment tool, the Program for Infant and Toddler Care Program Assessment Rating Scale (PITC PARS).

Introducing the PITC PARS

The PITC PARS was developed to assess the implementation of the PITC, which aims to improve quality by promoting responsive, relationship-based nurturance that supports young children's social-emotional, cognitive, language, and physical development (Bornstein & Bornstein, 1995; Lally & Mangione, 2006; Shonkoff & Phillips, 2000). At the outset of the PITC in 1986, a measure that emphasized interactions and relationships within a holistic view of infant and toddler care quality did not yet exist, which prompted the development of the PARS as a tool for self-study. As the definition of infant and toddler care quality has been refined over the past few decades, the PITC PARS continues to reflect the research literature's current conceptualization of quality and, we believe, can be used in broader quality improvement contexts. The five subscales of the PITC PARS represent domains of child care quality for infants and toddlers: (a) Quality of Adult's Interactions With Children; (b) Family Partnerships, Cultural Responsiveness, and Inclusive Care; (c) Organization of Group Care; (d) Physical Environment; and (e) Routines and Record Keeping. The PITC PARS features multimethod assessment, including direct observation, director interviews, and document review, to measure the caregiving interactions, care environment, program policies, and administrative structures that promote responsive, relationship-based care for infants and toddlers. The PITC PARS is designed to assess infant and toddler care quality across both family child care and center-based programs.

Defining infant and toddler care quality

In general, early care and education quality refers to "the aspects of the environment and children's experiences that nurture child development" (Layzer & Goodson, 2006, p. 558). The research literature has identified quality as global quality, structural quality, and process quality. Specifically, global quality has been conceptualized as a multidimensional construct encompassing both structural and process quality (Child Trends, 2009; Kreader et al., 2005). Structural quality includes the typically regulated features of child care classrooms, such as adult–child ratios, group size, and teacher education, whereas process quality refers to caregiving provided to the child in the form of sensitive adult–child interactions (Child Trends, 2009; Kreader et al., 2005). Structural quality provides the supports for process quality, which ultimately relates to improved child outcomes (Child Trends, 2009; Kreader et al., 2005; National Child Care Information and Technical Assistance Center, 2009). Although these components of quality most often are studied in the context of center-based care, they also apply when children receive care in family child care programs. Throughout this article, we use the term *care teacher* to emphasize the dual roles of caring and teaching for infants and toddlers, inclusive of both center-based teachers and family child care providers (California Department of Education, 2006). To remain consistent with the research literature, we use other terms, such as *caregiver, teacher*, or *adult*, interchangeably with *care teacher* as appropriate.

Previous research has documented links between structural and process quality. Aspects of structural quality such as teacher training, teacher wages, parent fees, teacher education, ratios, and group size correlate with process quality for infant and toddler center-based classrooms (Helburn et al., 1995; Howes, Whitebook, & Phillips, 1992; NICHD Early Child Care Research Network, 1996; Phillips et al., 2000). Similar associations between features of structural and process quality have been found in family child care programs (Doherty, Forer, Lero, Goelman, & LaGrange, 2006; Hughes-Belding, Hegland, Stein, Sideris, & Bryant, 2012). In addition to the link between structural and process quality, some studies suggest that process quality relates to children's developmental outcomes. In particular, indicators of process quality in both center-based and family child care programs such as positive caregiving and language stimulation during the first 3 years of life have been positively related to children's cognitive, language, and social-emotional outcomes (Forry et al., 2013; Loeb et al., 2004; NICHD Early Child Care Research Network, 2000).

Although numerous studies have shown the benefits of high-quality care on children's developmental outcomes, child care centers often fall short of the minimal recommendations for structural and process quality. Several studies have reported that infant and toddler classrooms serving families from diverse socioeconomic statuses do not meet state or other guidelines for adult–child ratios and group size, both essential features of structural quality (Phillips et al., 1994, 2000; Schmit & Matthews, 2013). Furthermore, the majority of center-based classrooms serving infants and toddlers demonstrate minimal to less than good process quality (i.e., caregiving and developmentally appropriate activities; Helburn et al., 1995; Howes, Whitebook, et al., 1992; Phillips et al., 1994; Pungello & Kurtz-Costes, 1999).

Measuring infant and toddler child care quality

Measures of early care and education quality have been developed and used for a variety of purposes in the contexts of research, practice, and policy. Originally, quality measures were developed by researchers to describe children's experiences in early care and education settings and identify aspects of the care environment that predicted children's developmental outcomes (Child Trends, 2009; Halle, Vick Whittaker, & Anderson, 2010; Zaslow, Tout, & Halle, 2011). Practitioners have also used quality measures as self-assessment tools to guide program improvement (Child Trends, 2009; Halle et al., 2010; Zaslow et al., 2011). Recently, quality measurement has entered the public policy context as it has been used to assess the impact of quality improvement initiatives, make programmatic decisions, and inform consumers (e.g., parents) about ratings of quality (Child Trends, 2009; Halle et al., 2010; Zaslow et al., 2011). Quality improvement initiatives include the national Race to the Top Early Learning Challenge, statewide and local Quality Rating and Improvement Systems, and other professional development efforts. Quality initiatives often use global and structural assessments of quality (Child Trends, 2009), though they have also recently added an emphasis on process quality (Zellman & Karoly, 2014).

The preponderance of quality improvement initiatives suggests the need for reliable and valid measures that document the multidimensional nature of child care quality across ages and settings (Bisceglia et al., 2009; Child Trends, 2009; Paulsell et al., 2013; Zaslow et al., 2010). In particular, the reliability of quality data obtained from surveys, document review, and observations needs to be assessed (Tout, Zaslow, Halle, & Forry, 2009). In response to this need, researchers have recently examined the psychometric properties of specific measures designed to assess program quality in infant and toddler settings (Bisceglia et al., 2009; Jamison, Cabell, LoCasale-Crouch, Hamre, & Pianta, 2014; Thomason & La Paro, 2009).

The Infant/Toddler Environment Rating Scale–Revised (ITERS-R) represents one of the most commonly used measures of global quality in practice, policy, and research contexts, including indicators of both structural and process quality (Burchinal, Cryer, Clifford, & Howes, 2002; Campbell & Milbourne, 2005; Harms, Cryer, & Clifford, 2003; Phillips et al., 2000). This rating scale can be used in classroom settings that serve children between the ages of birth and 30 months. The ITERS-R assesses space and furnishings, personal care routines, listening and talking, activities, interaction, program structure, and parents and staff. Previous research has shown that the ITERS-R items compose one dominant factor and that shorter subsets of both structural and process quality items of the ITERS-R can be used to measure quality (Bisceglia et al., 2009). In order to observe the quality of care provided to infants and toddlers in family child care homes, the sister tool, the Family Child Care Environment Rating Scale–Revised, is used (Harms, Cryer, & Clifford, 2007).

Other measures of infant and toddler child care quality focus predominantly on process quality. One of the earliest measures of process quality was the Arnett Caregiver Interaction Scale (CIS; Arnett, 1989). The CIS measures caregiving behaviors that fall into the following dimensions: sensitivity, harshness, detachment, and permissiveness (Arnett, 1989; Smart Start Evaluation Team, 2000). Although the CIS has been frequently used to assess quality, this instrument does not measure several important features of teacher–child interactions (Thomason & La Paro, 2009). For example, the CIS includes items that assess the caregiver's warmth and developmentally appropriate communication with children, but the CIS does not include items that focus on a caregiver's ability to sensitively respond to children's individual cues or a caregiver's ability to expand children's learning through interactions (Arnett, 1989). Although the CIS may not comprehensively measure current definitions of quality caregiving interactions, it is an instrument that has contributed to current approaches for measuring child care quality.

NICHD study investigators created the Observational Record of the Caregiving Environment (ORCE) to measure interactions between caregivers and children ages 6–54 months in nonmaternal care settings, including child care centers, family child care, and kith and kin settings (NICHD Early Child Care Research Network, 1996). The ORCE includes both behavioral frequency counts and qualitative ratings of caregiver stimulation, caregiver behavior management, caregiver language, child activity, child behavior, peer interactions, positive/negative affect, and activity setting. Infant and toddler child care quality as measured by the ORCE has predicted children's language and cognitive outcomes during the first 3 years of life, at school entry, and even through adolescence (NICHD Early Child Care Research Network, 2000, 2002; Vandell et al., 2010).

In addition, the Classroom Assessment Scoring System (CLASS) measures teacher–child interactions in center-based programs for infants between 0 and 18 months (Jamison et al., 2014) and toddlers between 18 and 36 months (Thomason & La Paro, 2009). The CLASS-Infant consists of one construct made up of the following four dimensions: relational climate, teacher sensitivity, facilitated exploration, and early language support (Jamison et al., 2014). The CLASS-Toddler comprises two constructs: emotional and behavioral support (positive climate, negative climate, teacher sensitivity, regard for child perspectives, behavior guidance) and engaged support for learning (facilitation of learning and development, quality of feedback, language modeling; La Paro, Hamre, & Pianta, 2012). Whereas the CLASS-PreK has been linked to preschool children's outcomes (Howes et al., 2008; Mashburn et al., 2008), the CLASS-Infant and CLASS-Toddler have yet to be used in studies of young children's developmental outcomes.

Describing the PITC PARS subscales

As a global measure that assesses both structural and process indicators across the entire birth-to-3 age period, the PITC PARS occupies a distinct position in the current landscape of infant and toddler assessments of quality. The following review of the literature describes the research evidence behind each of the PITC PARS subscales used to assess infant and toddler quality in both family child care and center-based programs.

Quality of Adult's Interactions With Children (Subscale I) assesses the responsiveness of individual teachers' interactions with the infants and toddlers in their care. Responsiveness and sensitivity are demonstrated when caregivers read a young child's emotional cues and respond appropriately to the child's needs in a timely manner (Shonkoff & Phillips, 2000). Responsive interactions between caregivers and children stimulate infants' brain development (Shore, 1997). In addition, responsiveness and sensitivity toward individual children contribute to social-emotional competence, secure attachment, language development, and cognition (Burchinal et al., 2000; Hirsh-Pasek & Burchinal, 2006; Howes, 1997; Howes, Matheson, & Hamilton, 1994; NICHD Early Child Care Research Network, 2002; Shonkoff & Phillips, 2000). In essence, the PITC considers the adult's interactions with infants and toddlers to include both a caring component and a teaching component. As adults care for infants, they provide guidance that helps children learn in all four developmental domains (i.e., social and emotional development, cognitive development, language development, and perceptual and motor development). In addition to responsiveness, Subscale I assesses the extent to which care teachers intentionally facilitate a child's cognitive and language development. When care teachers support infants' and toddlers' exploration, the children can investigate the physical environment, relationships, ideas, and symbols (Bransford, Brown, & Cocking, 2000). A rich language environment featuring aspects such as frequent talk at an appropriate pace with wait time (e.g., asking questions, responding to children's vocalizations, expanding and repeating children's words) and book reading predicts both language and cognitive outcomes (Dickinson & Tabors, 2001; Fowler, Ogston, Roberts-Fiati, & Swenson, 1997; NICHD Early Child Care Research Network, 2000; Nicholas, Lightbown, & Spada, 2001; Raikes et al., 2006; Risley & Hart, 2006).

Family Partnerships, Cultural Responsiveness, and Inclusive Care (Subscale II) assesses the extent to which caregiving practices, the classroom environment, and program policies are responsive to cultural and family practices as well as the unique needs of children. Building relationships with families allows parents to trust providers and enables care teachers to understand the child's home routines and parental childrearing values (Sandstrom et al., 2011). Caregivers and parents need to communicate about the child to ensure continuities across settings and full knowledge of the child's health, development, and daily routines (Arndt & McGuire-Schwartz, 2008; Harper-Browne & Raikes, 2012). Furthermore, this subscale addresses how programs meet diverse cultural, linguistic, and special needs. Programs promote cultural sensitivity by encouraging teachers to develop cultural knowledge; programs can also employ program staff and include classroom materials that are representative of the cultures and languages of children and families (Harper-Browne & Raikes, 2012; Lally, Torres, & Phelps, 1994). In addition to being culturally aware, high-quality programs have a set of policies in place that pertain to the inclusion of children with disabilities or special needs. Previous studies demonstrate many advantages to all children in inclusive early childhood settings (California Department of Education, 2009; Peck, Carlson, & Helmsetter, 1992). For example, typically developing children in inclusive settings have been observed to have more awareness of other children's needs, less discomfort with disability, and more acceptance of human differences, whereas children with disabilities have shown developmental gains in communication and social skills (California Department of Education, 2009; Odom & McEvoy, 1990; Peck et al., 1992).

The remaining three subscales of the PARS are made up of primary caregiving and many indicators of structural quality. The first items of Organization of Group Care (Subscale III) assess the extent to which caregiving practices and program procedures meet infants' and toddlers' individual needs through predictable and supportive relationships with one or two care teachers. Children form attachment relationships with care teachers, and these attachment relationships significantly affect children's development (Howes & Spieker, 2008). Primary caregiving facilitates caregivers' development of positive relationships with children and families and fosters a supportive environment for child development (Margetts, 2005). Limiting the number of adults with whom an infant interacts allows caregivers to learn the individual eating, sleeping, and diapering cues and routines of each child, which in turn helps children develop a sense of trust that caregivers will meet their physiological needs (Cassidy & Shaver, 2008; Zero to Three, 2008). Children demonstrate preference, positive emotions, exploration, and secure attachments when cared for by stable, long-term caregivers (Howes & Hamilton, 1992; Lamb & Ahnert, 2006; Raikes, 1993). The remaining items of Organization of Group Care include aspects of structural quality that provide the foundation for responsive caregiving, such as teacher–child ratios, group size, and physical space. Lower teacher–child ratios and group sizes have been related to higher ratings of caregiving practices, positive climate, competent peer play, and secure teacher–child relationships (Clarke-Stewart & Allhusen, 2002; Howes, Phillips, & Whitebook, 1992; Thomason & La Paro, 2009). Adequate physical space allows for children's movement and exploration and has been associated with fewer peer conflicts, positive peer interactions, and lower stress levels (American Academy of Pediatrics, 2002; Legendre, 1995, 2003).

Physical Environment (Subscale IV) assesses the extent to which a program provides indoor and outdoor environments that support infants' and toddlers' developmental needs. Well-designed environments affect children's learning and development by encouraging exploration, facilitating self-directed and regulated learning, fostering a sense of identity, and promoting both individual and peer play (Torelli, 2002). A variety of indoor and outdoor activities provide opportunities for fine motor, gross motor, cognitive, creative, social, emotional, and language skills (Essa, 2003; Frost, Wortham, & Reifel, 2008; Zero to Three, 2008). While the physical environment provides an array of interesting objects, textures, and physical challenges for active play, space should also be available for private and quiet activities (Curtis & Carter, 2003; Torelli & Durrett, 2001; Zero to Three, 2008). Finally, cleanliness and safety of the play materials and environment minimize the transmission of diseases or other threats to children's health and safety (Hale & Polder, 1997; National Resource Center for Health and Safety in Child Care, 2002).

Routines and Record Keeping (Subscale V) assesses the extent to which caregiving routines and program procedures promote infants' and toddlers' safety and health. High-quality settings feature health, safety, and nutrition standards to guide the basic routines of feeding, diapering, and napping (Sandstrom et al., 2011). Food preparation, service, and storage should meet national guidelines and parental or health care provider instructions (National Resource Center for Health and Safety in Child Care, 2002). Diapering and toileting routines should include proper sanitary and disinfecting practices for both adults and children, and children should play an active role in diapering and toileting routines in line with their developmental readiness (National Resource Center for Health and Safety in Child Care, 2002). Given the significance of sleep for physical, social-emotional, and cognitive development (Jung, Molfese, Beswick, Jacobi-Vessels, & Molnar, 2009; O'Callaghan et al., 2010; Scher, 2005; Spruyt et al., 2008), flexible nap scheduling and safe sleeping practices (e.g., putting infants to sleep on their backs) should be in place to respect children's sleep cycles (American Academy of Pediatrics Task Force on Infant Feeding and SIDS, 2000; Moon, Patel, & Shaefer, 2000; Pavia & Da Ros, 1997; Siren-Tiusanen & Robinson, 2001). Record keeping and information sharing allow caregivers to monitor the development of each individual child and maintain open lines of communication with parents.

The current study

The purpose of the current study is to explore the psychometric properties of the PITC PARS instrument. Specifically, this study provides information on the construct validity of the instrument, summarizing its background and development. In addition, this study illustrates concurrent validity with other commonly used measures of infant and toddler quality. Finally, the overall factor structure of the measure and the internal consistency of each individual subscale are presented.

Method

Sample

Between 2003 and 2007, two evaluation studies of a training and technical assistance initiative were conducted in California. The evaluations included both public and private programs operating on a not-for-profit basis, and all of the programs had subsidized slots serving low-income families. As part of the evaluations, PITC PARS assessments were conducted with a random sample of teachers in the programs served. The pool of teachers from which the random sample was drawn included 1,087 teachers of the following ethnicities: 44% Latino, 29% White, 12% Black/African American, 6% Asian, and 9% other. The teachers' educational attainment ranged from elementary to graduate school ($N = 1,087$ teachers): 15% completed a high school degree or less, 53% attended some college, 32% received a higher education degree (i.e., 2-year degree, 4-year degree, graduate degree). Thus, like the programs in which they worked, the teachers reflected the diversity of the infant and toddler care field.

The following psychometric information for the PITC PARS was based on data collected for the subset of programs and teachers with complete data for all items across all assessments. These criteria resulted in a sample of 101 infant center-based classrooms, 40 toddler center-based classrooms, and 81 family child care programs (59 small family child care homes and 22 large family child care homes). Within these 222 center-based classrooms and family child care programs, 330 individual teachers were observed, which was about 30% of the larger pool of teachers described in the previous paragraph. Among these classrooms and programs, 205 assessments were conducted in English, whereas the remaining 17 were conducted in Spanish.

Measures

CIS

The CIS describes different caregiving behaviors that can be categorized into four subscales: Sensitivity, Harshness, Detachment, and Permissiveness (Arnett, 1989; Smart Start Evaluation Team, 2000). The current study used the Sensitivity, Harshness, and Detachment subscales. The measure includes 26 items rated on a 4-point scale ranging from 1 = *not at all* to 4 = *very much*, based on how often the teacher exhibited each specific behavior. An infant care teacher at the highest level of quality would receive a rating of 4 on the sensitivity dimension and ratings of 1 on both the harshness and detachment dimensions. Although this measure is rarely used anymore because it lacks more recent conceptualizations of quality interactions, it was one of the few measures of caregiving interactions that had been used in studies of child care quality at the time the data were collected for the current study. In the current sample, Cronbach's alphas for each CIS subscale were .94 for Sensitivity, .82 for Harshness, and .83 for Detachment.

Environment Rating Scales (ERS)

The ERS are commonly used observational assessment tools that measure the global quality of the care environment. The ITERS-R measures the overall quality of the environment of center-based classrooms with children from birth to 30 months old (Harms et al., 2003). The Early Childhood Environment Rating Scale–Revised (ECERS-R) measures the quality of the environment of center-based classrooms with children from 30 months to 5 years old (Harms, Clifford, & Cryer, 1998). The Family Day Care Rating Scale (FDCRS) measures the quality of the environment of family child care programs caring for newborns to children age 5 (Harms & Clifford, 1989). The ITERS-R and ECERS-R each contain seven subscales: Space and Furnishings, Personal Care Routines, Language, Activities, Interaction, Program Structure, and Parents and Staff. The FDCRS consists of six subscales: Space and Furnishings, Basic Care, Language and Reasoning, Learning Activities, Social Development, and Adult Needs. All three instruments and their subscales are rated on a scale ranging from 1 = *inadequate* to 7 = *excellent*. In the current sample, Cronbach's alphas for each ERS instrument were as follows: .88 for ECERS-R, .92 for ITERS-R, and .90 for FDCRS. In the computation of the Cronbach's alphas some items were dropped because they were rated as not applicable to the majority of cases. The items that were dropped included staff continuity for the ECERS-R; use of TV, video, computer and provisions for children with disabilities for the ITERS-R; and all items in the Provisions for Exceptional Children subscale for the FDCRS.

PITC PARS

The PITC PARS measures the global quality of family child care programs and center-based classrooms serving infants and toddlers from birth up to 36 months of age. Through a combination of direct observation, administrator interview, and document review, the PITC PARS assesses the following five subscales: (a) Quality of Adult's Interactions With Children; (b) Family Partnerships, Cultural Responsiveness, and Inclusive Care; (c) Organization of Group Care; (d) Physical Environment; and (e) Routines and Record Keeping. Within each subscale, certain items or subitems were developed for the setting (i.e., family child care home or center) or the ages of children cared for in the setting (i.e., young infant, mobile infant/toddler, or older toddler) to assess the appropriateness and nuances of care for infants from birth up to 36 months in different care settings.

The PITC PARS takes a strengths-based perspective. In other words, all 27 PITC PARS items represent aspects of care that are supportive of children's positive development. Each item is further broken down into four subitems (see Table 1 for a sample item and subitems). To determine ratings on the PITC PARS,

Table 1. Sample item and subitems from the Program for Infant and Toddler Care Program Assessment Rating Scale.

Subscale	Item	Subitems
I. Quality of adult's interactions with children	F. Adult use of language and communication	1. The infant/toddler care teacher frequently talks with children at appropriate times and consistently gives the children opportunities to respond. 2. The infant/toddler care teacher uses parallel talk, commenting on the children's focus of interest or activity. 3. The infant/toddler care teacher regularly uses self-talk, commenting on his or her own actions. 4. The infant/toddler care teacher uses child-directed language.

the assessor first notes which subitems were observed by comparing the evidence gathered through observation, interview, or review of program materials to the rating guidance provided for each subitem. When the evidence sufficiently meets the criteria specified in the rating guidance, the subitem is rated as 1 = *observed;* otherwise, that subitem is given a 0 rating. The four subitem ratings for each item are summed to produce the item rating, which can range in value from 0 to 4. The item ratings for each subscale are then averaged to produce a subscale rating, which can also range in value from 0 to 4. These summary ratings averaged across the item ratings for each PITC PARS subscale fall within one of four ranges that indicate progress in implementing infant/toddler care quality. These ranges are interpreted as follows: 0–1.7 = "Beginning," 1.8–2.7 = "Emerging," 2.8–3.7 = "Developing," and 3.8–4 = "Refining."

Procedure

Prior to data collection, assessors were trained on each of the measures used in the study. Training and reliability procedures were followed according to the CIS and ERS instructions prescribed by the respective manuals and instrument authors. For the PITC PARS, assessor training consisted of classroom-style training to help participants become thoroughly familiar with the subitems and rating criteria. Assessors-in-training then shadowed a PITC PARS assessor during a classroom observation, followed by engaging in field training with a PITC PARS anchor. Each assessor was required to reach a minimum standard of exact agreement with a PITC PARS anchor for 80% of the subitems across three successive observations before conducting assessments on his or her own. To ensure rating consistency among assessors during periods of active PITC PARS data collection, assessors met regularly to discuss ratings and conducted interrater reliability checks after every 10–12 observations.

Assessors spent approximately 4 hr onsite at each child care program included in the present study. The onsite visit typically began around 7:30 a.m. or 8:00 a.m. so that assessors could collect program materials (e.g., parent handbook, program policy statements); ask about the group care arrangement; and begin to observe the environment, morning drop off, and staff interactions with children and family members. The observation was followed by an interview with the program director or family child care provider. During the classroom observation, the assessors concurrently collected the CIS, ERS, and observational portions of the PITC PARS. During the interview, information about the program's structure and policies was collected and used to complete corresponding sections of the PITC PARS and ERS instruments. On completion of an onsite visit, the assessor reviewed documentation gathered from the observation, interview, and program materials to determine ratings for all of the assessment instruments.

Results

Analytic procedures were conducted to establish the validity and reliability of the PITC PARS instrument in accordance with widely recognized recommended guidelines (American Educational

Construct validity

Construct validity of the PITC PARS subscales was established through a multistep development process. First, the constructs were drawn from the PITC strategies and recommendations, whose development was originally based on a thorough literature review of early childhood development and child care quality and guidance from a panel of national experts (Mangione, 1990). Second, a literature review update was conducted to ensure that the PITC-based constructs reflected current information on early childhood development and child care quality. Third, the ORCE and recommended practices of the American Academy of Pediatrics provided the foundation for several PITC PARS items. Next, the PITC PARS developers consulted with national experts in the fields of infant development, early care and education, and program quality assessment and evaluation when finalizing the instrument. Finally, extensive piloting resulted in the final version of the PITC PARS instrument.

Descriptive data

Means, standard deviations, ranges, and Cronbach's alphas for the PITC PARS items and subscales are displayed in Table 2. The means demonstrated that the PITC PARS subscales were all in the

Table 2. Descriptive statistics for Program for Infant and Toddler Care Program Assessment Rating Scale subscales and items ($N = 222$).

Subscale/Item	M	SD	Range	Cronbach's α
Subscale I: Quality of adult's interactions with children	2.61	0.94	(.14, 4.00)	.90
Item A: Responsiveness and sensitivity to children	2.90	1.43	(.00, 4.00)	
Item B: Positive tone and attentiveness	3.06	1.06	(.00, 4.00)	
Item C: Responsive engagement and intervention	2.97	1.22	(.00, 4.00)	
Item D: Respect for infants' initiative and choices	2.13	1.45	(.00, 4.00)	
Item E: Facilitation of cognitive development and learning	1.95	1.48	(.00, 4.00)	
Item F: Adult use of language and communication	2.46	1.08	(.00, 4.00)	
Item G: Adult support children's language development	2.82	1.01	(.00, 4.00)	
Subscale II: Family partnerships, cultural responsiveness, and inclusive care	2.18	0.74	(.60, 4.00)	.76
Item A: Relationships with families	2.08	1.08	(.00, 4.00)	
Item B: Communication with families	2.99	0.94	(.00, 4.00)	
Item C: Culturally responsive care	2.05	1.11	(.00, 4.00)	
Item D: Representative staffing	2.16	1.34	(.00, 4.00)	
Item E: Inclusion of children with disabilities or other special needs	1.63	1.24	(.00, 4.00)	
Subscale III: Organization of group care	2.26	0.85	(.00, 4.00)	.75
Item A: Primary caregiving	1.72	1.62	(.00, 4.00)	
Item B: Continuity of care	2.95	1.07	(.00, 4.00)	
Item C: Following children's individual schedules	2.79	1.20	(.00, 4.00)	
Item D: Group size and structure	1.58	1.27	(.00, 4.00)	
Subscale IV: Physical environment	2.26	0.71	(.43, 3.71)	.80
Item A: Room arrangement	2.42	1.08	(.00, 4.00)	
Item B: Opportunities for exploration	1.80	1.13	(.00, 4.00)	
Item C: Opportunities for movement	2.00	1.03	(.00, 4.00)	
Item D: Safety of play materials and environment	2.03	1.29	(.00, 4.00)	
Item E: Cleanliness of play materials and environment	2.53	1.16	(.00, 4.00)	
Item F: Comfort of infants and adults	2.31	1.02	(.00, 4.00)	
Item G: Reduced stimulation	2.74	1.09	(.00, 4.00)	
Subscale V: Routines and record keeping	2.21	0.75	(.50, 4.00)	.70
Item A: Healthful and safe feeding routines	2.29	1.19	(.00, 4.00)	
Item B: Healthful and safe diapering and toileting	1.36	1.27	(.00, 4.00)	
Item C: Healthful and safe napping	2.63	0.82	(.00, 4.00)	
Item D: Record keeping and information sharing	2.56	1.19	(.00, 4.00)	

Note. The possible range for summary subscale scores was 0 to 4.

Table 3. Bivariate correlations among Program for Infant and Toddler Care Program Assessment Rating Scale subscales ($N = 222$).

Subscale	I	II	III	IV	V
I. Quality of adult's interactions with children	—				
II. Family partnerships, cultural responsiveness, and inclusive care	.36***	—			
III. Organization of group care	.55***	.27***	—		
IV. Physical environment	.34***	.34***	.39***	—	
V. Routines and record keeping	.28***	.40***	.28***	.58***	—

***$p < .001$.

"Emerging" range, which suggests medium-low global quality. Programs were rated the highest on the Quality of Adult's Interactions With Children subscale. The ranges indicated that programs were rated across the full spectrum of global quality, with the exception that no program was rated at the highest level of 4 on Physical Environment. Subscale I was slightly negatively skewed (skewness = −.56), and Subscales II–V were approximately symmetric (skewness = −.23 to .26). The distributions for each of the subscales had a platykurtic kurtosis, ranging from −.68 to −.38, indicating that the distributions had a broader peak and shorter tails than would be observed in a normal distribution. Despite minor deviations from the normal distributions, the histograms demonstrated adequate variability on each of the subscales. Cronbach's alphas for the PITC PARS subscales ranged from .70 to .90, demonstrating preliminary evidence of the internal consistency of each subscale. Bivariate correlations among the PITC PARS subscales are presented in Table 3. The subscales were all positively and significantly intercorrelated. The moderate strength of correlations among most of the subscales suggests that these subscales assess related yet distinct aspects of child care quality. The strongest correlation was Physical Environment with Routines and Record Keeping ($r = .58$). The weakest correlation was Family Partnerships, Cultural Responsiveness, and Inclusive Care with Organization of Group Care ($r = .27$).

Concurrent validity

Concurrent validity was established by examining bivariate correlations between the PITC PARS and other commonly used measures of quality in infant and toddler environments. The first subscale of the PITC PARS, Quality of Adult's Interactions With Children, was correlated with the CIS because, like Subscale I of the PITC PARS, the CIS focuses on adult interactions with children. Correlations between PITC PARS Subscale I and the CIS were moderately high and in the expected direction: $r(330) = .64$, $p < .001$, with the Sensitivity subscale; $r(330) = -.62$, $p < .001$, with the Harshness subscale; and $r(330) = -.60$, $p < .001$, with the Detachment subscale. In addition, the overall PITC PARS summary rating was found to correlate highly with overall ratings of the ERS instruments: ITERS-R, $r(98) = .84$, $p < .001$; ECERS-R, $r(40) = .81$, $p < .001$; and FDCRS, $r(80) = .80$, $p < .001$.

To test for evidence of convergent and divergent validity, we examined the magnitude of correlations between individual PITC PARS subscales and the ERS subscales. We used Cohen's guidelines as a framework to interpret the strength of the correlations, with .10 as small, .30 as medium, and .50 as large (Cohen, 1988). In particular, we expected that the process quality subscales of both measures would correlate highly and that the structural quality subscales of both measures would correlate highly with each other. In addition, we anticipated that the associations between the process quality and structural quality subscales of each measure would be weaker in magnitude. The magnitudes of the correlations presented in Table 4 provide some support for these hypotheses. PITC PARS Subscale I, Quality of Adult's Interactions With Children, correlated more highly with the process quality subscales of the ERS, Support for Language Development and Interaction, than with the remaining structural quality subscales. PITC PARS Subscale IV, Physical Environment, correlated most highly with the corresponding structural quality ERS subscales, Space and Furnishings and Personal Care Routines. Similarly, PITC PARS Subscale V, Routines and Record

Table 4. Bivariate correlations between Program for Infant and Toddler Care Program Assessment Rating Scale subscales and Environment Rating Scale subscales ($N = 218$).

Subscale	Space and Furnishings	Personal Care Routines	Support for Language Development	Activities	Interaction	Program Structure	Parents and Staff
Quality of adult's interactions with children	.38**	.33**	.69**	.40**	.68**	.48**	.39**
Family partnerships, cultural responsiveness, and inclusive care	.36**	.16*	.46**	.44**	.48**	.44**	.40**
Organization of group care	.37**	.41**	.48**	.40**	.48**	.43**	.42**
Physical environment	.72**	.62**	.39**	.51**	.42**	.56**	.27**
Routines and record keeping	.52**	.57**	.39**	.33**	.40**	.52**	.14*

Note. Support for Language Development encompasses the ITERS Listening and Talking subscale, FDCRS Language and Reasoning subscale, and ECERS Language-Reasoning subscale. The Program Structure subscale was present in the ITERS and ECERS instruments but not in the FDCRS instrument ($N = 137$). The Parents and Staff subscale correlations included a smaller sample ($N = 215$). ITERS = Infant/Toddler Environment Rating Scale; FDCRS = Family Day Care Rating Scale; ECERS = Early Childhood Environment Rating Scale.
*$p < .05$. **$p < .01$.

Keeping, correlated most highly with three structural quality ERS subscales: Space and Furnishings, Personal Care Routines, and Program Structure. Finally, PITC PARS Subscale II, Family Partnerships, Cultural Responsiveness, and Inclusive Care, demonstrated small to medium correlations with all of the ERS subscales, likely because the individual items of PITC PARS Subscale II are distributed across multiple subscales of the ERS. PITC PARS Subscale III, Organization of Group Care, showed a similar pattern of medium correlations with all of the ERS subscales because most of the individual items of PITC PARS Subscale III are not specifically represented in the ERS. The higher magnitude correlations across similar subscales and weaker magnitude correlations across dissimilar subscales provide some evidence for the PITC PARS's convergent and divergent validity with the ERS.

Factor analysis

Because the PITC PARS items and subitems were developed to address nuances in key aspects of care by program type and the age of children, we conducted a principal component analysis on the largest subsample of our data: infant center-based programs ($N = 101$). Principal component analysis is a multivariate technique used to identify the linear components of a set of variables (Field, 2009). The Kaiser–Meyer–Olkin measure verified the sampling adequacy for the analysis, KMO = .83, which was above the acceptable limit of .50 (Field, 2009). Bartlett's test of sphericity indicated that correlations between items were sufficiently large for principal component analysis, $\chi^2(351) = 1,186$, $p < .001$, $N = 101$. Based on the five conceptual subscales of the PITC PARS, an initial analysis was run with five factors, which yielded unclear results. Two-, three-, four-, and six-factor solutions were then examined using varimax rotation of the factor loading matrix. This method provides for efficient orthogonal rotation that clearly delineates variable loadings onto individual factors. The three-factor solution, which explained 47% of the variance, was preferred because of the conceptual underpinnings, point of inflexion on the scree plot, amount of variance explained, and difficulty interpreting additional factors. We used .40 as our cutoff for acceptable factor loadings (Field, 2009).

Table 5 presents the factor loadings after rotation for the final three-factor solution, and Table 6 lists the items by factor. All of the items from Subscale I and one additional item from Subscale III loaded together on the first factor, which represented the quality of the adult's interactions with children. The first factor included the following items: responsiveness and sensitivity (I), positive tone and attentiveness (I), responsive engagement and intervention (I), respect for infants' initiative and choices (I), facilitation of cognitive development and learning (I), adult use of language and communication (I), adult support of children's language development (I), and following children's

Table 5. Summary of factor analysis with varimax rotation of Program for Infant and Toddler Care Program Assessment Rating Scale subscales ($N = 101$).

Item	Factor 1	Factor 2	Factor 3
I.A. Responsiveness and sensitivity to children	.78	.22	.13
I.B. Positive tone and attentiveness	.78	.13	.09
I.C. Responsive engagement and intervention	.81	.24	.03
I.D. Respect for infants' initiative and choices	.67	.15	.12
I.E. Facilitation of cognitive development and learning	.80	.12	.01
I.F. Adult use of language and communication	.80	.13	.06
I.G. Adult support children's language development	.64	.25	.15
II.A. Relationships with families	.34	.62	.11
II.B. Communication with families	.36	.61	−.09
II.C. Culturally responsive care	.22	.59	.21
II.D. Representative staffing	.01	.70	−.20
II.E. Inclusion of children with disabilities or other special needs	−.10	.64	−.22
III.A. Primary caregiving	.14	.43	.18
III.B. Continuity of care	.14	−.01	.62
III.C. Following children's individual schedules	.58	.11	.39
III.D. Group size and structure	.25	.38	.29
IV.A. Room arrangement	.11	.06	.60
IV.B. Opportunities for exploration	.18	.59	.35
IV.C. Opportunities for movement	.25	.42	.45
IV.D. Safety of play materials and environment	.01	−.17	.74
IV.E. Cleanliness of play materials and environment	.11	−.03	.72
IV.F. Comfort of infants and adults	.32	.41	.41
IV.G. Reduced stimulation	.19	.35	.44
V.A. Healthful and safe feeding routines	.10	.46	.62
V.B. Healthful and safe diapering and toileting	.14	.28	.31
V.C. Healthful and safe napping	−.07	.05	.49
V.D. Record keeping and information sharing	.20	.52	.04
Eigenvalue	5.08	3.99	3.70
Percent variance	18.81	14.79	13.69
Cronbach's α	.90	.74	.80

Table 6. Summary of items by factor.

Factor 1	Factor 2	Factor 3
Responsiveness and sensitivity to children (I)	Relationships with families (II)	Continuity of care (III)
Positive tone and attentiveness (I)	Communication with families (II)	Room arrangement (IV)
Responsive engagement and intervention (I)	Culturally responsive care (II)	Opportunities for movement (IV)
Respect for infants' initiative and choices (I)	Representative staffing (II)	Safety of play materials and environment (IV)
Facilitation of cognitive development and learning (I)	Inclusion of children with disabilities or other special needs (II)	Cleanliness of play materials and environment (IV)
Adult use of language and communication (I)	Primary caregiving (III)	Comfort of Infants and adults (IV)
Adult support children's language development (I)	Opportunities for exploration (IV)	Reduced stimulation (IV)
Following children's individual schedules (III)	Record keeping and information sharing (V)	Healthful and safe feeding routines (V)
		Healthful and safe napping (V)

individual schedules (III). All of the items from Subscale II loaded together, along with a few additional items from other subscales, on the second factor, representing program policies that address responsiveness to the needs of children and families. The second factor included the following items: relationships with families (II), communication with families (II), culturally responsive care (II), representative staffing (II), inclusion of children with disabilities or other special needs

(II), primary caregiving (III), opportunities for exploration (IV), and record keeping and information sharing (V). Finally, most of the items from Subscales IV and V loaded onto the third factor, representing the physical environment and daily routines. The third factor included the following items: continuity of care (III), room arrangement (IV), opportunities for movement (IV), safety of play materials and environment (IV), cleanliness of play materials and environment (IV), comfort of infant and adults (IV), reduced stimulation (IV), healthful and safe feeding routines (V), and healthful and safe napping (V). Opportunities for movement (IV), comfort of infants and adults (IV), and healthful and safe feeding routines loaded onto Factors 2 and 3, but these items fit better conceptually with the other items from Factor 3. Two items, group size and structure (III) and healthful and safe diapering and toileting (V), did not load strongly onto any one factor. All three factors of the PITC PARS had high scale reliabilities as measured by Cronbach's alpha: Factor 1 = .90, Factor 2 = .74, Factor 3 = .80.

Discussion

This study examined the psychometric properties of the PITC PARS. Careful development of this instrument included consulting both the existing literature and national experts regarding infant/toddler child care quality to establish construct validity. Examination of the bivariate correlations with other commonly used measures of infant and toddler child care quality provided evidence of concurrent validity. Finally, the factor analysis suggested that the PITC PARS measures three distinct yet related dimensions of global child care quality.

Validity of the PITC PARS

The iterative development process of creating the PITC PARS helped ensure adequate construct validity. Informed by both the research literature and national experts, the PITC PARS subscales comprehensively address the breadth of infant/toddler child care quality. Pilot testing shaped refinements to the instrument, and the results of the current study suggest that the PITC PARS assesses conceptually and empirically meaningful aspects of infant/toddler child care quality. In addition, the descriptive data illustrated that the PITC PARS captures adequate variability, which serves as an important feature of a quality measure. For example, policymakers need quality measures that can validly and reliably assess varying levels of quality, whereas practitioners can use measures with adequate variability to assess their programs and set goals for improvement. Researchers also require quality measures with adequate variability in order to identify predictors of quality or to predict child outcomes. The ranges and distributions of the data presented in this study demonstrated that programs were rated across the full range of the program quality scale, from 0 ("Beginning") to 4 ("Refining"). On average, programs achieved "Emerging" quality between 2.18 and 2.61, which falls in the middle of the range for all subscales.

To assess whether the PITC PARS taps into the same construct as other current assessments of quality, we examined several sets of bivariate correlations. PITC PARS Subscale I, Quality of Adult's Interactions With Children, had moderately high correlations with the CIS. The moderately high correlation suggests that PITC PARS Subscale I captures something unique and distinct from the CIS. This moderately high correlation makes sense because the CIS captures affect, communication, and level of involvement in interactions (Arnett, 1989), whereas PITC PARS Subscale I focuses more on responsiveness and facilitation of children's development and learning. Lastly, it is important to note the negative correlation between two of the CIS dimensions (Harshness and Detachment) and PITC PARS Subscale I. The PITC PARS takes a strengths-based perspective and focuses on positive behaviors that are supportive of children's development and learning rather than on negative care teacher practices. In addition, the PITC PARS overall rating was highly correlated with the ERS overall ratings. As the overall ratings of both the PITC PARS and the ERS instruments provide an indication of global quality, the relatively high bivariate correlations suggest that the instruments assess similar aspects of global quality, though with some variation. Taken together, these associations provide evidence of concurrent validity.

Preliminary evidence for convergent and divergent validity was examined using the correlations between the individual PITC PARS subscales and ERS subscales. Because the PITC PARS and ERS were correlated at the overall rating level, we would expect to find low to high correlations among all of the subscales. The magnitude of these correlations supported our hypotheses. The PITC PARS Quality of Adult's Interactions With Children (Subscale I) correlated more highly with the process quality subscales of the ERS, Support for Language Development and Interaction. The PITC PARS Physical Environment (Subscale IV) correlated more highly with the corresponding structural quality subscales of the ERS, Space and Furnishings and Personal Care Routines. The PITC PARS Routines and Record Keeping (Subscale V) correlated more highly with the corresponding structural quality subscales of the ERS, Space and Furnishings, Personal Care Routines, and Program Structure. Because some of the individual items are distributed differently across the measures' subscales, the PITC PARS Family Partnerships, Cultural Responsiveness, and Inclusive Care (Subscale II) did not map directly onto particular ERS subscales. For example, PITC PARS Subscale II includes items on culturally responsive care and the inclusion of children with disabilities or other special needs, whereas the ERS has an inclusion item in the Program Structure subscale and a diversity item in the Activities subscale. Similarly, the PITC PARS Organization of Group Care (Subscale III) demonstrated medium correlations with all of the ERS subscales because most of the individual items of PITC PARS Subscale III undergird the ERS constructs, even though they are not specifically assessed by the ERS subscales.

Factor structure of the PITC PARS

Overall, the factor analysis indicated that three factors likely underlie the global quality assessed through the PITC PARS. The factor analysis suggested that process quality items loaded together, items on program policies addressing responsiveness to the needs of children and families loaded together, and structural quality items loaded together. Factor 1 comprises the process quality items: responsiveness and sensitivity (I), positive tone and attentiveness (I), responsive engagement and intervention (I), respect for infants' initiative and choices (I), facilitation of cognitive development and learning (I), adult use of language and communication (I), adult support of children's language development (I), and following children's individual schedules (III). These items represent the various aspects of process quality (i.e., adults' interactions with children that are thought to affect children's attachment to their caregivers and stimulate developmental outcomes; Hirsh-Pasek & Burchinal, 2006; Loeb et al., 2004; NICHD Early Child Care Research Network, 2000, 2002; Shonkoff & Phillips, 2000; Vandell et al., 2010). Based on this literature that links child care quality with child outcomes, we would expect that PITC PARS Factor 1 would most likely predict positive child outcomes because of its focus on responsiveness and sensitivity, facilitation of cognitive development, and support for language development. Future research should test this hypothesis to shed light on the predictive validity of the PITC PARS.

Factor 2 represents program policies that address responsiveness to the needs of children and their families, including cultural sensitivity, inclusion, and family engagement. Factor 2 comprises the following items primarily from Subscale II and a few additional items from other subscales: relationships with families (II), communication with families (II), culturally responsive care (II), representative staffing (II), inclusion of children with disabilities or other special needs (II), primary caregiving (III), opportunities for exploration (IV), and record keeping and information sharing (V). All of the original items from Subscale II explicitly focus on being responsive to families, culture, and children's special needs. Primary caregiving (III) measures the extent to which one or two teachers primarily care for a child and communicate with that child's family, which provides a strong foundation for responsiveness to the needs of individual children and their families. Record keeping and information sharing (V) includes subitems that focus on the various types of documentation teachers use to share information with parents about their child's daily routines and developmental progress, which clearly relates to the items on relationships and communication with families of Factor 2. The item opportunities for exploration (IV) fits better conceptually with the physical environment items of Factor 3, but it loaded onto Factor 2. Even when we removed opportunities for exploration (IV) from Factor 2, Cronbach's alpha did not improve, which suggests that it does belong with the other items from Factor 2. This item assesses the variety of activities and materials available in the environment that support children's exploration. Perhaps cultural differences in providing opportunities for exploration or the role of inclusive environments in promoting children's exploration accounts for this item's loading on Factor 2. Further study should investigate how practices that foster cultural continuity and inclusion may relate to those that promote opportunities for exploration.

Factor 3 comprises items representing the structural indicators of quality: continuity of care (III), room arrangement (IV), opportunities for movement (IV), safety of play materials and environment (IV), cleanliness of play materials and environment (IV), comfort of infant and adults (IV), reduced stimulation (IV), healthful and safe feeding routines (V), and healthful and safe napping (V). Opportunities for movement (IV), comfort of infants and adults (IV), and healthful and safe feeding routines (V) loaded onto Factors 2 and 3. The factor loadings are comparable across factors, and these items fit better conceptually with the other physical environment and daily routine items of Factor 3. Even though the PITC PARS separates these structural quality items into multiple subscales for ease of data collection and measurement, these items load together, which suggests their conceptual connectedness.

Two items, group size and structure (III) and healthful and safe diapering and toileting (V), did not load strongly onto any one factor. Group size and structure (III) had low loadings on all factors. The subitems of group size and structure likely provide the foundation for many of the items across the three factors. For example, low teacher–child ratios and smaller group sizes allow for responsive relationships and interactions with individual children and families represented by Factors 1 and 2. The space requirements provide the foundation for the physical environment items of Factor 3. Healthful and safe diapering and toileting (V) similarly had low loadings across all three factors. Healthful and safe diapering and toileting (V) seems to be pulled across multiple factors because conceptually this item can fit with the different factors. For example, diapering and toileting represents one daily routine that maps onto the third factor of the physical environment and daily routines. Yet diapering routines also offer opportunities for rich interactions between care teachers and children (Factor 1) and have strong cultural underpinnings (Factor 2).

Significance of the PITC PARS

In addition to the psychometric properties presented previously, the PITC PARS was designed with several important features to measure infant and toddler child care quality. The infant/toddler period represents a unique stage of development, and care environments require a different set of standards than prekindergarten or kindergarten through Grade 12 environments (Lally, 2010). The PITC PARS was established specifically for use in infant and toddler programs rather than as a measure of programs serving older children adapted to younger classrooms. Furthermore, the PITC PARS can be used across family child care and center-based programs serving children from birth to 36 months. The option of using one instrument across settings and age groups may make this tool particularly helpful in practice, policy, or research that considers infants and toddlers in different program types. It is important to note that the PITC PARS includes specific items that are differentiated by program type and child age to ensure that the measure assesses appropriate indicators of quality for the various care settings.

Furthermore, the content of the PITC PARS reflects what the developmental literature shows as important dimensions of quality for infants and toddlers. Recent reviews on infant and toddler child care quality have focused either on the various components of global quality (Harper-Browne & Raikes, 2012; Sandstrom et al., 2011) or specifically on caregiver–child interactions of process quality (Elicker, Ruprecht, & Anderson, 2014; Halle, Anderson, Blasberg, Chrisler, & Simkin, 2011). Components of global quality include a wide range of indicators, such as positive caregiver–child relationships and interactions, appropriate cognitive and language stimulation, physical environment, schedules and routines, health and safety, staff qualifications, and family engagement (Harper-Browne & Raikes, 2012; Sandstrom et al., 2011). Other reviews have discussed dimensions of caregiver–child interactions such as sensitive responsiveness, cognitive/language stimulation, support for autonomy, positive emotional tone, behavior guidance, and support for peer interactions (Elicker et al., 2014; Halle et al., 2011). The current measurement of infant/toddler child care quality reflects this distinction. The ITERS-R measures global quality with an emphasis on the physical aspects of the environment (Bisceglia et al., 2009), whereas the CIS, CLASS, and ORCE focus exclusively on adult–child interactions (Arnett, 1989; Jamison et al., 2014; La Paro et al., 2012; NICHD Early Child Care Research Network, 1996). In contrast to these existing measures, the five subscales of the PITC PARS encompass the breadth of infant/toddler child care quality. Subscale I includes several items focusing on most of the important aspects of adult–child interactions, whereas the remaining subscales include the other components of global quality (e.g., physical environment, schedule and routines, health and safety, family engagement). The PITC PARS also uniquely includes a subscale to assess family partnerships, cultural responsiveness, and inclusive care. The research literature cites the importance of these practices (Harper-Browne & Raikes, 2012), but the current assessments of quality that are widely used do not assess these constructs. As an instrument that assesses the multidimensional nature of child care quality, the PITC PARS offers infant and toddler care programs an efficient means of documenting their efforts to improve quality.

Limitations

Although this study provides preliminary evidence of the psychometric properties of the PITC PARS, some limitations exist. The data used in these analyses were collected for evaluation purposes and consequently represent a convenient sample for the purposes of this psychometric study. Limited information was available on teacher demographic, classroom, and program characteristics; the study sample was drawn from a pool of public and private infant/toddler programs representing a range of quality with diverse teachers in California. Given these characteristics, the data likely apply to other diverse, not-for-profit programs. The PITC PARS has been effectively used as a self-study tool by programs in other states, such as Arizona, New York, and Ohio. Even so, studies that investigate the use of the PITC PARS in other contexts should test its general applicability. In addition, the modest sample size for the factor analysis may have limited the detection of stable factors. In particular, these data did not include large enough sample sizes to apply the factor analysis to all possible subsamples of PITC PARS. Future work with larger and more diverse samples would allow more in-depth investigation of the stability of the factor structure. Finally, the same observers collected the PITC PARS, CIS, and ERS data, which may have influenced the concurrent validity findings. Correlations of measures completed by independent assessors would strengthen the validity findings that resulted in the present analysis.

Practice, policy, and research implications

Increased formal training and professional development have been associated with more supportive caregiving practices, improved classroom quality, and positive child development outcomes (Blau, 2000; Burchinal et al., 2002; Burchinal, Roberts, Nabors, & Bryant, 1996; Campbell & Milbourne, 2005; Clarke-Stewart & Allhusen, 2002; Howes, Whitebook, et al., 1992). The PITC PARS has previously been used in such practice contexts as a self-assessment and coaching tool. It has also been used in combination with other assessments to evaluate training and technical assistance provided by PITC. These evaluations have shown that the programs' PITC PARS rating scores were higher after participating in PITC onsite training and technical assistance (Kriener-Althen & Mangione, 2007; Mangione, 2003). Such findings indicate the potential utility of this measure in quality improvement initiatives such as multifaceted Quality Rating and Improvement Systems endeavors that aim to improve both structural and process indicators of quality. Because the PITC PARS assesses global quality and has been effectively used as a coaching tool, this instrument may play an important role in quality improvement or professional development policy initiatives. In particular, the PITC PARS user's guide is currently being developed to help coaches provide guidance and support to infant and toddler care teachers. The results of the PITC PARS indicate to care teachers and their coaches which specific areas of quality need to be strengthened (e.g., physical environment, facilitation of cognitive development, cultural responsiveness). Care teachers and their coaches can refer to the user's guide for an elaboration of the items with specific examples of what the recommended practice looks like. Care teachers can use these descriptions to reflect on their own practices. To further support efforts to improve the quality of caregiving practices, the user's guide provides links to resources with information on additional training. As part of a comprehensive approach to quality improvement, the PITC PARS can provide a broad measure of infant and toddler care quality and be used as a tool to identify specific practices that programs and care teachers can work on strengthening.

Although the PITC PARS can continue to be used for these practical purposes, we anticipate future research applications for this instrument. Additional research can be conducted to continue to validate the psychometric properties of the PITC PARS (American Educational Research Association, American Psychological Association, & National Council on Measurement in Education, 2014). For example, future research could compare the PITC PARS with additional measures of infant and toddler care quality, such as the CLASS. Future research also might consider whether the PITC PARS can meaningfully assess varying levels of quality and predict child outcomes. The extent to which the PITC PARS can detect varying levels of quality and predict child outcomes will shed light on its usefulness in policy contexts concerned with improving child care quality. Because the PITC PARS assesses the full breadth of infant and toddler child care quality, it may be particularly useful in research to study how different dimensions of quality relate to children's developmental outcomes. As measures of infant and toddler care quality continue to be developed and refined, future research needs to study the relationships between measures and identify which ones best apply in different practice, policy, and research contexts.

Funding

This research was supported in part by contracts with the California Department of Education.

References

American Academy of Pediatrics. (2002). *Caring for our children: National health and safety performance standards: Guidelines for out-of-home child care programs* (2nd ed.). Elk Grove Village, IL: Author.

American Academy of Pediatrics Task Force on Infant Feeding and SIDS. (2000). Changing concepts of sudden infant death syndrome: Implications for infant sleeping environment and sleep position. *Pediatrics, 105,* 650–656. doi:10.1542/peds.105.3.650

American Educational Research Association, American Psychological Association, & National Council on Measurement in Education. (2014). *The standards for educational and psychological testing.* Washington, DC: AERA Publications.

Arndt, J. S., & McGuire-Schwartz, M. E. (2008). Early childhood school success: Recognizing families as integral partners. *Childhood Education, 84,* 281–285. doi:10.1080/00094056.2008.10523025

Arnett, J. (1989). Caregivers in day-care centers: Does training matter? *Journal of Applied Developmental Psychology, 10,* 541–552. doi:10.1016/0193-3973(89)90026-9

Bisceglia, R., Perlman, M., Schaak, D., & Jenkins, J. (2009). Examining the psychometric properties of the Infant-Toddler Environment Rating Scale-Revised edition in a high stakes context. *Early Childhood Research Quarterly, 24,* 121–132. doi:10.1016/j.ecresq.2009.02.001

Blau, D. M. (2000). The production of quality in child-care centers: Another look. *Applied Developmental Science, 4,* 136–148. doi:10.1207/S1532480XADS0403_3

Bornstein, M., & Bornstein, H. (1995). Caregiver's responsiveness and cognitive development. In P. L. Mangione (Ed.), *Infant/toddler caregiving: A guide to learning and cognitive development* (pp. 12–21). Sacramento: California Department of Education.

Bransford, J. D., Brown, A. L., & Cocking, R. R. (2000). *How people learn: Brain, mind, experience, and school.* Washington, DC: National Academies Press.

Burchinal, M., Cryer, D., Clifford, R., & Howes, C. (2002). Caregiver training and classroom quality in child care centers. *Applied Developmental Science, 6,* 2–11. doi:10.1207/S1532480XADS0601_01

Burchinal, M., Roberts, J. E., Nabors, L. A., & Bryant, D. M. (1996). Quality of center child care and infant cognitive and language development. *Child Development, 67,* 606–620. doi:10.2307/1131835

Burchinal, M., Roberts, J. E., Riggins, R., Ziesel, S. A., Neebe, E., & Bryant, D. (2000). Relating quality of center-based child care to early cognitive and language development longitudinally. *Child Development, 71,* 339–357. doi:10.1111/cdev.2000.71.issue-2

California Department of Education. (2006). *Infant/toddler learning and development program guidelines.* Sacramento, CA: Author.

California Department of Education. (2009). *Inclusion works! Creating child care programs that promote belonging for children with special needs.* Sacramento, CA: Author.

Campbell, P. H., & Milbourne, S. A. (2005). Improving the quality of infant-toddler care through professional development. *Topics in Early Childhood Special Education, 25,* 3–14. doi:10.1177/02711214050250010101

Cassidy, J., & Shaver, P. R. (2008). *Handbook of attachment: Theory, research, and clinical applications* (2nd ed.). New York, NY: Guilford Press.

Child Trends. (2009). *What we know and don't know about measuring quality in early childhood and school-age care and education settings.* Washington, DC: Author.

Clarke-Stewart, K. A., & Allhusen, V. D. (2002). Nonparental caregiving. In M. H. Bornstein (Ed.), *Handbook of parenting: Being and becoming a parent* (Vol. 3, pp. 215–252). Mahwah, NJ: Erlbaum.

Cohen, J. (1988). *Statistical power analysis for the behavioral sciences* (2nd ed.). Hillsdale, NJ: Erlbaum.

Curtis, D., & Carter, M. (2003). *Designs for living and learning: Transforming early childhood environment.* St. Paul, MN: Redleaf Press.

Dickinson, D. K., & Tabors, P. O. (2001). *Beginning literacy with language: Young children learning at home and school.* Baltimore, MD: Brookes.

Doherty, G., Forer, B., Lero, D. S., Goelman, H., & LaGrange, A. (2006). Predictors of quality in family child care. *Early Childhood Research Quarterly, 21,* 296–312. doi:10.1016/j.ecresq.2006.07.006

Elicker, J., Ruprecht, K., & Anderson, T. (2014). Observing infants' and toddlers' relationships and interactions in group care. In L. J. Harrison & J. Sumison (Eds.), *Lived spaces of infant-toddler education and care* (pp. 131–145). Dordrecht, The Netherlands: Springer Netherlands.

Essa, E. L. (2003). *Introduction to early childhood education* (4th ed.). Clifton Park, NY: Thomson Delmar Learning.

Field, A. (2009). *Discovering statistics using SPSS* (3rd ed.). Los Angeles, CA: Sage.

Forry, N., Iruka, I., Tout, K., Torquati, J., Susman-Stillman, A., Bryant, D., & Daneri, M. P. (2013). Predictors of quality and child outcomes in family child care settings. *Early Childhood Research Quarterly, 28,* 893–904. doi:10.1016/j.ecresq.2013.05.006

Fowler, W., Ogston, K., Roberts-Fiati, G., & Swenson, A. (1997). The effects of enriching language in infancy on the early and later development of competence. *Early Child Development and Care, 135,* 41–77. doi:10.1080/0300443971350105

Frost, J. L., Wortham, S. C., & Reifel, S. (2008). *Play and child development.* Upper Saddle River, NJ: Merrill Prentice Hall.

Hale, C. M., & Polder, J. A. (1997). *The ABCs of safe and healthy child care: A handbook for child care providers.* Washington, DC: Centers for Disease Control and Prevention.

Halle, T., Anderson, R., Blasberg, A., Chrisler, A., & Simkin, S. (2011). *Quality of Caregiver-Child Interactions for Infants and Toddlers (Q-CCIIT): A review of the literature.* Washington, DC: Administration for Children and Families.

Halle, T., Vick Whittaker, J., & Anderson, R. (2010). *Quality in early childhood care and education: A compendium of measures* (2nd ed.). Washington, DC: Child Trends.

Harms, T., & Clifford, R. M. (1989). *Family Day Care Rating Scale.* New York, NY: Teachers College Press.

Harms, T., Clifford, R. M., & Cryer, D. (1998). *Early Childhood Environment Rating Scale-Revised edition.* New York, NY: Teachers College Press.

Harms, T., Cryer, D., & Clifford, R. M. (2003). *The Infant/Toddler Environment Rating Scale-Revised edition.* New York, NY: Teachers College Press.

Harms, T., Cryer, D., & Clifford, R. M. (2007). *Family Child Care Environment Rating Scale-Revised edition.* New York, NY: Teachers College Press.

Harper-Browne, C., & Raikes, H. A. (2012). *Essential elements of quality infant-toddler programs.* Retrieved from the University of Minnesota, Center for Early Education and Development, website: http://www.cehd.umn.edu/ceed/projects/essentialelements/EssentialElementsOfInfantsAndToddlersReportNov2012.pdf

Helburn, S., Culkin, M. L., Morris, J., Mocan, N., Howes, C., Phillipsen, L. C., & Rustici, J. (1995). *Cost, quality, and child outcomes in child care centers: Executive summary.* Denver, CO: University of Colorado at Denver.

Hirsh-Pasek, K., & Burchinal, M. (2006). Mother and caregiver sensitivity over time: Predicting language and academic outcomes with variable- and person-centered approaches. *Merrill-Palmer Quarterly, 52*, 449–485.

Howes, C. (1997). Teacher sensitivity, children's attachment and play with peers. *Early Education & Development, 8*, 41–49. doi:10.1207/s15566935eed0801_4

Howes, C., Burchinal, M., Pianta, R., Bryant, D., Early, D., Clifford, R., & Barbarin, O. (2008). Ready to learn? Children's pre-academic achievement in pre-kindergarten programs. *Early Childhood Research Quarterly, 23*, 27–50. doi:10.1016/j.ecresq.2007.05.002

Howes, C., & Hamilton, C. E. (1992). Children's relationships with child care teachers: Stability and concordance with parental attachments. *Child Development, 63*, 867–878. doi:10.2307/1131239

Howes, C., Matheson, C. C., & Hamilton, C. E. (1994). Maternal, teacher, and child care history correlates of children's relationships with peers. *Child Development, 65*, 264–273. doi:10.2307/1131380

Howes, C., Phillips, D. A., & Whitebook, M. (1992). Thresholds of quality: Implications for the social development of children in center-based child care. *Child Development, 63*, 449–460. doi:10.2307/1131491

Howes, C., & Spieker, S. (2008). Attachment relationships in the context of multiple caregivers. In J. Cassidy & P. R. Shaver (Eds.), *Handbook of attachment: Theory, research, and clinical applications* (2nd ed., pp. 317–332). New York, NY: Guilford Press.

Howes, C., Whitebook, M., & Phillips, D. (1992). Teacher characteristics and effective teaching in child care: Findings from the National Child Care Staffing Study. *Child and Youth Care Forum, 21*, 399–414. doi:10.1007/BF00757371

Hughes-Belding, K., Hegland, S., Stein, A., Sideris, J., & Bryant, D. (2012). Predictors of global quality in family child care homes: Structural and belief characteristics. *Early Education & Development, 23*, 697–712. doi:10.1080/10409289.2011.574257

Jamison, K. R., Cabell, S. Q., LoCasale-Crouch, J., Hamre, B., & Pianta, R. (2014). CLASS-Infant: An observational measure for assessing teacher-infant interactions in center-based child care. *Early Education & Development, 25*, 553–572. doi:10.1080/10409289.2013.822239

Jung, E., Molfese, V. J., Beswick, J., Jacobi-Vessels, J., & Molnar, A. (2009). Growth of cognitive skills in preschoolers: Impact of sleep habits and learning-related behaviors. *Early Education & Development, 20*, 713–731. doi:10.1080/10409280802206890

Kreader, J. L., Ferguson, D., & Lawrence, S. (2005). *Infant and toddler child care quality.* Alhambra, CA: National Center for Children in Poverty.

Kriener-Althen, K., & Mangione, P. L. (2007). *Monitoring PITC partners for quality training and technical assistance.* Sausalito, CA: WestEd Center for Child and Family Studies.

Lally, J. R. (2010). School readiness begins in infancy. *Phi Delta Kappan, 92*(3), 17–21. doi:10.1177/003172171009200305

Lally, J. R., & Mangione, P. L. (2006). The uniqueness of infancy demands a responsive approach to care. *Young Children, 61*(4), 14–20.

Lally, J. R., Torres, Y., & Phelps, P. (1994). Caring for infants and toddlers in groups: Necessary considerations for emotional, social, and cognitive development. *Zero to Three, 14*(5), 1–11.

Lamb, M. E., & Ahnert, L. (2006). Nonparental child care: Context, concepts, correlates, and consequences. In K. A. Renninger, I. E. Sigel, W. Damon, & R. M. Lerner (Eds.), *Handbook of child psychology* (Vol. 4, 6th ed., pp. 950–1016). Hoboken, NJ: Wiley.

La Paro, K. M., Hamre, B. K., & Pianta, R. C. (2012). *Classroom Assessment Scoring System (CLASS) manual-toddler.* Baltimore, MD: Brookes.

Layzer, J. I., & Goodson, B. D. (2006). The "quality" of early care and education settings: Definitional and measurement issues. *Evaluation Review, 30*, 556–576. doi:10.1177/0193841X06291524

Legendre, A. (1995). The effects of environmentally modulated visual accessibility to caregivers on early peer interactions. *International Journal of Behavioral Development, 18*, 297–313. doi:10.1177/016502549501800207

Legendre, A. (2003). Environmental features influencing toddlers' bioemotional reactions in day care centers. *Environment & Behavior, 35*, 523–549. doi:10.1177/0013916503035004005

Loeb, S., Fuller, B., Kagan, S. L., & Carrol, B. (2004). Child care in poor communities: Early learning effects of type, quality, and stability. *Child Development, 75*, 47–65. doi:10.1111/cdev.2004.75.issue-1

Mangione, P. L. (1990). A comprehensive approach to using video for training infant and toddler caregivers. *Infants & Young Children, 3*, 61–68. doi:10.1097/00001163-199007000-00009

Mangione, P. L. (2003). *Impact of PITC training on quality of infant/toddler care.* Sausalito, CA: WestEd Center for Child and Family Studies.

Margetts, K. (2005). Responsive caregiving: Reducing the stress in infant toddler care. *International Journal of Early Childhood, 37,* 77–84. doi:10.1007/BF03165748

Mashburn, A. J., Pianta, R. C., Hamre, B. K., Downer, J. T., Barbarin, O. A., Bryant, D., ... Howes, C. (2008). Measures of classroom quality in prekindergarten and children's development of academic, language, and social skills. *Child Development, 79,* 732–749. doi:10.1111/j.1467-8624.2008.01154.x

Moon, R. Y., Patel, K. M., & Shaefer, S. M. (2000). Sudden infant death syndrome in child care settings. *Pediatrics, 106,* 295–300. doi:10.1542/peds.106.2.295

National Child Care Information and Technical Assistance Center. (2009). *Research and standards on child-staff ratios and group size.* Washington, DC: Author.

National Institute of Child Health and Human Development Early Child Care Research Network. (1996). Characteristics of infant child care: Factors contributing to positive caregiving. *Early Childhood Research Quarterly, 11,* 296–306.

National Institute of Child Health and Human Development Early Child Care Research Network. (2000). The relation of child care to cognitive and language development. *Child Development, 71,* 960–980.

National Institute of Child Health and Human Development Early Child Care Research Network. (2002). Early child care and children's development prior to school entry: Results from the NICHD Study of Early Child Care. *American Educational Research Journal, 39,* 133–164. doi:10.3102/00028312039001133

National Resource Center for Health and Safety in Child Care. (2002). *Caring for our children: National health and safety performance standards guidelines for out-of-home child care* (2nd ed.). Denver, CO: Author.

Nicholas, H., Lightbown, P. M., & Spada, N. (2001). Recasts as feedback to language learners. *Language Learning, 51,* 719–758. doi:10.1111/lang.2001.51.issue-4

O'Callaghan, F. V., Al Mamun, A., O'Callaghan, M., Clavarino, A., Williams, G. M., Bor, W., ... Najman, J. M. (2010). The link between sleep problems in infancy and early childhood and attention problems at 5 and 14 years: Evidence from a birth cohort study. *Early Human Development, 86,* 419–424. doi:10.1016/j.earlhumdev.2010.05.020

Odom, S. L., & McEvoy, M. A. (1990). Mainstreaming at the preschool level: Potential barriers and tasks for the field. *Topics in Early Childhood Special Education, 10,* 48–61. doi:10.1177/027112149001000205

Paulsell, D., Tout, K., & Maxwell, K. L. (2013). Evaluating implementation of quality rating and improvement systems. In T. Halle, A. Metz, & I. Martinez-Beck (Eds.), *Applying implementation science in early childhood programs and systems* (pp. 269–293). Baltimore, MD: Brookes.

Pavia, L. S., & Da Ros, D. (1997). Choice: A powerful tool in caring for toddlers. *Early Childhood Education Journal, 25,* 67–69. doi:10.1023/A:1025646217709

Peck, C. A., Carlson, P., & Helmsetter, E. (1992). Parent and teacher perceptions of outcomes for typically developing children enrolled in integrated early childhood programs: A statewide survey. *Journal of Early Intervention, 16,* 53–63. doi:10.1177/105381519201600105

Phillips, D., Mekos, D., Scarr, S., McCartney, K., & Abbott-Shim, M. (2000). Within and beyond the classroom door: Assessing quality in child care centers. *Early Childhood Research Quarterly, 15,* 475–496. doi:10.1016/S0885-2006(01)00077-1

Phillips, D., Voran, M., Kisker, E., Howes, C., & Whitebook, M. (1994). Child care for children in poverty: Opportunity or inequity? *Child Development, 65,* 472–492. doi:10.2307/1131397

Pungello, E. P., & Kurtz-Costes, B. (1999). Why and how working women choose child care: A review with a focus on infancy. *Developmental Review, 19,* 31–96. doi:10.1006/drev.1998.0468

Raikes, H. A. (1993). Relationship duration in infant care: Time with high-ability teacher and infant-teacher attachment. *Early Childhood Research Quarterly, 8,* 309–325. doi:10.1016/S0885-2006(05)80070-5

Raikes, H., Luze, G., Brooks-Gunn, J., Raikes, H. A., Pan, B. A., Tamis-LeMonda, C. S., & Rodriguez, E. T. (2006). Mother-child bookreading in low-income families: Correlates and outcomes during the first three years of life. *Child Development, 77,* 924–953. doi:10.1111/j.1467-8624.2006.00911.x

Risley, T. R., & Hart, B. (2006). Promoting early language development. In N. F. Watt, F. Ayoub, R. H. Bradley, J. E. Puma, & W. A. Leboeuf (Eds.), *The crisis in youth mental health: Critical issues and effective programs* (Vol. 4, pp. 83–88). Westport, CT: Praeger.

Sandstrom, H., Moodie, S., & Halle, T. (2011). Beyond classroom-based measures for preschoolers: Addressing the gaps in measures for home-based care and care for infants and toddlers. In M. Zaslow, I. Martinez-Beck, K. Tout, & T. Halle (Eds.), *Quality measurement in early childhood settings* (pp. 317–343). Baltimore, MD: Brookes.

Scher, A. (2005). Infant sleep at 10 months of age as a window to cognitive development. *Early Human Development, 81,* 289–292. doi:10.1016/j.earlhumdev.2004.07.005

Schmit, S., & Matthews, H. (2013). *Better for babies: A study of state infant and toddler child care policies.* Washington, DC: Center for Law and Social Policy.

Shonkoff, J. P., & Phillips, D. A. (2000). *From neurons to neighborhoods: The science of early childhood development.* Washington, DC: National Academies Press.

Shore, R. (1997). *Rethinking the brain: New insights into early development.* New York, NY: Families and Work Institute.

Siren-Tiusanen, H., & Robinson, H. A. (2001). Nap schedules and sleep practices in infant-toddler groups. *Early Childhood Research Quarterly, 16*, 453–474. doi:10.1016/S0885-2006(01)00119-3

Smart Start Evaluation Team. (2000). *Caregiver Interaction Scale Arnett, 1989*. Retrieved from the Frank Porter Graham Child Development Institute website: http://fpg.unc.edu/sites/fpg.unc.edu/files/resources/assessments-and-instruments/SmartStart_Tool6_CIS.pdf

Spruyt, K., Aitken, R. J., So, K., Charlton, M., Adamson, T. M., & Horne, R. S. (2008). Relationship between sleep/wake patterns, temperament and overall development in term infants over the first year of life. *Early Human Development, 84*, 289–296. doi:10.1016/j.earlhumdev.2007.07.002

Thomason, A. C., & La Paro, K. M. (2009). Measuring the quality of teacher-child interactions in toddler child care. *Early Education & Development, 20*, 285–304. doi:10.1080/10409280902773351

Torelli, L. (2002). Enhancing development through classroom design in Early Head Start. *Children and Families, 16*(2), 44–51.

Torelli, L., & Durrett, C. (2001). Landscape for learning: The impact of classroom design on infants and toddlers. Retrieved from the *Early Childhood News* website: http://www.earlychildhoodnews.com/earlychildhood/article_view.aspx?ArticleID=238

Tout, K., Zaslow, M., Halle, T., & Forry, N. (2009). *Issues for the next decade of quality rating and improvement systems*. Washington, DC: Child Trends.

Vandell, D. L., Belsky, J., Burchinal, M., Steinberg, L., & Vandergrift, N. (2010). Do effects of early child care extend to age 15 years? Results from the NICHD Study of Early Child Care and Youth Development. *Child Development, 81*, 737–756. doi:10.1111/cdev.2010.81.issue-3

Zaslow, M., Tout, K., & Halle, T. (2011). Differing purposes for measuring quality in early childhood settings: Aligning purpose with procedures. In M. Zaslow, I. Martinez-Beck, K. Tout, & T. Halle (Eds.), *Quality measurement in early childhood settings* (pp. 389–410). Baltimore, MD: Brookes.

Zaslow, M., Tout, K., & Martinez-Beck, I. (2010). *Measuring quality of early care and education programs at the intersection of research, policy, and practice*. Washington, DC: Administration for Children and Families.

Zellman, G. L., & Karoly, L. A. (2014). Improving QRISs through the use of existing data: A virtual pilot of the California QRIS. *Early Childhood Research Quarterly, 30*(Part B), 241–254.

Zero to Three. (2008). *Caring for infants and toddlers in groups* (2nd ed.). Washington, DC: National Center for Infants, Toddlers, and Families.

A Mixed Methods Investigation of Maternal Perspectives on Transition Experiences in Early Care and Education

Rebecca Anne Swartz, Katherine Elizabeth Speirs, Amy Johnson Encinger, and Nancy L. McElwain

ABSTRACT

Research Findings: Strong relationships among children, families, and early care and education (ECE) providers are key to quality infant–toddler care. These relationships are shaped during the initial transition period to group care. We used a mixed methods approach to (a) assess maternal perspectives on the transition to group care, (b) explore mothers' perceptions of factors that made for easy or difficult transitions, and (c) examine associations between maternal and child characteristics and the ease of the transition. Through qualitative interviews, mothers identified factors that played a role in their child's transition, including the child's age, the ECE provider's support, and the number of transitions the child experienced. For mothers, an easy transition was characterized by ease of child adjustment to group care, comfort with nonparental care and returning to work, and being able to exercise some control over the transition. Quantitative analyses revealed that an easy child transition was associated with younger child age, low maternal distress reactions to child distress, and low child social fearfulness. Higher maternal depressive symptoms and maternal distress reactions to child distress were associated with mothers having a difficult transition. *Practice or Policy*: Implications of the findings for ECE provider training and ECE policy development related to transitions are discussed.

In the United States, child care provided by nonparental caregivers in group settings has become a common experience for infants, toddlers, and their families. In 2005, the National Household Education Survey indicated that nonparental care arrangements were utilized by families of 42% of infants younger than the age of 1 year, 53% of 1-year-olds, and 73% of 2-year-olds (Halle et al., 2009). Accumulating research points toward the importance of *high-quality* care in promoting positive child outcomes as well as fostering economic stability for families (Belsky et al., 2007; Forry et al., 2013; National Institute of Child Health and Human Development Early Child Care Research Network, 2004; Phillips, McCartney, & Sussman, 2006). Strong relationships among parents, children, and early care and education (ECE) providers are an essential component of high-quality care (Baker & Manfredi-Petitt, 2004; Honig, 2002). For instance, children who experience warm and secure relationships with their ECE providers show more positive developmental trajectories in cognitive, social, and emotional domains and greater success as they enter the primary grades (Ahnert, Pinquart, & Lamb, 2006; Kryzer, Kovan, Phillips, Domagall, & Gunnar, 2007; Peisner-Feinberg et al., 2001). One context in which strong parent–provider and provider–child relationships are formed is during the initial transitions to the group care setting. During these transitions, ECE providers, parents, and children are communicating, learning about one another, and laying a foundation for future interactions. These moments are foundational in shaping relationships that promote positive child and family trajectories in the ECE years and merit closer investigation (Fiese, Eckert, & Spagnola, 2006; Knopf & Swick, 2007).

The strategies that ECE providers use to support children and families (Bromer & Henly, 2009; Klein, Kraft, & Shohet, 2010) and the reasons parents choose particular child care arrangements are varied (Meyers & Jordan, 2006; Raikes, Torquati, Wang, & Shjegstad, 2012; Sosinsky & Kim, 2013) and may influence mothers' and children's experiences during the transition period. However, researchers know very little about mothers' understanding of the transition period and how individual differences in maternal and child functioning, especially in the affective domain, may shape transition experiences. Thus, the objectives of the current study were to (a) assess maternal perspectives of the ease or difficulty of the transition to child care for both the mother and her child, (b) explore mothers' perceptions about the factors that made for easy or difficult transitions, and (c) assess the extent to which maternal and child characteristics were related to maternal perceptions of the ease or difficulty of the transition experience.

Transitions in ECE settings

In the United States much of the discourse related to educational transitions focuses on the transition to formal schooling (Ladd & Price, 1987; Rimm-Kaufman, Pianta, & Cox, 2000; Rous, Hallam, McCormick, & Cox, 2010). Readiness for kindergarten is clearly important, yet success during this transition period may rest in part on the foundation that is laid by earlier experiences in ECE settings (Kontos & Wilcox-Herzog, 1997; Peisner-Feinberg et al., 2001). Furthermore, the ECE transition experience of infants and toddlers needs to be considered in the context of the rapid and immense development of physical, emotional, and social capacities over the first years of life (Brownell & Kopp, 2010). The development of these capacities is embedded in the child's close relationships with primary caregivers, especially the mother. Moreover, of particular relevance to ECE transitions is that the infant's negative emotions are coregulated in the context of face-to-face interactions with the mother. These mutually regulated interactions form the building blocks of the child's regulatory capacities and provide a foundation for subsequent social and emotional development (Sroufe, 1996; Tronick, 1989). By the end of the first year, the child–mother attachment relationship has fully emerged, and this development coincides with the infant's increased separation anxiety from the mother and wariness of strangers (see Cassidy, 2008; Sroufe, 1996). Therefore, we situate our investigation of maternal perspectives of the ECE transition in the context of these developmental themes that may be especially salient for mothers of infants and toddlers.

Although standards from the National Association for the Education of Young Children and Head Start call attention to the importance of family participation in planning for successful transitions into child care (Copple & Bredekamp, 2009; Head Start Program Performance Standards, 2009), the U.S. ECE community may benefit from a better understanding of the ways in which families perceive the transition to ECE and the related challenges and opportunities this transition presents. More targeted investigations of these experiences could strengthen ECE provider training and increase providers' success in supporting families during ECE transitions.

With this objective in mind, we look to practices from other countries, in which approaches to transitioning infants and toddlers into group care settings are more clearly articulated. In the municipal child care centers in Italy, for instance, the time period of transitioning to child care is known as *inserimento*, which is loosely translated as the period of "settling in" (Bove, 2001). In this approach, time is provided for families to gradually transition their child into the care setting, and the focus is on welcoming the family and building new relationships. The relationship between the child's family and nonfamilial caregivers is also a key component of *inserimento*, as these relationships lay a foundation for partnerships that are seen as essential for promoting the child's development. Each family's *inserimento* unfolds in a unique narrative, and such diversity of experiences is valued and expected. A great emphasis is placed on the image of the child in the Italian centers; for example, the teachers providing care devote energy and time to representing the child through documentation in photos, narratives, and other media. Because there is a strong emphasis on the child being rooted within the relationship context of the family and neighborhood, these aspects of the child's life are reflected within this documentation. The documentation of the child's experience within and outside the child care center in turn creates a space for shared communication and dialogue about the child and family's experience transitioning into the center and becoming a part of the center's community of families. This documentation is part of the curricular practice and is located in places for the adults and children to see and dialogue about during daily routines. This process is intended to help families and children feel valued and supported during their transition to, and time in, the center.

Likewise, in New Zealand, the focus of the transition period is on understanding the child and family's unique experience as they together discover new physical and social spaces in the child care setting. The family is considered a critical partner in the child care setting, and clearly articulated practices for transitioning children into the care setting are used and stated in the national ECE guidelines (Carr & May, 1993; Dalli, 1999; Jovanovic, 2011; New Zealand Ministry of Education, 1996). In particular, the national guidelines frame the transition period as a time when young children are actively learning about the relationship-building process (Dalli, 2000). As in the programs of Italy, there is great emphasis on the child and family belonging to the community of the child care center. A clear definition of belonging is articulated in the guidelines for ECE from the Ministry of Education. The definition refers to children and families gaining a sense of security and valuing the contributions they will bring to the community of the child care center that will lay a foundation for the child's future contribution to the community at large. The guidelines emphasize the importance of families and children seeing the child care center as embedded within the wider community, becoming comfortable with the routines of the child care setting, and feeling that they have a place in the center as full participants. The learning guidelines also state specific age-appropriate practices for child care providers to use within their settings to create these communities in which children and families can experience belonging. The guidelines articulate best practices for various age groups as well as reflection questions to assist child care providers in evaluating their own practices. In sum, the relationally focused perspectives of Italy and New Zealand that value the unique narratives of families and their experiences shaped the current study. We aimed to assess mothers' perspectives of the transition period, as well as factors that may be associated with the ease or difficulty of the transition, so that our findings might be used to inform articulation of transition practices in U.S. policy and practice statements in the future.

Maternal and child characteristics as correlates of transition experiences

The ease or difficulty of the transition to group care is likely influenced by a variety of factors related to the child, mother, family situation, and ECE caregiving setting (Swartz & Easterbrooks, 2014). Transitioning to child care can be an emotional time for both parents and children. Thus, our study was guided by Dix's (1991) model of the affective organization of parenting. This model focuses on cognitive and emotional factors that influence parents' responses to children's emotions and, in doing so, outlines a complex, multidirectional process in which parents and children exercise mutual influence on each other's experience and expression of emotions. In this study, we focused on the extent to which the child's temperamental characteristics (i.e., social fearfulness, anger proneness, and pleasure) and the mother's emotional functioning (i.e., maternal depressive symptoms, maternal general personal distress, and maternal distress in the face of child distress) were associated with whether the transition was easy or difficult for the child as well as for the mother.

Child temperament has emerged as an important predictor of children's ease or difficulty in settling into a new child care arrangement. In particular, higher levels of teacher-reported social fearfulness have been associated with cortisol elevation in toddlers in child care settings (Watamura, Donzella, Alwin, & Gunnar, 2003), and anger proneness has been associated with lower social competence among children in preschool classrooms (Diener & Kim, 2004). In contrast, children with "easy" temperaments tend to experience smoother transitions to center-based care, lower levels of problem behaviors, and greater well-being (Ahnert, Gunnar, Lamb, & Barthel, 2004; Crockenberg, 2003; De Schipper, Tavecchio, Van IJzendoorn, & Van Zeijl, 2004; Phillips, Fox, & Gunnar, 2011). Dix (1991) also considered child temperament and its contribution to *parental* feelings and behavior in emotionally challenging parent–child interactions, such as those that might occur during the period of transition to child care. Emotions are elicited when the child and parent experience separation and reunion as part of the child care day. We therefore examined the degree to which aspects of the child's temperament were related to the mother's perceptions of the child's and mother's ease or difficulty during the transition period.

Maternal emotional functioning may also influence the ease or difficulty of transitioning to the child care setting. Greater maternal distress in the face of child emotional distress has been associated with less supportive responses to children's emotional displays (Clark, Kochanska, & Ready, 2000; Wong, McElwain, & Halberstadt, 2009) and lower levels of child social competence (Fabes, Poulin, Eisenberg, & Madden-Derdich, 2002). Maternal depressive symptoms have also been associated with lower levels of sensitivity to young children as well as lower levels of socioemotional functioning among infants and toddlers (Gravener et al., 2012; Huang, Lewin, Mitchell, & Zhang, 2012; Miklush & Connelly, 2013). These factors may further intensify the difficulty that the mother and child experience during the transition to child care because depressive symptoms may inhibit the mother's ability to support her child's emotional experience and emerging emotional competence (Kujawa et al., 2014). In light of these findings, we examined the mother's personal distress in response to others' distress—both to general others and specifically to her child's negative emotions—and maternal depressive symptoms as correlates of the child's and the mother's ease or difficulty in the transition to child care.

The current study

The current study aimed to illuminate the experience of the initial transition period into group care for mothers and their young children by drawing on conceptualizations of the transition period found in the literatures from Italy and New Zealand (Gandini & Edwards, 2001; New Zealand Ministry of Education, 1996) as well as Dix's (1991) model of the affective organization of parenting. We defined the initial transition period as the first weeks and months after a child began attending a nonparental care arrangement. For families who had used more than one nonparental care arrangement, we considered the child's initial transition period for each care arrangement that the mother described. In general, the mothers in our sample also discussed the daily transitions into and out of the place where care was provided as well as their feelings about using nonparental care.

We used a mixed methods approach in which both quantitative and qualitative data were examined. A mixed methods approach was well suited for addressing the aims of this study. We used a qualitative approach to explore mothers' perceptions of the transition period because there are no existing quantitative measures and because this is an understudied area that would benefit from the identification of core constructs. We assessed maternal and child characteristics using established and psychometrically sound measures of maternal depressive symptoms, maternal personal distress, and child temperament. Taking a quantitative approach in this way allowed us to make connections between our qualitative assessments of mothers' perspectives on the transition to child care and larger bodies of literature on maternal and child emotional functioning, thereby providing insight into how mothers' understanding of their transition experience may be related to established concepts.

We utilized a convergence design to allow qualitative interview data and quantitative questionnaire data to simultaneously co-inform our understanding of the transition to child care (Creswell & Plano Clark, 2007). In this design, the qualitative and quantitative data were collected at the same time point. During the analysis phase, each type of data was analyzed separately. The findings from the qualitative data were then examined in conjunction with the quantitative data to provide a more complete picture of the experiences of our participants. In short, bringing together mothers' understanding of the transition period with well-established quantitative assessments of commonly studied maternal and child characteristics enabled us to draw a rich picture of the diverse experiences of individual families and better understand congruencies and differences between group-level trends and individual family experiences (Yoshikawa, Weisner, Kalil, & Way, 2008).

Method

Participants

The data for this study came from a larger study of parent–toddler relationships. A total of 66 mother–child dyads from a mid-size midwestern city volunteered to participate in the current study. Families were recruited via informational flyers distributed through local organizations and child care centers as well as through online announcements and were eligible to participate if they had a toddler-age child who was in nonmaternal care for at least 10 hr per week. Three mothers were missing data on the maternal interview because of technical difficulties. Thus, this article is based on data from 63 families.

Procedure overview

Mother–child dyads participated in a 90-min visit to a university laboratory that resembled a home environment (e.g., living room, dining area, and functional kitchen). Dyads were observed for approximately 1 hr during a series of interactive tasks (e.g., play and clean-up session; see Emery, McElwain, Groh, Haydon, & Roisman, 2014, for further details). Following the mother–child tasks, the lead research assistant interviewed the mother about her perceptions of the child and his or her child care arrangements while a second research assistant administered social-cognitive and language assessments to the child. Mothers and fathers also independently completed a series of parent questionnaires, including items capturing child temperament and parental emotional functioning. For this article, data from the maternal interview session and parent questionnaires were examined.

Maternal interview

Interview protocol and procedure

The semistructured interview protocol included 14 open-ended questions about the mother–child relationship and the child's transition into and experiences in child care setting(s). For this article, we examined maternal responses to six questions about child care that were designed specifically for the current study and informed by prior literatures on the affective processes of parenting (Dix, 1991) and child care transitions (Gandini & Edwards, 2001) as well as the first author's professional experience working with families in toddler programs. Each mother was asked about (a) her current child care arrangement, (b) her child's first days and weeks in the child care setting, (c) what a typical drop-off or pick-up time was like for her and her child, (d) how the mother felt during her child's transition to care, (e) communication with the child's ECE provider, and (f) advice the mother would give to other families about starting child care. Probes were used to encourage mothers to elaborate on emotions (their own and their child's) and thoughts during the transition time as well as to gain greater depth about contextual details of the care arrangement and family situation (Rubin & Rubin, 2005). Interviews were digitally recorded, and verbatim transcripts of the entire interview protocol were completed by trained research assistants and checked for accuracy. Three research assistants were engaged in transcription and received intensive training and practice before completing official transcripts of the interviews. Rules for verbatim transcription indicated that every word spoken by both the interviewer and interviewee should be transcribed exactly, including stammering, indications of assent or dissent (e.g., "mm-hmm"), and placeholders. All transcripts were checked (and checked a second time, if revisions were needed) by an advanced research assistant with more than 5 years of experience carrying out transcription and coding of interview protocols to ensure accuracy and adherence to the transcription guidelines.

Parent questionnaires

Maternal depressive symptoms
Mothers completed the Center for Epidemiological Studies–Depression scale (Radloff, 1977). The scale consists of 20 items, and mothers rated the frequency of depressive symptoms experienced during the past week on a 4-point scale ranging from 0 (*less than once a week*) to 3 (*5 to 7 days a week*). Items were summed (with reverse-scoring as appropriate) to create a total depressive symptoms score ($\alpha = .85$). The Center for Epidemiological Studies–Depression scale has good reliability and validity and is widely used as a measure of depressive symptoms among community samples (Radloff, 1977).

Maternal personal distress
Two subscales captured mothers' feelings of personal distress. First, a 7-item personal distress subscale from the Interpersonal Reactivity Index (Davis, 1994) assessed the mother's feelings of distress in response to others' distress generally (e.g., "When I see someone who badly needs help in an emergency, I go to pieces"). Items were rated on a 5-point scale ranging from 0 (*does not describe me well*) to 4 (*describes me very well*), and a personal distress score was created by averaging ratings across items ($\alpha = .80$). We refer to this measure as *general personal distress*.

Second, a 12-item subscale from the Coping with Toddlers' Negative Emotions Scale (Spinrad, Eisenberg, Kupfer, Gaertner, & Michalik, 2004) captured the mother's distress reactions when her child displays negative emotions (e.g., "If my child is participating in some group activity with his/her friends and proceeds to make a mistake and then looks embarrassed and on the verge of tears, I would feel uncomfortable and embarrassed myself"). Items were rated on a 7-point scale ranging from 1 (*very unlikely*) to 7 (*very likely*). Items were averaged to create a composite score of *personal distress reactions to child's distress* ($\alpha = .73$). The measures of personal distress used in this study have each demonstrated acceptable levels of internal reliability, high test–retest reliability over several months, and good construct validity (Davis, 1994; Spinrad et al., 2004).

Child temperament
Mothers and fathers independently completed portions of the Toddler Behavior Assessment Questionnaire (Goldsmith, 1996). For this study, we examined data from three subscales: (a) anger proneness (e.g., "When it was time for bed or a nap and your child did not want to go, how often did s/he protest by crying loudly?" 19 items, $\alpha s = .88$ and $.87$, mothers and fathers, respectively), (b) social fearfulness (e.g., "If a stranger came to your home or your apartment, how often did your child cling or hold on to you and not want to let go?" 19 items, $\alpha s = .90$ and $.85$), and (c) pleasure (e.g., "When playing quietly with one of his/her favorite toys, how often did your child smile?" 19 items, $\alpha s = .86$ and $.84$). Parents rated how often in the past month their child had exhibited specific behaviors. Items were rated on a 7-point scale ranging from 1 (*never*) to 7 (*always*), and a "does not apply" response option was also available. Subscales were computed by averaging ratings (with reverse-scoring when appropriate) across items. Associations between mothers' and fathers' subscale scores were moderate to strong ($rs = .57, .58$, and $.26$, $ps < .05$, for anger, fear, and pleasure, respectively). To obtain more reliable measures of temperament, we computed a composite score for each subscale by averaging across mother and father reports. The Toddler Behavior Assessment Questionnaire has well-established reliability and validity, and Goldsmith (1996) reported substantial convergence between parental reports on this questionnaire and parent and teacher reports of other conceptually related child behaviors.

Analytic strategy

Phase 1: qualitative analyses classifying the cases for ease or difficulty of transition
Coding was conducted in two phases by the second and third authors. In the first phase, the coders each independently classified the transition to child care as easy or difficult for (a) the child and (b) the mother

for all interview protocols ($N = 63$). Given that our questions and probes aimed at capturing both the mother's and the child's transition experience, mothers typically evaluated the transition for themselves and their child separately. To make these classifications, the coders started with the mother's explicit evaluations of the transitions (i.e., if the mother described a transition using words such as *easy* or *difficult*, the transition was classified as such). If the mother did not explicitly describe the transition as easy or difficult, the coders classified it as *easy for the child* if the mother reported that the child (a) was excited to go to child care, (b) easily left the mother at drop off, and/or (c) cried at drop off for 2 weeks or less and the crying was not intense enough to upset the mother. The transition was classified as *difficult for the child* if the mother reported that the child (a) refused to go to child care or clung to the mother at drop off and/or (b) cried at drop off for more than 2 weeks or to a degree that upset the mother. Likewise, in the absence of an explicit description of the transition as easy or difficult, the coders classified the transition as *easy for the mother* if the mother reported feeling good about leaving her child with the ECE provider and/or excited about returning to work or not providing full-time care for her child. Transitions coded as *difficult for the mother* were those for which the mother reported distress after or in anticipation of leaving her child with the ECE provider.

The two coders reviewed the interview transcripts and independently coded all mothers and children as having either an easy or difficult transition. The two coders then compared their coding. When there were differences, the two coders, working together, reviewed the interview transcripts again and came to a consensus about whether the transitions should be classified as easy or difficult. During this process it was decided that a third code—"difficult at first"—should be added for the mothers. This code captured mothers who at first had trouble with their child's transition to child care but quickly became comfortable leaving their child with the ECE provider. This code was also assigned to mothers who anticipated that the transition would be difficult (and for this reason worried about it) but quickly found the actual transition to be easy.

Phase 2: qualitative analyses examining maternal perspectives

In the second phase of coding, the coders reviewed the interview transcripts for maternal statements describing why the transition to child care was easy or difficult for the mother and her child. This coding moved through three stages: open, axial, and selective coding (LaRossa, 2005). During open coding, the coders read through the transcripts and compiled a list of factors that made the transitions easy or difficult. For instance, some of the factors that made the transition easier for the child were the ECE provider holding the child, playing with the child, hugging the child, or providing an activity for the child.

During axial coding, the coders grouped the factors identified during open coding into categories, defined the categories, and determined the relations among them. Axial coding also involved moving back and forth between the codes and the interview data to test and revise the codes and deepen understanding of the data. For example, we grouped the open codes listed previously under a category labeled "ECE provider supports the child's transition" because all of these open codes described something the ECE provider did to ease the transition for the child. We divided the open codes under the category "ECE provider supports the child's transition" into two subcategories, "ECE provider distracts the child" and "ECE provider comforts the child," to describe the two ways the ECE provider supported the transition. We then returned to the data to ensure that our two subcategories fully captured what the ECE providers did to support the child's transition. In doing this we found that some of the mothers felt that their child's transition was easier because their ECE provider attempted to make the child's schedule at the center match his or her schedule at home. We added this as a third subcategory.

Finally, selective coding involved bringing together the categories that were created through axial coding to tell a coherent story (Daly, 2007). For instance, in the example described previously, we combined the category "ECE provider supports the child's transition" with two other categories to describe the factors that made the child's transition easy or difficult. The computer program NVivo 10 was used to organize coding.

Phase 3: quantitative analyses
We first assessed key demographic variables as potential covariates, and we examined intercorrelations among the measures of maternal emotional functioning and child temperament to assess the extent to which they were tapping distinct constructs. Next, a series of analysis of covariance (ANCOVA) models were tested to assess whether maternal emotional functioning and child temperament differed as a function of the child and maternal transition groups that emerged from the Phase 1 qualitative analyses.

Results

First, we present findings from the qualitative analysis of the maternal interview responses, in which the transition period was categorized as easy or difficult for both the child and the mother (or difficult at first for mothers only). Second, we present findings from the second phase of our qualitative analysis, in which we explored mothers' perceptions about why transitions were easy or difficult. Third, we present results from the quantitative analyses, in which we investigated differences in maternal and child transition groups (i.e., easy, difficult, difficult at first) on maternal (i.e., depressive symptoms and distress to others' distress) and child (i.e., child temperament) characteristics assessed via parent questionnaires.

Phase 1: qualitative analyses classifying the cases for ease or difficulty of transition

As a first step in the qualitative analyses, the interview protocols were each classified for the child's and the mother's ease or difficulty with the child's transition to child care. Among the children, 51 (80.9%) were classified as experiencing an easy transition and 12 (19.0%) were classified as experiencing a difficult transition (total $N = 63$). Among the mothers, 37 (58.7%) were classified as having an easy transition, 15 (23.8%) were classified as having a difficult transition, and 10 (15.9%) were classified as experiencing a difficult transition that became easier with time. In one case, the mother could not be categorized into one of the three groups because she described her experience as easy at first but then increasingly difficult. This case was dropped for the analyses involving the mother transition groups (total $N = 62$).

Phase 2: qualitative analyses examining maternal perspectives

We conducted our Phase 2 analyses of the interview data to explore maternal perceptions of the factors that made the child's transition to child care easy or difficult for the mother herself and for her child. In exploring mothers' descriptions of why the child had an easy or difficult transition, we found that mothers identified three main factors: the child's age, assistance from the child's ECE provider, and the number of transitions the child made.

The child's ease of transition
First, 30 mothers (48% of the sample[1]) suggested the importance of their child's age in determining how easily their child transitioned to nonparental care. For instance, several mothers reported that their child easily transitioned because the child was too young to be upset by being separated from his or her parents. Jessica[2] explained, "When we first did the day care in someone's home, totally easy. I forget what age she was, like 5 months. We handed her off and she didn't even notice." Conversely, some mothers felt that older children had trouble transitioning because they struggled with separation anxiety. When asked to describe her son's transition into child care, Carrie said, "When he was really little, I think he was okay. But then,

---

[1] Please note that the percentages in this section do not sum to 100% and represent only the proportion of mothers in the sample who stated a particular reason.
[2] All names used in this article are pseudonyms.

pretty quickly, when the separation anxiety did start up, we would always have a hard time on Mondays, after a weekend, or after a break." Other mothers reported that their children experienced more difficult transitions as they aged. Audra explained,

> He was 12 weeks old when he went into day care, thankfully it wasn't too traumatic for him ... he seemed to do fairly well ... he's always done well, but now that he's getting kind of old enough to understand, you know, Mom and Dad are leaving and things like that, we are going through, we're actually now going through a transition where he's not exactly keen on us leaving him at day care.

Second, 21 mothers (34%) commented that transitions were easy because the ECE provider did something to either distract or comfort their child while the mother was leaving in the morning. In response to a question about what her ECE providers did to support her daughter's transition into child care, Alison said,

> They were really good ... during the drop-off transition, they would try to find an activity for her to participate in, or they would hold her and give her some extra hugs while I was leaving ... Her old teachers would come and visit her in the toddler room ... They were on break or running an errand, they would just poke their heads in and visit with her for a few minutes and try to ease that transition so she was still seeing a familiar face.

In contrast, one mother reported that she wished her ECE providers would more actively engage her child when she was leaving in the morning to help ease the daily transition.

In addition, a few mothers reported that their child's transition was easy because their ECE provider attempted to make the child's schedule at the center match his or her schedule at home. Julie explained that her ECE provider asked for information about her daughter's schedule at home so she could replicate it:

> She had us stop by during the day before [Julie's daughter] started coming and got us the details about when she ate and how often, you know, how much, and would give me reports on what she did during the day and try to keep things as normal—as close to what they would be at home, her schedule and everything.

In these ways many of the mothers who felt their children had an easy transition saw their ECE providers as important partners in helping them transition their children.

Third, five of the mothers (8%) reported that their children had difficult transitions because they had to make multiple transitions. Haley reported,

> I think it is harder for [my daughter] because I'm a teacher so I would have my summers off. So she has a huge break in the summer and then she has to go back and so every year ... it's a whole process again.

For some mothers the initial transition into child care was easy for their child, but a change in classroom or caregiver within the center was more difficult. Tina explained,

> Since she's started they've had five new teachers in her classroom, but they've just now started to settle into one teacher who has been here for a while, she's getting to know her, getting to have a good time with her. For a while she was just kind of confused every day she would go in and there was a different teacher, different things going on.

Some mothers also felt their children struggled with multiple transitions when their children did not attend care every day of the week.

The mother's ease of transition
We also explored mothers' understanding of why child care transitions were easy or difficult for the mothers themselves. We identified four main factors that made the transition easier or more difficult.

First, for 18 of the mothers (29%), their experience transitioning their child to nonparental care was driven by how well their child adjusted to being in care. Mothers whose children had a difficult time also had a difficult transition. Danielle explained,

She's excited all the way there ... but as soon as we get there, she wraps her hands around whatever part of my body she can get to and latches on, and she doesn't want me to leave. So, unfortunately, I feel very frustrated and stressed when I leave right now because I feel badly that I'm leaving her when she's that worried and sad about it.

Conversely, some mothers who had anticipated having a difficult time leaving their children in nonparental care found it to be easier than they thought it would be when their children seemed to enjoy spending time with their ECE provider. When asked about transitioning her daughter to child care, Stacy responded,

It was harder on me. I wasn't ready for my baby to go to school, at all. I was probably the one who was restless about it, not her. But it's good now, 'cause I see how happy she is. She's excited to go and she gets herself dressed.

Second, 35 of the mothers (56%) had an easier transition when they felt good about leaving their child with the ECE provider, either because they trusted the ECE provider or because they felt their child benefited from spending time with the ECE provider. Elizabeth explained, "I wasn't anxious to leave him with her; I knew he was in good hands. That wasn't an issue. I totally trusted her, more so than myself, at that point." The mothers who trusted their ECE providers during the initial transition into care—when they did not know the ECE provider well—did so because the ECE provider had been referred to them by friends or family or an initial interaction with the ECE provider suggested that she was trustworthy. Alissa explained,

She let us come over and check out the place, let us play. We spent like an hour there like one day before we took him ... and [she] gave us the toys that they would be playing with and let us really look around and chat with her. And I have a 13-year-old helper who comes to my house sometimes ... And that girl went to this day care when she was a baby, so I knew the lady from the neighbors and this babysitter that I have, so I felt really comfortable. I didn't call any references or anything 'cause I didn't need to.

In addition to trusting their ECE provider, mothers also found it easy to leave their child with an ECE provider if they felt their child benefited from spending time in nonparental care. In general, mothers valued the opportunities that ECE provided for social interaction, early learning, structured play, and emotional development. Shannon explained that even though it was challenging to leave her child in child care, she felt good about it because she knew "it's good for her to have all the social experiences and—I've seen her developmentally just really—explode in the last few months from the opportunities that she's had [while in child care]."

Third, 11 of the mothers (18%) stated that they were certain that they wanted to return to work, and this certainty seemed to make the child's transition to child care easier for these mothers. Furthermore, some of these mothers discussed their enjoyment and satisfaction in their work, whereas others suggested that they did not perceive themselves as well suited to being home and caring for their children full time. Ashley expressed the latter of these sentiments:

I honestly feel that the separation that we have during the day is good for both of us. It teaches her to be more independent, and I think more social. And, it's good for me to have that break too. I think that maybe I don't have enough patience as I should. So I think if I were home all day that would be very difficult. So, transitioning her to day care wasn't difficult for me because I knew that was kind of the best thing for everybody, all around.

For mothers who were uncertain about returning to work or who indicated feelings of guilt about using nonparental child care, the transition was more difficult. When asked to give advice to parents who are looking for child care for the first time, Vanessa replied,

It's hard. You know, there's nothing you can do ... the guilt. I just still feel the guilt ... I would like to be a stay-at-home mom. I would love to be a stay-at-home mom. I'd absolutely—I love my work, I love going [to work] ... But, I think I could find that outlet even if I stayed at home.

Fourth, 18 of the mothers (29%) found the transition to child care easier when they were able to have some control over the transition. Mothers exerted control in a few different ways. Some mothers were able to take advantage of schedule flexibility offered by their employers to slowly begin using nonparental care. For instance, Tabby described,

> Where I work, they were very helpful because they let me start back at work part time and those days that I was, those days that I was working part time I was working from home so it was nice, kinda easing back into it and so they [her children] went part time for a couple weeks.

In addition to working part time for a few weeks before returning to a full-time schedule, mothers also reported that transitions were easier when they could leave work and pick up their children from child care in the early afternoon.

These mothers' experiences can be contrasted with those of mothers who had difficulty transitioning because they wanted to spend more time with their children but did not have the work flexibility to do so. After stating that she was not "a big fan of full-time day care," Nicole explained that when she had to return to work full time "that was really hard ... we don't want her there full time, but our schedules are such that we always need it."

Another way that mothers gained some control over the transition to nonparental care was to request information about their child's time in the child care setting, especially during the first days or weeks in a new care arrangement. Being able to call their ECE provider to find out what their child had done during the day was described as an important support during transitions by several mothers. Other mothers reported watching their children at child care through a webcam their ECE provider had set up.

Finally, mothers exerted control over the transition by selecting an ECE provider who was close enough to their place of employment that they could see their child during the day. Tiffany explained,

> [Her daughter] handled it completely fine. She was 7 months when she went there and it was hard for me, the first week or so, but it was nice because I was still coming over and nursing during the day and I could see her, and I was so close, and it just, it helped make a smooth transition.

This can be contrasted with the concern that Megan felt when she was not able to visit her son's child care center as often as she would have liked. She said that she "was worried. He'd been at a relative's. We'd pop in any time, and we can pop in here [the child care center] any time, but it's a little bit more distracting to their structure." Overall, when mothers had some control over the transition in ways that worked for their family, the child's transition to nonparental care was viewed as easier for the mother than when mothers were required to leave their child in care before they were ready or were not able to have as much access to their child during the day as they would have liked.

Phase 3: quantitative analyses comparing transition groups on maternal and child characteristics

Using the categorization of children and mothers in their respective transition groups from the first phase of our qualitative analysis, we examined whether the child and maternal transition groups differed on key maternal or family demographics (i.e., maternal age, maternal education, and family income) or child care characteristics (i.e., child's current age, age at first entry into child care, type of current child care arrangement, number of children in the child care setting, and hours per week in child care). Descriptive statistics for the demographic and child care characteristics are shown in Table 1 for the full sample and by child and mother transitions group. Comparisons (t tests for independent samples and chi-square tests, as appropriate) indicated group differences on one characteristic: child age at initial entry into child care. For the child transition groups, the easy group was younger at age of initial entry on average compared with children in the difficult group, $t(61) = -4.79$, $p < .001$ (see Table 1). The maternal transition groups also differed on child age at initial entry, $F(2, 59) = 3.90$, $p = .026$. Mothers in the difficult-at-first group tended to have

Table 1. Descriptive statistics for the study measures for the full sample and by child and mother transition groups.

Study measure	Full sample	Child transition groups Easy	Child transition groups Difficult	Mother transition groups Easy	Mother transition groups Difficult	Mother transition groups Difficult at first
Child gender (female), n (%)	32 (50.8)	25 (49.0)	7 (58.3)	18 (48.6)	7 (46.7)	6 (60.0)
Child birth order (first born), n (%)	36 (57.1)	28 (54.9)	8 (66.7)	20 (54.1)	9 (60.0)	7 (70.0)
Maternal education (4-year college degree), n (%)	24 (38.1)	22 (43.1)	2 (16.7)	14 (37.8)	4 (26.7)	6 (60.0)
Type of CC, n (%)						
Center	32 (50.8)	24 (47.1)	8 (66.7)	23 (62.2)	7 (46.7)	2 (20.0)
Family	22 (34.9)	20 (39.2)	2 (16.7)	10 (27.0)	6 (40.0)	6 (60.0)
Other[a]	9 (14.3)	7 (13.7)	2 (16.7)	4 (10.8)	2 (13.3)	2 (20.0)
Child age (in months), M (SD)	27.30 (5.43)	26.84 (5.16)	29.25 (6.34)	27.43 (5.13)	27.20 (5.56)	25.80 (5.67)
Maternal age, M (SD)	32.02 (3.97)	31.78 (4.00)	33.00 (3.93)	32.78 (3.82)	31.20 (3.80)	30.40 (4.53)
Family income[b], M (SD)	7.26 (2.48)	7.37 (2.34)	6.83 (3.04)	7.5 (2.43)	7.33 (2.61)	6.30 (2.45)
Child age at first entry into CC, M (SD)	9.17 (8.02)	*7.16 (6.41)*	*17.75 (8.73)*	*9.49 (8.32)*	*12.33 (8.19)*	*3.60 (2.99)*
Hours per week in CC, M (SD)	34.97 (9.88)	35.41 (9.69)	33.08 (10.88)	35.95 (10.58)	32.80 (9.04)	35.70 (8.43)
Number of children in CC, M (SD)	9.69 (4.92)	9.15 (4.96)	11.83 (4.32)	10.80 (4.56)	9.14 (5.02)	7.11 (5.06)
Maternal depressive symptoms, M (SD)	10.68 (6.89)	10.35 (6.53)	12.18 (8.49)	9.91 (6.35)	14.33 (8.12)	7.90 (4.77)
Maternal distress (general), M (SD)	1.46 (0.72)	1.42 (0.69)	1.65 (0.81)	1.41 (0.702)	1.67 (0.75)	1.36 (0.73)
Maternal distress to child distress, M (SD)	3.10 (0.83)	*2.99 (0.80)*	*3.56 (0.80)*	*3.04 (0.76)*	*3.57 (0.71)*	*2.61 (0.96)*
Child pleasure, M (SD)	5.48 (0.62)	5.48 (0.62)	5.50 (0.65)	5.44 (0.61)	5.60 (0.75)	5.44 (0.50)
Child anger proneness, M (SD)	3.93 (0.67)	3.91 (0.69)	4.02 (0.60)	3.96 (0.65)	4.15 (0.73)	3.48 (0.48)
Child social fearfulness, M (SD)	4.06 (0.81)	*3.97 (0.81)*	*4.45 (0.70)*	4.05 (0.91)	4.10 (0.74)	4.07 (0.54)

Note. Means in italics indicate significant differences between groups based on analyses reported in the text. CC = child care.
[a] Other child care typically reflected a mix of arrangements, such as 3 days at a child care center and 2 days in relative care.
[b] In reporting on family income, parents selected from income increments that ranged from less than $10,000 to greater than $100,000. A value of 7 on the income scale reflected a family income between $71,000 and $80,000.

children who were younger in age at their initial entry to child care compared with mothers in the difficult or easy groups. To assess the degree to which our quantitative measures were distinct, we present intercorrelations among measures of maternal and child characteristics, as well child age at initial entry into child care, in Table 2. Associations across measures were weak to moderate, indicating that our measures captured distinct constructs. Because one family was missing all questionnaire data and two additional mothers did not complete the depressive symptoms scale, Ns ranged from 60 to 62 for the analyses reported here.

Table 2. Intercorrelations among the study measures.

Study measures	1	2	3	4	5	6	7
1. Child age of entry into child care	—	−.01	−.08	.06	.32*	.11	−.06
2. Maternal depressive symptoms		—	.29*	.30*	.07	.37**	−.02
3. Maternal distress (general)			—	.23	−.03	.20	.10
4. Maternal distress to child distress				—	−.06	.26*	.20
5. Child pleasure					—	−.01	−.44**
6. Child anger proneness						—	.12
7. Child social fearfulness							—

*$p < .05$. **$p < .01$.

Child transition groups

A series of one-way ANCOVAs (adjusting for child age at initial entry into child care) was conducted to assess whether the child transition groups (easy vs. difficult) differed in turn on measures of maternal emotional functioning (depressive symptoms, general personal distress, personal distress reactions to child distress) and child temperament (pleasure, anger proneness, social fearfulness). Analyses revealed that compared with the difficult transition group, the easy transition group was lower on maternal personal distress reactions to child distress (M_{adj} = 2.97 vs. 3.66, respectively) and child social fearfulness (M_{adj} = 3.92 vs. 4.66): maternal personal distress reactions to child distress, $F(1, 59) = 5.19$, $p = .026$; child social fearfulness, $F(1, 59) = 6.27$, $p = .015$. No group differences emerged for maternal depressive symptoms, maternal general personal distress, or child anger proneness or pleasure.

Mother transition groups

We conducted a series of one-way ANCOVAs (adjusting for child age at initial entry into child care) to assess whether the maternal transition groups (easy vs. difficult vs. difficult at first) differed on the maternal emotional functioning and child temperament measures. The mother transition groups differed on maternal depressive symptoms and maternal personal distress reactions to child distress: maternal depressive symptoms, $F(2, 56) = 3.79$, $p = .029$; maternal personal distress reactions to child distress, $F(2, 58) = 4.82$, $p = .012$. Pairwise comparisons indicated that on average the difficult transition group was higher on depressive symptoms (M_{adj} = 14.66) and personal distress reactions to child distress (M_{adj} = 3.60) compared with the easy transition group (M_{adj} = 9.94 and 3.04, depression and personal distress, respectively) and the difficult-at-first transition group (M_{adj} = 7.33 and 2.57). The easy and difficult-at-first groups did not differ on these measures. No group differences emerged for maternal general personal distress or child temperament.

Discussion

Transitions into group child care and to new classroom groups within child care centers are important times for relationship building among parents, children, and ECE providers (Baker & Manfredi-Petit, 2004; Honig, 2002). Our overall goal was to better understand how mothers perceive transitions to and within child care for their infants and toddlers. We also aimed to explore how individual differences among mothers and children were associated with transition experiences. To provide a rich picture of families' varied experiences, we used a mixed methods approach in which qualitative interview data on mothers' perspectives about transitions to and within child care were paired with quantitative assessments of mothers' emotional functioning and children's temperament characteristics. Here we interpret the findings from the qualitative and quantitative data jointly to provide a comprehensive overview of our findings.

Overall frequency of ease versus difficulty in transitions

During our first phase of qualitative analysis, we classified the transitions for mothers and children as easy or difficult based on maternal descriptions of the transition experience. In our sample, the majority (80.9%) of children were classified as having an easy transition, whereas just more than half (58.7%) of the mothers were classified as having an easy transition. We also noted that among the mothers, a larger group described some difficulty with their own transition (39.7%) than difficulty for their child (19.0%). We suspect that children experienced less difficulty in the transition in our sample due to the fact that children in our sample were relatively young at the time of the initial transition. Our sample also included a group of families of relatively high socioeconomic status in high-quality care with providers who may have had greater skill in assisting children in having a smooth transition to care. Nevertheless, we were intrigued by these differences between mothers and children, and therefore we looked more deeply at the overall experience of the family in transitioning. We focused our analysis and interpretation on the intersection of child and maternal characteristics and explored mothers' perspectives on children's experience in addition to their perspectives on their own experiences. These findings may inform family-centered practices that address the needs of the entire family unit, which are a key component of high-quality child care (Baker & Manfredi-Petit, 2004; Raikes & Edwards, 2009).

Child age at entry into child care

Child age at initial entry to child care was significantly associated with ease or difficulty of the transition for mothers and children in the quantitative analyses. Children who had an easier transition were younger at initial entry than those who had a difficult transition, and mothers whose transitions were difficult at first had younger children at initial entry than mothers who had easy or difficult transitions. This pattern of findings was also reflected in the qualitative data. Mothers described transitions with younger children as easier. It is possible that in cases in which the child was a young infant when first entering child care, mothers did not perceive their child as having difficulty because they believed their child was unaware of the transition. It is also possible that mothers with older toddlers transitioning to care experienced a more difficult transition to nonparental care. Older children may have a more difficult transition because the attachment relationship is more developed and the presence of unfamiliar caregivers may cause older infants and toddlers to be wary. (Field et al., 1984). In addition, for children entering child care at later ages, peers may play a role in the ease or difficulty of the transition.[3] Classrooms serving older infants or young toddlers (vs. young infants) may have more children overall and higher child-to-teacher ratios. If so, these children may experience stress via interactions with peers, especially during the toddler period when verbal communication and social skills are still rudimentary.

One notable exception to the trend that earlier transitions were easier was reflected in the qualitative data. Mothers who expressed guilt or sadness at leaving their infants described difficulty in the transition. In these cases, other factors may have contributed to the mother's difficulty during the transition period. Therefore, we turn our attention to specific maternal and child characteristics that emerged in both data sources and how, beyond the age of the child at entry, these characteristics may influence transition experiences.

Child temperament and transitions

Child characteristics appeared to influence the child's ease or difficulty in transition. In particular, children in the easy transition group were lower on social fearfulness than those in the difficult transition group. Our findings are consistent with previous literature that indicates that children with more difficult temperaments, such as higher levels of social fearfulness, experience more difficulty in transitioning and adjusting to the child care setting (e.g., Watamura et al., 2003). Children with lower levels of social fearfulness may experience an easier transition because of their general comfort in new situations. Children with high levels of social fearfulness are likely to respond to new social situations with wariness, which may make it difficult for them to settle into a group care setting and develop rapport with caregivers and peers. Our finding that high levels of social fearfulness were associated with the child's transition difficulty was echoed in the qualitative

---

[3] We thank an anonymous reviewer for calling our attention to this possible explanation. Although we did not ask the mothers about the quality of the child's experiences with peers in the ECE setting, we did ask about the number of peers in the setting. Thus, we further explored the association between transition and number of peers in the ECE setting for children who entered child care at an older age. We found that older children (based on a median split on age of entry, $Mdn = 4.0$ months) who experienced a difficult transition ($n = 10$) had significantly more peers in the child care arrangement than did older children who had an easy transition ($n = 22$), $Ms = 12.4$ and 8.3, respectively, $t(28) = -2.39$, $p = .024$. Among the younger children (i.e., below the median on age of entry), only two were classified as having a difficult transition, and thus comparisons were not conducted for this group.

data. Namely, mothers who anticipated or experienced their child having separation anxiety—descriptions consistent with children who are more socially fearful—also found the transition to be more difficult.

Child anger proneness and pleasure were not associated with the child's ease or difficulty in child care transitions. It is possible that these particular temperament characteristics are not as critical as social fearfulness to understanding the child's transition experience. Instead, these aspects of child temperament may be associated with other aspects of children's experience in child care, such as their ability to form positive relationships with ECE providers and peers over the long term. It is also possible that child anger proneness and pleasure exhibit relatively small effects on children's transition experiences or may interact with other factors (e.g., maternal emotional functioning or ECE provider characteristics) to predict children's ease or difficulty in transitioning to child care. In sum, further investigation of an array of child temperament characteristics and their associations with children's experiences in child care is warranted.

Maternal emotional functioning and transitions

It is important to note that the ease or difficulty of the child's transition was also related to the mother's emotional functioning. Specifically, the quantitative analyses revealed that children who were classified as having a difficult versus easy transition had mothers who reported higher levels of personal distress reactions in response to their child's distress. These findings are consistent with prior theory (Dix, 1991) and empirical findings (e.g., Fabes et al., 2002) suggesting that parents who experience more distress in the face of their child's distress may provide less optimal responses to their child's distress in challenging moments. Although we cannot draw causal conclusions from our data, we speculate that the child's difficulty during transition periods may become intensified when the mother finds it more difficult to be emotionally available to her child's distress, as she may be preoccupied with her own distress. In contrast, mothers who reported lower distress reactions to their child's distress may have been able to respond more calmly and reassuringly at signs of child distress, and such responses could serve to lessen or de-escalate the child's distress or anxiety surrounding the transition period. This finding was echoed in the qualitative data, in which mothers cited the importance of feeling that their child was "settled" into the arrangement and that their ECE provider actively comforted or engaged their child during daily transitions. Mothers also reported feeling distressed when their ECE provider did not attempt to actively engage or distract their child during daily transitions, especially when the child was upset or hesitant to separate from the mother. In sum, the ECE provider's ability to tune into the mother's response to the child and respond sensitively to them as a dyad is likely to be an important skill in facilitating successful transitions for families.

We also found that maternal emotional well-being, as indexed by maternal depressive symptoms, was correlated with maternal ease or difficulty in transition. Among mothers, the difficult transition group was higher on depressive symptoms compared with the easy and difficult-at-first transition groups. Prior research indicates that mothers with high levels of depressive symptoms respond less sensitively to their children's distress and that infants and toddlers of mothers with depressive symptoms display lower levels of socioemotional functioning (Gravener et al., 2012; Miklush & Connelly, 2013). Findings from the qualitative data also corroborated this quantitative finding. Namely, mothers who discussed feeling more positive about returning to work generally reported an easy time transitioning their child to out-of-home care. Mothers who either were conflicted about returning to work or discussed feelings of guilt about leaving their child generally reported having a difficult transition. It is possible that some of these mothers were also experiencing elevated depressive symptoms, which would be consistent with feelings of guilt and conflict in facing the transition to care. Future research should investigate further parents' emotion-related functioning, as challenges in this domain may intensify difficulties for families during the transition period.

Limitations

We note several limitations of our study. First, we assessed only mothers' perspectives. Future studies should explore the perspectives of ECE providers, center directors, and fathers during the transition to nonfamilial care. Considering such perspectives could provide important insights into whether mothers and other caregivers of infants and toddlers have similar or different perspectives about a child's transition. Second, our participating families made up a convenience sample, and the mothers largely represented middle- to high-income families. It is highly likely that low-income families have different experiences transitioning to nonfamilial care. For example, paying for care with child care subsidy money or using other public assistance programs may constrain mothers' choices when selecting an ECE provider. Thus, it will be important for future investigations to capture maternal perspectives of child care transitions among more representative samples. Third, small cell sizes for some of the child and mother transition groups may have limited our statistical power to detect weak effects. Furthermore, because of the small cell sizes, we were unable to test factors (e.g., child gender or type of child care arrangement) that may moderate associations between maternal or child characteristics and the transition groups. Lastly, our concurrent study design does not permit conclusions about the direction of effects between maternal and child characteristics and mothers' perspectives about the ease or difficulty of their and their child's transition. Constellations of different factors (including child, mother, nonfamilial caregiver, and situational factors) may combine to create ease or difficulty in the transition to child care. Our overall analysis suggests that in understanding the transition to nonfamilial care for infants and toddlers, it is important to consider maternal and child psychological characteristics as well as examine the social relationships and contextual factors that may converge to promote greater ease versus difficulty in the transition. Intensive longitudinal study designs in which maternal perspectives and maternal and child behaviors (e.g., child separation distress, maternal depressive symptoms) are assessed at frequent intervals before, during, and after the transition to child care would provide a rich window into the dynamics that result in more difficult transitions for some families.

Recommendations for policy and practice

Despite these limitations, this study provides information that may be valuable for practitioners and policymakers. Our findings underscore the need to strengthen ECE professional development training with respect to child developmental changes as well as parents' emotional functioning. ECE training should teach providers to be attuned to individual differences and to implement specific strategies to help families transition to group care (e.g., regular communication with parents, planning with parents about their child's transition needs, knowledge of a variety of strategies for managing child and parent distress during transitions). In particular, ECE providers should receive training that bolsters their knowledge and awareness of the different transition needs of children and parents that may vary by the child's age. To better understand child needs, ECE providers should also have awareness of the specific needs of children who are fearful in new social situations and be prepared to have conversations with parents about their child's temperamental characteristics so that the parent and provider can strategize about how to best meet the child's needs.

For these early transitions in infancy and toddlerhood, an individualized approach to supporting families may be especially important when considering the experiences of specific subgroups of families, such as in the case of mothers experiencing depressive symptoms or a great deal of distress in the face of their child's distress during the transition. These parents may require extra support from nonfamilial caregivers to promote a positive settling in period.

The Italian approach to ECE emphasizes the importance of teachers engaging in active inquiry about experiences in the child care setting and using these findings to inform daily practices. Greater use of this type of inquiry could be a mechanism that enables knowledge building at the intersection of practice and research. The work of Dalli (1999, 2000) and Edwards and Rinaldi (2009) provide in-depth narratives of the settling in process of individual children and families and use qualitative case methods. The stories told by these researchers reflect the experiences of diverse families and children. This information is useful in research but, most important, it can be used as the basis for professional development for child care providers to aid in their development of reflective capacities that can support their work with children and families during challenging transitions. These narratives place emphasis on the child and family's belonging to and being reflected within the child care center community. These documented narratives and photo displays may provide opportunities for dialogue among adults and children. The careful arrangement of photos is especially useful for infants and toddlers because they are limited in their ability to articulate how their experiences unfold and affect them socially, emotionally, and cognitively. Children may use these displays to prompt communication with both parents and providers. For example, children may be able to point to and seek out the documentation in the context of routines such as looking at family pictures with a child care provider, providing an opportunity for the child to indicate to child care providers that the child is thinking about his or her connections to his or her home and family. A child may be eager to show a parent (during drop off and pick up) photographs of an experience he or she has had in the center, which indicates to the parent that the child is having exciting experiences and developing a sense of belonging in the child care center community. As the adults discuss these experiences together, they may be better able to work through difficulties and celebrate the successes of the transition process.

Our findings also bolster the argument that focusing on the needs of parents in the ECE setting is critical for successful transitions. ECE providers should be given opportunities to build their knowledge of parental emotional needs and how to support them, especially for families experiencing distress. This could involve helping ECE providers develop strategies for communicating with parents about their adult emotional experiences and awareness of support services in the community that can provide additional support for parents experiencing emotional distress during the transition. Programs may also want to take a team approach and involve other members of the ECE community, such as center directors and family support and engagement specialists, in supporting families experiencing high levels of distress during transition periods. In particular, researchers should aim to understand how maternal depressive symptoms affect the transition to group care because postpartum depression (considered to be a depressive episode within the first year following childbirth) is a relatively common experience for new mothers (estimated at 21.9% in the United States; Gaynes et al., 2005). This is especially important because for many families, the initial connections with the ECE system are built during infancy and early toddlerhood when mothers may be experiencing postpartum depression.

Lastly, the mothers in our study reported easier transitions when they were able to have some control over the transition experience. Workplace and ECE center policies can be written to allow parents some control. In particular, allowing parents flexible leave times and the ability to visit their child within the child care center and be part of their child's new experience in the child care setting could support successful transitions for infants and toddlers. Our findings related to multiple transitions within a particular child care center or to another care setting being difficult for children may also have implications for child care subsidy policy. For example, policies may be developed to allow families utilizing subsidies to maintain their child care placements even when experiencing a shift in employment in order to allow them to maintain continuous relationships with their child's ECE caregivers.

In sum, the period of transitioning to child care is a special time for families with infants and toddlers. The expansion of the child's relationship circle to include new caregivers beyond his or her family is filled with opportunities for promoting child growth but also challenges as the child, family, and nonfamilial caregivers build relationships and new experiences together. We suggest that the ECE field focus on building resources and policies that strengthen the relationship context that supports infants and toddlers and enhance providers' ability to recognize different strengths and challenges across families to help parents and children make successful transitions to group care.

Acknowledgments

We are grateful to the families who participated in this research. We also thank Mallory Mudra, Ashley Holland, Rita Botbol, Jason Burgus, Kate Jeselnick, and Christina Linden for their help with data collection, management, and transcription.

Funding

This study was supported by funds from the Family Resiliency Center at the University of Illinois at Urbana-Champaign and from the U.S. Department of Agriculture National Institute of Food and Agriculture (ILLU-793-362) to the fourth author.

References

Ahnert, L., Gunnar, M. R., Lamb, M. E., & Barthel, M. (2004). Transition to child care: Associations with infant–mother attachment, infant negative emotion, and cortisol elevations. *Child Development, 75*, 639–650. doi:10.1111/j.1467-8624.2004.00698.x

Ahnert, L., Pinquart, M., & Lamb, M. E. (2006). Security of children's relationships with nonparental care providers: A meta-analysis. *Child Development, 77*, 664–679. doi:10.1111/j.1467-8624.2006.00896.x

Baker, A. C., Manfredi-Petitt, L. A., & National Association for the Education of Young Children. (2004). *Relationships, the heart of quality care: Creating community among adults in early care settings*. Washington, DC: National Association for the Education of Young Children.

Belsky, J., Burchinal, M., McCartney, K., Vandell, D. L., Clarke-Stewart, K. A., Owen, M. T., & the NICHD Early Child Care Research Network. (2007). Are there long-term effects of early child care? *Child Development, 78*, 681–701. doi:10.1111/j.1467-8624.2007.01021.x

Bove, C. (2001). Inserimento: A strategy for delicately beginning relationships and communications. In I. L. Gandini & C. P. Edwards (Eds.), *Bambini: The Italian approach to infant/toddler care* (pp. 109–123). New York, NY: Teachers College Press.

Bromer, J., & Henly, J. R. (2009). The work–family support roles of child care providers across settings. *Early Childhood Research Quarterly, 24*, 271–288. doi:10.1016/j.ecresq.2009.04.002

Brownell, C. A., & Kopp, C. B. (2010). Transitions in toddler socioemotional development: Behavior, understanding, relationships. In C. A. Brownell & C. B. Kopp (Eds.), *Socioemotional development in the toddler years: Transitions and transformations* (pp. 1–40). New York, NY: Guilford Press.

Carr, M., & May, H. (1993). Choosing a model. Reflecting on the development process of Te Whariki: National early childhood curriculum guidelines in New Zealand. *International Journal of Early Years Education, 1*, 7–22. doi:10.1080/0966976930010302

Cassidy, J. (2008). The nature of the child's ties. In J. Cassidy & P. R. Shaver (Eds.), *Handbook of attachment: Theory, research, clinical applications* (pp. 3–22). New York, NY: Guilford Press.

Clark, L. A., Kochanska, G., & Ready, R. (2000). Mothers' personality and its interaction with child temperament as predictors of parenting behavior. *Journal of Personality and Social Psychology, 79*, 274–285. doi:10.1037/0022-3514.79.2.274

Copple, C., & Bredekamp, S. (2009). *Developmentally appropriate practice in early childhood programs serving children from birth through age 8*. Washington, DC: National Association for the Education of Young Children.

Creswell, J. W., & Plano Clark, V. (2007). *Designing and conducting mixed methods research*. Thousand Oaks, CA: Sage.

Crockenberg, S. C. (2003). Rescuing the baby from the bathwater: How gender and temperament (may) influence how child care affects child development. *Child Development, 74*, 1034–1038. doi:10.1111/1467-8624.00585

Dalli, C. (1999). Learning to be in childcare: Mothers' stories of their child's "settling-in." *European Early Childhood Education Research Journal, 7*, 53–66. doi:10.1080/13502939985208401

Dalli, C. (2000). Starting child care: What young children learn about relating to adults in the first weeks of starting child care. *Early Childhood Research and Practice, 2*(2), 1–31.

Daly, K. J. (2007). *Qualitative methods for family studies and human development*. Los Angeles, CA: Sage.

Davis, M. H. (1994). *Empathy: A social psychological approach*. Boulder, CO: Westview Press.

De Schipper, J., Tavecchio, L. C., Van IJzendoorn, M. H., & Van Zeijl, J. (2004). Goodness-of-fit in center day care: Relations of temperament, stability, and quality of care with the child's adjustment. *Early Childhood Research Quarterly, 19*, 257–272. doi:10.1016/j.ecresq.2004.04.004

Diener, M. L., & Kim, D.-Y. (2004). Maternal and child predictors of preschool children's social competence. *Journal of Applied Developmental Psychology, 25*, 3–24. doi:10.1016/j.appdev.2003.11.006

Dix, T. (1991). The affective organization of parenting: Adaptive and maladaptative processes. *Psychological Bulletin, 110*(1), 3–25. doi:10.1037/0033-2909.110.1.3

Edwards, C. P., & Rinaldi, C. (Eds.). (2009). *The diary of Laura: Perspectives on a Reggio Emilia diary*. St. Paul, MN: Redleaf Press.

Emery, H. T., McElwain, N. L., Groh, A. M., Haydon, K. C., & Roisman, G. I. (2014). Maternal dispositional empathy and electrodermal reactivity: Interactive contributions to maternal sensitivity with toddler-aged children. *Journal of Family Psychology, 28*, 505–515. doi:10.1037/a0036986

Fabes, R. A., Poulin, R. E., Eisenberg, N., & Madden-Derdich, D. A. (2002). The Coping with Children's Negative Emotions Scale (CCNES): Psychometric properties and relations with children's emotional competence. *Marriage & Family Review, 34*, 285–310. doi:10.1300/J002v34n03_05

Field, T., Gewirtz, J. L., Cohen, D., Garcia, R., Greenberg, R., & Collins, K. (1984). Leave-takings and reunions of infants, toddlers, preschoolers, and their parents. *Child Development, 55*, 628–635. doi:10.2307/1129974

Fiese, B. H., Eckert, T., & Spagnola, M. (2006). Family context in early childhood: A look at practices and beliefs that promote early learning. In B. Spodek & O. N. Saracho (Eds.), *Handbook of research on the education of young children* (2nd ed., pp. 393–409). Mahwah, NJ: Erlbaum.

Forry, N., Iruka, I., Tout, K., Torquati, J., Susman-Stillman, A., Bryant, D., & Daneri, M. P. (2013). Predictors of quality and child outcomes in family child care settings. *Early Childhood Research Quarterly, 28*, 893–904. doi:10.1016/j.ecresq.2013.05.006

Gandini, L., & Edwards, C. P. (Eds.). (2001). *Bambini: The Italian approach to infant/toddler care*. New York, NY: Teachers College Press.

Gaynes, B. N., Gavin, N., Meltzer-Brody, S., Lohr, K. N., Swinson, T., Gartlehner, G., ... Miller, W. C. (2005). Perinatal depression: Prevalence, screening accuracy, and screening outcomes. *Evidence Report/Technology Assessment, 119*. Retrieved from http://archive.ahrq.gov/downloads/pub/evidence/pdf/peridepr/peridep.pdf

Goldsmith, H. H. (1996). Studying temperament via construction of the Toddler Behavior Assessment Questionnaire. *Child Development, 67*, 218–235. doi:10.2307/1131697

Gravener, J. A., Rogosch, F. A., Oshri, A., Narayan, A. J., Cicchetti, D., & Toth, S. L. (2012). The relations among maternal depressive disorder, maternal expressed emotion, and toddler behavior problems and attachment. *Journal of Abnormal Child Psychology, 40*, 803–813. doi:10.1007/s10802-011-9598-z

Halle, T., Hair, M., Weinstein, D., Vick, J., Forry, N., & Kinukawa, A. (2009). *Primary child care arrangements of US infants: Patterns of utilization by poverty status, family structure, maternal work status, maternal work schedule, and child care assistance* (OPRE Research Brief, No. 1). Washington, DC: Office of Planning Research and Evaluation, Administration for Children and Families.

Head Start Program Performance Standards. (2009). *Federal Register, No. 217*. Vol. 76. Washington, DC: US Department of Health and Human Services, Administration for Children and Families, Office of Head Start.

Honig, A. S. (2002). *Secure relationships: Nurturing infant/toddler attachment in early care settings*. Washington, DC: National Association for the Education of Young Children.

Huang, Z. J., Lewin, A., Mitchell, S. J., & Zhang, J. (2012). Variations in the relationship between maternal depression, maternal sensitivity, and child attachment by race/ethnicity and nativity: Findings from a nationally representative cohort study. *Maternal and Child Health Journal, 16*, 40–50. doi:10.1007/s10995-010-0716-2

Jovanovic, J. (2011). Saying goodbye: An investigation into parent–infant separation behaviours on arrival in childcare. *Child Care in Practice, 17*, 247–269. doi:10.1080/13575279.2011.571237

Klein, P. S., Kraft, R. R., & Shohet, C. (2010). Behaviour patterns in daily mother–child separations: Possible opportunities for stress reduction. *Early Child Development and Care, 180*, 387–396. doi:10.1080/03004430801943290

Knopf, H. T., & Swick, K. J. (2007). How parents feel about their child's teacher/school: Implications for early childhood professionals. *Early Childhood Education Journal, 34*, 291–296. doi:10.1007/s10643-006-0119-6

Kontos, S., & Wilcox-Herzog, A. (1997). Influences on children's competence in early childhood classrooms. *Early Childhood Research Quarterly, 12*, 247–262. doi:10.1016/S0885-2006(97)90002-8

Kryzer, E. M., Kovan, N., Phillips, D. A., Domagall, L. A., & Gunnar, M. R. (2007). Toddlers' and preschoolers' experience in family day care: Age differences and behavioral correlates. *Early Childhood Research Quarterly, 22*, 451–466. doi:10.1016/j.ecresq.2007.08.004

Kujawa, A., Dougherty, L., Durbin, C. E., Laptook, R., Torpey, D., & Klein, D. N. (2014). Emotion recognition in preschool children: Associations with maternal depression and early parenting. *Development and Psychopathology, 26*, 159–170. doi:10.1017/S0954579413000928

Ladd, G. W., & Price, J. M. (1987). Predicting children's social and school adjustment following the transition from preschool to kindergarten. *Child Development, 58*, 1168–1189. doi:10.2307/1130613

LaRossa, R. (2005). Grounded theory methods and qualitative family research. *Journal of Marriage and Family, 67*, 837–857. doi:10.1111/jomf.2005.67.issue-4

Meyers, M. K., & Jordan, L. P. (2006). Choice and accommodation in parental child care decisions. *Community Development, 37*, 53–70. doi:10.1080/15575330609490207

Miklush, L., & Connelly, C. D. (2013). Maternal depression and infant development: Theory and current evidence. *MCN: The American Journal of Maternal/Child Nursing, 38*, 369–374.

National Institute of Child Health and Human Development Early Child Care Research Network. (2004). Type of child care and children's development at 54 months. *Early Childhood Research Quarterly, 19,* 203–230. doi:10.1016/j.ecresq.2004.04.002

New Zealand Ministry of Education. (1996). *Te Whàriki He Whàriki Màtauranga mò ngà Mokopuna o Aotearoa* [An early childhood curriculum for inclusion in New Zealand] (Item No. 02980). Wellington, New Zealand: Learning Media. Retrieved from http://www.educate.ece.govt.nz/learning/curriculumAndLearning/TeWhariki.aspx

Peisner-Feinberg, E. S., Burchinal, M. R., Clifford, R. M., Culkin, M. L., Howes, C., Kagan, S. L., & Yazejian, N. (2001). The relation of preschool child-care quality to children's cognitive and social developmental trajectories through second grade. *Child Development, 72,* 1534–1553. doi:10.1111/1467-8624.00364

Phillips, D. A., Fox, N. A., & Gunnar, M. R. (2011). Same place, different experiences: Bringing individual differences to research in child care. *Child Development Perspectives, 5*(1), 44–49. doi:10.1111/j.1750-8606.2010.00155.x

Phillips, D., McCartney, K., & Sussman, A. (2006). Child care and early development. In K. McCartney & D. Phillips (Eds.), *The handbook of early child development* (pp. 471–489). Malden, MA: Blackwell.

Radloff, L. S. (1977). The CES-D scale: A self-report depression scale for research in the general population. *Applied Psychological Measurement, 1,* 385–401. doi:10.1177/014662167700100306

Raikes, H., & Edwards, C. P. (2009). *Extending the dance in infant and toddler caregiving: Enhancing attachment and relationships.* Baltimore, MD: Brookes.

Raikes, H., Torquati, J., Wang, C., & Shjegstad, B. (2012). Parent experiences with state child care subsidy systems and their perceptions of choice and quality in care selected. *Early Education & Development, 23,* 558–582. doi:10.1080/10409289.2011.574268

Rimm-Kaufman, S. E., Pianta, R. C., & Cox, M. J. (2000). Teachers' judgments of problems in the transition to kindergarten. *Early Childhood Research Quarterly, 15,* 147–166. doi:10.1016/S0885-2006(00)00049-1

Rous, B., Hallam, R., McCormick, K., & Cox, M. (2010). Practices that support the transition to public preschool programs: Results from a national survey. *Early Childhood Research Quarterly, 25,* 17–32. doi:10.1016/j.ecresq.2009.09.001

Rubin, H., & Rubin, I. (2005). *Qualitative interviewing* (2nd ed.). Thousand Oaks, CA: Sage.

Sosinsky, L. S., & Kim, S.-K. (2013). A profile approach to child care quality, quantity, and type of setting: Parent selection of infant child care arrangements. *Applied Developmental Science, 17,* 39–56. doi:10.1080/10888691.2013.750196

Spinrad, T. L., Eisenberg, N., Kupfer, A., Gaertner, B., & Michalik, N. (2004, May). *The Coping with Toddlers' Negative Emotions Scale.* Poster session presented at the Biennial International Conference on Infant Studies, Chicago, IL.

Sroufe, L. A. (1996). *Emotional development: The organization of emotional life in the early years.* New York, NY: Cambridge University Press.

Swartz, M. I., & Easterbrooks, M. A. (2014). The role of parent, provider, and child characteristics in parent–provider relationships in infant and toddler classrooms. *Early Education & Development, 25,* 573–598. doi:10.1080/10409289.2013.822229

Tronick, E. Z. (1989). Emotions and emotional communication in infants. *American Psychologist, 44,* 112–119. doi:10.1037/0003-066X.44.2.112

Watamura, S. E., Donzella, B., Alwin, J., & Gunnar, M. R. (2003). Morning-to-afternoon increases in cortisol concentrations for infants and toddlers at child care: Age differences and behavioral correlates. *Child Development, 74,* 1006–1020. doi:10.1111/cdev.2003.74.issue-4

Wong, M. S., McElwain, N. L., & Halberstadt, A. G. (2009). Parent, family, and child characteristics: Associations with mother- and father-reported emotion socialization practices. *Journal of Family Psychology, 23,* 452–463. doi:10.1037/a0015552

Yoshikawa, H., Weisner, T. S., Kalil, A., & Way, N. (2008). Mixing qualitative and quantitative research in developmental science: Uses and methodological choices. *Developmental Psychology, 44,* 344–354. doi:10.1037/0012-1649.44.2.344

Experiences of Parents and Professionals in Well-Established Continuity of Care Infant Toddler Programs

Mary Benson McMullen, Na Ra Yun, Alina Mihai, and Hyojin Kim

ABSTRACT

Research Findings: A qualitative descriptive study was conducted to look at the nature of continuity of care by examining the perspectives of those who lived it in 2 programs in which it was a well-established practice. The 35 participants included infant toddler caregivers, parents, preschool teachers, and administrators. Findings are organized around 8 features of continuity of care revealed in the study: increased knowledge (increased understanding of child development and individual children), stable relationships (decreased disruption associated with frequent transitions), a family-type atmosphere (trust, warmth, and affection promoted), primary caregiving (changing nature of roles over time), family-centeredness (mutual empowerment of parents and caregivers), effective caregiver partnerships (caregiving relationships among caregivers), the transition to preschool (higher levels of ability in social and self-help skills among children), and recommendations for improvement. *Practice or Policy*: We discuss implications for practitioners, teacher educators and policymakers, including further consideration of parental/caregiver empowerment, the maintenance of continuity across members of caregiving teams, and keeping children ages birth to 5 together in 1 setting. Also, findings suggest differences in the nature of primary caregiving in continuous versus discontinuous care settings. Finally, we conclude that continuity is beneficial, but complex, and more likely to succeed in programs already committed to engagement in strong, relationship-based practice.

Increased focus on the infant toddler period across multiple fields of study (e.g., psychology, neuroscience, sociology, and education) and families' increased need for care have elevated the birth-to-3 period as a specialized field of study within early childhood education. The provision of professional group care for infants and toddlers is now widely acknowledged in the early childhood field to be different from preschool and Kindergarten-primary education in at least three key ways: (a) the specialized knowledge needed by caregivers[1] to support the tremendous growth, development, and learning unique to individual infants and toddlers during this period (Institute of Medicine & National Research Council, 2012; National Scientific Council on the Developing Child, 2004); (b) the specific and highly individualized practices recommended for working with infants and toddlers and their families in group care (Goldstein, Hamm, & Schumacher, 2007; Lally & Mangione, 2008); and (c) how the nature of the care experienced by the child in the first 3 years has the potential for life-long impact (National Institute of Child Health and Human Development, 1996; Phillips & Lowenstein, 2011; Vandell, Belsky, Burchinal, Steinberg, & Vandergrift, 2010). These special features speak to the need for all adults who care for infants and toddlers—parents and

---

[1]We embrace the term *caregiver* as our preferred term for professionals who work with young children, birth to age 3, elevating the role of 'care' within the field of early childhood care and education.

professionals—to work together to optimize experiences, relationships, and environments during the first 3 years.

Recommendations for practices such as continuity of care (COC), the assignment of primary caregivers, and a commitment to family-centeredness in infant toddler child care are based primarily on scholarship related to developmental and relational theories (Copple, Bredekamp, Koraleck, & Charner, 2013; Cryer, Hurwitz, & Wolery, 2000; Zero to Three, 2008). Basically, these widely endorsed practices are designed to facilitate caregivers' acquisition of knowledge concerning general expectations for children's growth and development and to facilitate caregivers' ability to focus in depth on the unique growth and development unfolding in individual infants and toddlers (Aguillard, Pierce, Benedict, & Burts, 2005; Copple et al., 2013; Horm, Goble, & Branscomb, 2011; Zero to Three, 2008).

There is significant support for COC, primary caregiving, and family-centered practices in the field. Leading early childhood education and birth-to-3 professional organizations and policy groups endorse COC, in particular Zero to Three (2008), the Program for Infant Toddler Care (2015), the National Association for the Education of Young Children (NAEYC; Copple et al., 2013), the National Head Start Association's Early Head Start–Child Care Partnership (National Head Start Association, 2014), EDUCARE (2015), High/Scope (Snyder, 2011), the Ounce of Prevention Fund (2015), Childcare Aware of America (2015), and the Center for Law and Social Policy (2015), among others.

The problem

COC has received little of the attention from research scholars that is necessary to validate its widespread endorsement within the profession (Elicker, Ruprecht, & Anderson, 2014). Much of the research literature touting the benefits of COC appears anecdotal or suppositional rather than empirical and objective. Similarly, much of the literature written for practitioners includes little or no substantiation and focuses on one of two extremes—the status of COC as essential to best practice or COC as an unattainable standard. This sets up an unnecessary and unhealthy tension in the field between those who take a highly idealistic stance and those who engage in what amounts to a discourse of fear—fear that COC is too difficult to implement; fear that it will make caregivers unhappy, resulting in turnover; and fear that it will be disliked by parents, who may feel stuck with the same caregivers over a number of years (Aguillard et al., 2005; Cryer et al., 2000; Essa, Favre, Thweatt, & Waugh, 1999).

Questions and purpose

Current understandings and misunderstandings about COC led us to ask the following: What does COC look like in infant toddler programs in which COC is a well-established, long-running practice? After we reviewed the existing research literature on COC, we generated three additional questions: What do adults who experience well-established COC in infant toddler programs say about its benefits and challenges? What is the nature of primary caregiving and family-centered care in well-established, long-running infant toddler COC? And what happens when the children from COC in these groups turn 3 and transition to preschool? We addressed these questions by examining the perspectives of parents and early childhood professionals in two infant toddler child care settings in which COC had been a well-established practice for many years. We believed that seeing COC by listening to the perspectives of those who lived it would not only be the most authentic way to understand it but best help other infant toddler professionals to see themselves within a COC environment.

We considered it important to examine COC as it exists in a model program, one in which these practices have been the norm for a number of years. The assumption was that examining COC in such an environment would facilitate researchers' understanding of what, why, and how COC works when fully implemented as recommended or in what ways it does not demonstrate assumed effects or outcomes. Thus, the study was conducted in two accredited child care programs in which COC had been standard practice for several years. The nature of both programs was known to us as the settings were part of a previous observation study in which infants' perspectives and lived experience in full-time child care were examined (see McMullen et al., 2009; McMullen & Lash, 2012).

Thus, the purpose of this study was to look at the nature of COC and related practices (i.e., primary caregiving and family-centered practices) within two well-established infant toddler programs and to do so by examining the perspectives of the adults who lived it. Along with this, we intended to uncover benefits and challenges to the successful implementation of COC in center-based child care.

The theoretical foundation of this study is presented next followed by an overview of practices examined in this study as they are defined within the early childhood education field. Research and theory that informs these practices is then examined. Findings are organized around themes that emerged from the data that could be said to describe special features of COC, and these features are presented using the words of the participants.

Theoretical foundation

Infants and toddlers learn what it means to care, what it means to be cared for, and that they themselves are worthy of care within relationships with those surrounding them (Eisenberg, 1992). Bronfenbrenner's bioecological systems theory helped us think about the nature of the important caring relationships surrounding and including infants and toddlers in child care settings and the relative impact of relationships based on proximity (Bronfenbrenner & Morris, 2006). This model informed our design of the study, in particular in deciding who and for what reason various participants should be selected.

Bronfenbrenner asserted that children's growth, development, and learning is impacted by, and simultaneously impacts, individuals and factors both proximal and distal to them within a system (Bronfenbrenner & Morris, 2006). Depictions of his systems model typically show a series of nested subsystems surrounding a central core in which a child is positioned. Surrounding and encompassing the core is one or more subsystems or *microsystems* consisting of individuals in close relationship to the child. The closer the subsystem is positioned in relation to the child, the stronger the mutual influence that members of that subsystem and the child have on each other. In interpreting and translating Bronfenbrenner's model for this study, we positioned primary participants in the study, including children's parents and professionals within the children's caregiving teams, in what was labelled *Microsystem I*. These participants were considered to have the most significant close relationships with the infants and toddlers in this study, as they engaged with them on a day-to-day basis. A secondary level, or *Microsystem II*, surrounds the first, and it includes the secondary participants in the study, including other infant toddler caregivers in the settings, preschool teachers in affiliated programs, and program administrators.

A *mesosystem* defines factors that interconnect children at the core of the system with the microsystems (Bronfenbrenner & Morris, 2006). We conceptualized the practices of interest in this study—COC, primary caregiving, and family-centered care—as elements within the mesosystem. In addition, we placed the factors influencing and influenced by the mesosystem, such as child care licensing regulations, local and state policies, and the state's Quality Rating Improvement Systems (QRIS), within the subsystem surrounding the mesosystem, or the *exosystem*. Finally, community and program values and cultures, the social-emotional climate, and socioeconomic status were placed in the most distal level, or the *macrosystem*.

The literature

Four bodies of literature are relevant to this study and are presented here. First a review of how COC, primary caregiving, and family-centered practices are characterized in scholarly literature and general best practice publications is presented. This is followed by a consideration of attachment theory as it informs these practices. Then research about both the benefits of and challenges to COC as a practice with infants and toddlers is summarized.

Description of practices

COC

COC is the practice of keeping groups of children together with their caregiving team over an extended period of time, typically for 2 to 3 years. Two popular forms of achieving COC include the use of (a) multiage groupings, consisting of infants, 1-year-olds, and 2-year-olds together in a mixed group; and (b) the looping model, in which same-age children begin a program together, usually in infancy, and remain together until they graduate and go to preschool. In both forms of COC, children and families remain with their key caregivers for up to 3 years (Lally & Mangione, 2008).

In COC, furnishings, equipment, materials and supplies, and sometimes the rooms themselves may change, but the group of individuals, and thus the relationships, remains intact. A major premise of COC is that if groups of children and caregiving adults stay together for an uninterrupted, extended period of time, the knowledge and understanding of caregivers about individual children and their families will grow and deepen. Staying together over time allows trust to form, to be nurtured, and to flourish between and among all within the group—caregivers, children, and families—facilitating caregivers' ability to work with families to optimize the daily experience of child care as well as outcomes that impact children's growth and development (Essa et al., 1999; Theilheimer, 2006).

Primary caregiving

In primary (or key person) caregiving, one caregiver becomes principally but not exclusively responsible for a small number of children within the group with the goal of forming trusting, secure attachment relationships with each infant toddler in the group and strong working partnerships with toddlers' families (Bary, 2010; Bernhardt, 2000; Elfer, Goldschmied, & Selleck, 2003; Lally & Mangione, 2008; Zero to Three, 2008). Primary caregivers are responsible for addressing the majority of individualized care needs in their small group, as well as for keeping records and working directly with the families of their assigned children. Primary caregiving can and does occur in programs not practicing COC, but it is presumed that those engaging in COC also assign primary caregivers.

Family-centered care

It is important for caregivers to commit to creating trusting, mutually supportive, reciprocal relationships with parents. Family-centered care is not simply parent involvement, participation, or the welcoming of families to visit anytime; it involves caregivers and families working in partnership around common goals supporting the child (Gonzalez-Mena, 2012; Keyser, 2006; Pianta, Barnett, & Justice, 2012). It requires intentional investment in the relationships between parents and caregivers by all parties involved. Essa et al. (1999) found that COC facilitated trusting relational bonds between caregivers and parents, a bond built on mutual respect for the knowledge and expertise each partner brings.

COC and attachment

Support for COC is found in attachment theory (Ainsworth, Blehar, Waters, & Wall, 1978; J. Bowlby, 1969). From the vast body of research on attachment, two key findings are most relevant to this study: Children can and do form important attachments with more than one caregiver (R. Bowlby, 2007; Goossens & van Ijzendoorn, 1990; Howes, 1999; Howes & Hamilton, 1992); and the security of attachment during the first 3 years is related to both short- and long-term positive and negative outcomes in multiple developmental domains, in particular in terms of social-emotional development (Cummings & Davies, 1996; Howes & Hamilton, 1993; Mann & Carney, 2008; Waters, Weinfield, & Hamilton, 2000; Whitaker, Orzol, & Kahn, 2006).

Secure attachment results from, and occurs within, trusting relationships (J. Bowlby, 1988; Honig, 2002; 2010; Raikes, 1993, 1996; Raikes & Edwards, 2009; Riley, San Juan, Klinkner, & Ramminger, 2008). Specifically, when adult caregivers (parents and professionals) engage in sensitive, individually responsive interactions with infants and toddlers, these babies learn that caregivers can be trusted to meet their needs in kind and predictable ways. The trust born of predictability facilitates attachment; the experience of trust over time facilitates security (Ebbeck & Yim, 2008; Elicker & Fortner, 1995). Recommendations for COC arise from an understanding of the importance of secure attachment and how it develops over time within key relationships (Institute of Medicine & National Research Council, 2012), along with acknowledgment of the potential danger associated with the disruption of attachment relationships that occurs with frequent changes of trusted caregivers (Cryer et al., 2005).

Continuity of care
Benefits
Beneficial outcomes for infants and toddlers in COC appear to be dependent on the length of time in high-quality care settings (i.e., quality as defined by accreditation standards and state quality criteria) and with high-ability caregivers (e.g., those who are highly responsive and sensitive in caregiving interactions). Raikes (1993) examined length of time with high-ability caregivers as an indicator of the quality of infant–caregiver relationships. She found that among the infants in her study who had spent more than 12 months together with their high-ability caregivers, 91% developed secure attachments to the caregiver, whereas only 50% of infants who had spent less time (5 to 8 months) did.

The Raikes (1993) study examined the interdependence of time (duration) and caregiver ability as they relate to security of attachment. Security is a product of relationship; relationships are built on knowledge of one another formed over time. It is important for caregivers to have the time and opportunity to get to know each infant or toddler well so that they may respond sensitively and with an appropriate individualized response (Elicker et al., 2014). This is inherently difficult in group care. Primary caregiving was designed specifically to promote relational bonds between the caregiver and a small subset of children within a larger group in a caregiving setting (Theilheimer, 2006).

Responsiveness of care within COC was linked to positive outcomes in a study by Ruprecht, Elicker, and Choi (in press), who found that the toddlers in their sample who were in continuous versus discontinuous care experienced more sensitively responsive caregiving and displayed fewer behavioral concerns as rated by their caregivers. Similarly, an earlier study by Essa et al. (1999) found benefits to children in COC, reporting that babies with close, secure relationships with their caregivers engaged more actively in exploring their environments.

Challenges
Although supported by researchers and policy analysts (e.g., see Schumacher, Hamm, Goldstein, & Lombardi, 2006; Schumacher & Hoffmann, 2008), COC is still not a widely adopted practice (Ackerman, 2008; Cryer et al., 2000). Most infants and toddlers in group child care in the United States experience multiple transitions resulting in changes in physical setting, ever-changing caregivers, and new groups of peers several times between birth and age 3. Discontinuous care is experienced when children transition from room to room based on birthday or the attainment of a developmental milestone or because of space considerations (Cryer et al., 2000; Essa et al., 1999). The practice of frequent transitioning is the norm despite research indicating that the disruption and constant negotiation of new relationships can be harmful to the developing sense of self, and it has also been linked to distress and problem behaviors (Cryer et al., 2005; de Schipper, Van Ijzendoorn, & Tavecchio, 2004; Hegde & Cassidy, 2004; Howes & Hamilton, 1993).

Aguillard et al. (2005) examined general barriers to implementing COC perceived by child care program directors. A total of 42% of directors in their study attributed the low adoption rates of COC to the attitudes of caregivers, whereas 24% indicated that they were due to the caregivers' capabilities as professionals. In particular, Aguillard and her colleagues found that infant caregivers were reluctant to continue working with children when they became toddlers and that there was a reluctance among administrators to force the issue. Similarly, in their interview study of caregivers,

Hegde and Cassidy (2004) uncovered dispositional resistance at the heart of a reluctance to adopt COC. They credited this to caregivers' preferences to work with certain age groups and conviction that they were more skilled with one age over another.

Such challenges to COC suggest that caregivers may need more supportive administrative structures or perhaps more professional development opportunities to help facilitate full adoption. Ackerman (2008) and Norris (2010) reported the benefits of transitioning to COC concurrent with engagement in ongoing professional development. Not only does this provide structure to facilitate the process of change, but Ackerman's work suggests that it may enhance the professional community overall within the setting. Supportive professional communities enrich caregivers' relationships in a setting (Grodsky & Gamoran, 2003) and encourage meaningful, reflective dialogue among professional caregivers (Louis & Marks, 1998). These studies are encouraging in that they highlight the roles of recursive reflection and supportive relationships in COC during and perhaps beyond implementation.

Hegde and Cassidy (2004) studied perspectives of caregivers and families soon after the adoption of COC in a high-quality university-affiliated program. Both the Hegde and Cassidy study and the work reported in this article involved COC in university-affiliated programs by considering the perspectives of those who implemented it daily. In the present study, the university-affiliated programs were ones that had gone through several 3-year looping cycles with infants and toddlers. The current study also included voices of participants beyond parents and primary caregivers, which were the primary informants in the Hegde and Cassidy study.

Recchia (2012) included the perspectives of preschool teachers in their study of toddler boys as they transitioned to preschool. She examined the relationships with caregivers and teachers before, during, and after the boys' transition from infant toddler care to preschool. The very stability inherent in COC, concluded Recchia, may make children's transition to preschool from COC programs more difficult compared to that of children from discontinuous care programs. Her work made us wonder whether COC matters less than the nature of caring relationships. Recchia indicated that sensitively responsive, caring support from both previous and new caregivers can act as "a bridge" (p. 155) allowing children to more easily adapt to the new setting. Recchia's work informed us of the importance of considering relational aspects of care over time and suggested the inclusion of preschool teachers in our COC study.

Conclusion

Attachment theory and the available research on COC show general support for the field's recommendations of COC as a practice to foster secure care relationships important to infants and toddlers. Within the scholarship, however, it is suggested that most U.S. infants and toddlers remain in discontinuous child care settings (Aguillard et al., 2005; Cryer et al., 2000; Essa et al., 1999; Hegde & Cassidy, 2004). Clearly, the implementation of COC lags behind current recommendations, and the gap between what is known and what is done suggests that more research is warranted. The purpose of this study is to contribute to the literature reported here by focusing on the nature of relationships in COC, the benefits and challenges related to COC, the role of primary caregiving and family-centeredness in COC, and what happens to all involved during the transition to preschool. In addition, it uses a wider variety of participant perspectives to tell the story. In addition, the study contributes by examining programs in which COC is well established. The four research questions addressed are as follows: (a) What does COC look like in infant toddler programs in which COC is a well-established, long-running practice? (b) What do adults who experience well-established COC in infant toddler programs say about its benefits and challenges? (c) What is the nature of primary caregiving and family-centered care in well-established, long-running infant toddler COC? and (d) What happens when the children from COC in these groups turn 3 and transition to preschool?

Method

We used a qualitative descriptive method for the study. The study has elements of phenomenology in that it seeks understanding of the shared experiences of several individuals around a common phenomenon, in this case COC (Moustakas, 1994). Elements of grounded theory are present in our method to help generate general explanations or theories as they are shaped by the various perspectives of the participants (Charmaz, 2000). In short, we use the data (i.e., the words of those who lived the experience of relationship-based care) to tell the story of COC practices as directly experienced to generate understanding of the phenomenon.

Sandelowski (2010) said, "The value of qualitative description lies not only in the knowledge its use can produce, but also as a vehicle for presenting and treating research methods as living entities that resist simple classification" (p. 83). She argued that qualitative description goes beyond the simple presentation of the data, stressing the role the researcher has in the interpretation and organization of the findings. In the case of this study, foundational research and theory were considered in constructing protocols for the collection and interpretation of the data (Tobin, 2010), and multiple sources of data were used to examine perspectives of COC as experienced by those who lived it. Perspectives of adults both proximal and distal to the day-to-day experience of relational practices, as well as informational documents describing policies, philosophies, and practices, were included as data (Yin, 2012). Emergent patterns and themes from the data were examined to interpret the findings (Hatch, 2002). Sandelowski described this method as producing findings "closer to the data as given or data-near" (p. 78).

Settings

Two programs were included in this study, designated as the B-5 and B-3 + P programs. The B-5 program includes infants, toddlers, and preschoolers in one building (i.e., ages birth to 5), whereas B-3 + P has one building for infants toddlers and an affiliated preschool in a separate facility. Thus, participants in this study were in one of two university-affiliated programs housed in three separate buildings located on the same research-based university campus. The university is located in the midwestern United States in a small urban community.[2]

The programs are state licensed and nationally accredited through NAEYC. Licensing regulations in this state require primary caregiving and reasonable attempts to implement COC. In addition, the programs have achieved the highest level of quality rating for licensed child care programs through their state's QRIS.[3] Strict adult-to-child ratios and group size requirements are maintained in these sites, specifically a minimum of two adults with eight infants, two adults for 10 toddlers, and two adults for the preschool rooms, which had 16–20 children. In all cases, there is usually a third adult present, a caregiving aide or teacher's aide. All professional staff (lead caregivers/teachers) had bachelor's degrees, the minimum requirement in these programs, and many had master's degrees or were working toward them. Finally, these programs have existed on the campus for more than 30 years.

Quality assurance based on ratings and adherence to standards was not the only concern in selecting settings for the study, however. Relationship focus was an additional criterion. Owen, Klausli, Mata-Otero, and Caughy (2008) differentiated relationship-focused settings from non-relationship-focused settings among NAEYC-accredited settings, finding more positive outcomes in the former. We had prior experience in the chosen settings and considered them relationship focused based on their commitment to primary caregiving, family-centered practices, and engagement in COC.

---

[2] Pseudonyms are used for the names of individuals and places.
[3] The highest QRIS rating in this state is Level 4. This level requires documentation and assessment of the numerous standards and requires that the child care center achieve and maintain national recognition by an accrediting body recognized by the state, typically NAEYC.

The campus child care system uses a co-lead structure for its infant toddler caregivers and preschool teachers, meaning that two professional practitioners work together as co-leads rather than as one lead with an assistant. Staff schedules are arranged so that families always have one of the co-lead practitioners available when they arrive, whether at the beginning or end of the day. The system also places a value on caregiving teams, making every effort to keep co-leads together with the same aides, part-time hourly workers, and substitute caregivers over the 3 years of the continuity cycle. To this end, infant toddler caregivers and preschool teachers in this university system have staggered 2-hr breaks in the middle of the day during which they must remain in their buildings—1 hr for lunch and 1 hr for planning—with 1 hr overlapping so professionals can plan as teams.

Birth-to-5 program (B-5)
The B-5 program has five classrooms for children ages 6 weeks to age 5. They utilize a looping model of COC for infants and toddlers. The caregiving team remains with a group from infancy until the children have all had their third birthday. The group remains in the same room for the first 2 years of the program, and changes are made in furnishings and materials to accommodate changing growth and development. After 2 years, the entire group of children and caregivers transitions together into a more spacious room specifically designed for big, active 2-year-olds. The summer following their third birthdays, the group of children is divided roughly in half and transitioned into one of two multiage preschool classrooms in the same building. During the daily 2-hr midday breaks in this center, infant toddler caregivers from the three infant toddler rooms and the preschool teachers from the two preschool rooms have an opportunity to meet together, plan, and discuss issues of practice.

Birth-to-3 with separate preschool program (B-3 + P)
In this program, infants and toddlers are housed in a building with four rooms, one each for infants, ones, young twos, and older 2-year-olds. This program also follows a looping model, with adults and children moving through the rooms together until, in the late summer after the children turn 3, children transition to the preschool up the hill. Three-year-olds who transition into the preschool part of the program are dispersed across three multiage classrooms. As in the B-5 program, caregivers and teachers in the B-3 + P program have a 1-hr lunch and 1-hr planning time. However, unlike the B-5 caregivers, the infant toddler caregivers in the B-3 + P program rarely interact with, and even more rarely plan with, preschool teachers.

Participants
There were 35 participants in total in this study, including 14 primary and 21 secondary participants. Primary participants were members of the professional caregiving team ($n = 6$) and parents ($n = 8$) considered most proximally related, in Microsystem I, to infants and toddlers in the two child care centers in their respective rooms. Six of the parent participants had children currently cared for in one of the two rooms ($n = 6$), whereas two had children who had recently transitioned into preschool classrooms ($n = 2$). Summary descriptions of primary participants in Microsystem I are shown in Tables 1 and 2.

There were 21 secondary participants, positioned in Microsystem II, including one campus-wide administrator and three program directors, infant toddler co-lead caregivers from rooms in the program other than the two of central focus ($n = 8$), and preschool teachers in the classrooms into which children typically transition from infant toddler COC ($n = 9$). A summary description of the secondary participants is shown in Table 3.

Participant selection
Among the primary participants were caregiving teams from two child care rooms, consisting of co-lead caregivers and their caregiving aides. These two teams of caregivers were purposefully selected because

TABLE 1. Summary Description of Primary Informants in Microsystem I: Caregiving Teams.

Setting and Caregiver	Highest Degree and Field of Study	Years in Program	Years in Profession	Experience With Continuity of Care
B-5 program (n = 3)				
Lilly Grace, co-lead caregiver	MS and EdD in ECEC	17	22	7 years (in third 3-year looping cycle)
Jack, co-lead caregiver	BS in political science and CDA (preschool)	3	7	5 years (in second 3-year looping cycle)
Buket, caregiving aide	BS in physics (from native Afghanistan) and infant toddler CDA	10	11	7 years (in third 3-year looping cycle)
B-3 + P program (n = 3)				
Lucy, co-lead caregiver	BA psychology and sociology; MS in ECEC nearly completed	7	11	8 years (in third 3-year looping cycle)
Viviane, co-lead caregiver	BA sociology, family studies; MS in ECEC nearly completed	10	18	9 years (in third 3-year cycle in current program; experience in previous program)
Ceylan, aide	BA in teacher training (from native Afghanistan)	6	32	6 years (in second 3-year looping cycle)

Note. B-5 = birth-to-5 program; MS = master of science degree; EdD = doctorate in education; ECEC = early childhood education and care; BS = bachelor of science; CDA = Child Development Associate credential; B-3 + P = birth-to-3 with separate preschool program; BA = bachelor of arts degree.

TABLE 2. Description of Primary Informants in Microsystem I: Parents.

Program and Parent Pseudonym	Family Description	Experience With COC
B-5 program ($n = 4$)		
Meredith (mother)	Three sons, ages 17 months, 5 years, and 9 years, live with two professionally employed parents	Two youngest sons in COC from 3 and 6 months; oldest son moved to COC from discontinuous program at age 2
Monica (mother)	One daughter, age 18 months, lives with two parents, both professionally employed	Daughter in COC in B-5 program since 6 months
Maryanne (mother)	Three sons, ages 8, 4½, and 2, live with two professionally employed parents	Two youngest sons in COC from 5 months; oldest son in discontinuous care most of his first 3 years
Madeleine (mother)	One child, a daughter, age 3, lives with two professionally employed parents	Daughter in COC in B-5 program since early infancy, now in preschool in B-5
B-3 + P program ($n = 3$)		
Demetri (father)	Two daughters, ages 4½ and 9, live with two professionally employed parents; family from Russia	Younger daughter in COC from ages 1 to 3½, now in preschool; first daughter in discontinuous care as an infant toddler
Dionne (mother)	Two sons, ages 5 and 6 months, live with two parents, one professionally employed and one a graduate student	Oldest son in B-3 + P program for 2 years before preschool; second son just started COC program
Debra (mother)	One son, age 2½, lives with two professionally employed parents	Son transitioned into COC program at 18 months from a discontinuous program
B-5 and B-3 + P program ($n = 1$)		
Dao-Ming (mother)	Two sons, ages 5 and 1½, live with two parents, both graduate students (from Taiwan)	Oldest son in COC in B-3 + P program 3 years, now preschool, B-5 program; youngest son in COC in B-5 program

Note. COC = continuity of care; B-5 = birth-to-5 program; B-3 + P = birth-to-3 with separate preschool program.

TABLE 3. Summary Description of Secondary Informants in Microsystem II.

Program and Setting	Pseudonym	Highest Degree and Field of Study	Years in Program	Years in Profession
B-5 program				
Other B-3 caregivers (*n* = 4)	Becky, Betty, Beth, Belle	One MS and one EdD in ECEC; one BS and one in process of earning MS in ECEC	17	22
Preschool teachers (*n* = 4)	Tatsu, Tracy Tammy, Tara	Three with master's degrees in ECEC and one in process of earning master's	*M* = 8; range = 4–13	*M* = 13; range = 10–19
Administrator (*n* = 1)	Abby	MS in ECEC	9	20
B-3 + P program				
Other B-3 caregivers (*n* = 4)	Cybil, Chelsea, Clara, Caitlin	BA in psychology and sociology; MS in ECEC nearly completed	7	11
Preschool teachers (*n* = 5)	Paul, Phoebe Peggy, Pavla, Patricia	Four with bachelor's degrees in ECEC and one with an MFA	*M* = 15; range = 7–21	*M* = 12; range = 2–16
Infant toddler director (*n* = 1)	Anna	Master's in ECEC	5	30
Preschool director (*n* = 1)	Alexis	Master's in ECEC	13	34
University system				
Administrator (*n* = 1)	Andy	Master's in ECEC	16	38

Note. B-5 = birth-to-5 program; MS = master of science degree; EdD = doctorate in education; ECEC = early childhood education and care; BS = bachelor of science; B-3 + P = birth-to-3 with separate preschool program; BA = bachelor of arts degree; MFA = master of fine arts degree.

these individuals (a) were well-educated, veteran early childhood infant toddler professionals; (b) had experienced continuity in their programs for several years; (c) had been caregivers in the programs before continuity was implemented and participated in their programs' transition to COC; (d) had been part of an earlier study in which extensive observations had been conducted in their rooms 5 years earlier (McMullen & Lash, 2012; McMullen et al., 2009); and (e) had classrooms within programs recognized as exhibiting a high level of quality on state and national measures. Six professionals (two teams) were invited to be part of the study, and all agreed.

Parents in the study were also considered primary participants and considered positioned in Microsystem I with the caregiving team from the two rooms; they constituted a convenience sample of individuals who were referred to us by participating caregiving professionals. Caregivers provided names and e-mail addresses of 16 current and recent parents, who were then contacted and invited to participate. Six parents (38%) never responded, whereas two who agreed to participate were not interviewed because of time constraints and difficulties scheduling the interviews. In agreeing to participate, the final sample of eight parents indicated understanding that quotations might be taken from transcripts of their audiotaped interviews, were assured of anonymity, and were informed that pseudonyms would be used in place of their names. As shown in Table 2, all of the participating parents worked in professional positions ($n = 6$) or were graduate students ($n = 2$). Nearly all were White and U.S. citizens ($n = 7$), whereas one mother was Taiwanese.

As noted earlier, secondary participants included administrators, preschool teachers, and infant toddler caregivers other than those in the two rooms examined, and they were positioned within Microsystem II in our conceptualization of Bronfenbrenner's model (Bronfenbrenner & Morris, 2006). Although not involved each and every day with infants and toddlers, they were selected because they were highly involved with and influenced by those within Microsystem I.

Procedure

We met weekly during one academic semester to discuss the research literature, consider the theoretical framing of the study, determine the appropriate methodology, plan interview protocols, and examine various documents available about the selected early childhood programs. After securing permission from our institution's Human Subjects Committee, we invited participants. For a period of 20 weeks, three researchers conducted interviews using the protocols found in the Appendix as guides. Observations of the settings had been done in a study that had been conducted 4 years earlier concerning infants' experiences in group care.

Individual interviews were conducted with each primary participant (Microsystem I), including the members of the infant toddler caregiving teams and parents from the two focus rooms. Each interview lasted 60 to 90 min and was conducted in a setting selected by the respondent. For these interviews, we sought general impressions of COC from the perspectives of the participants, specifically concerning the nature of COC, the role of relationships in caregiving, how primary caregiving was practiced and understood, and to what extent families were incorporated into decision making and goal setting.

Secondary participants were interviewed in three small groups, formed according to program affiliation and professional role. Thus, there were four groups as follows: B-3 + P preschool teachers, B-5 preschool teachers, other infant toddler caregivers in the programs, and all administrators. Preschool teachers were interviewed primarily about their perceptions of the children and families who transitioned into their classrooms, in particular about any differences perceived in the children or families from COC versus those with other experiences before entering preschool. The group interviews of preschool teachers lasted about 45 min. The four administrators were interviewed as a group in a 90-min meeting focusing on the background of COC on campus and in the programs, issues of staffing, unique cultures within each building, and the administrators' thoughts about benefits and challenges related to the implementation of COC.

Lead infant toddler caregivers (primary participants) and administrators were interviewed by Researcher 1, preschool teachers and caregiving aides by Researcher 2, and parents by Researcher 3. With the exception of the focus group, which was videotaped and transcribed by Researcher 4, all individual and group interviews were audio-recorded and transcribed by a professional secretary. The interviewers reviewed transcripts for accuracy and edited and annotated as needed for clarity. The final transcripts were then posted to a secure shared online work site for analysis. After several meetings discussing our preliminary interpretations, we held a 90-min focus group discussion with the four infant toddler co-lead caregivers who were primary participants and three other infant toddler caregivers from the two programs. The purpose of the focus group was to discuss our preliminary findings and initial interpretations.

Analysis

We met frequently to review incoming data and discuss upcoming interviews based on what we saw as emerging ideas and patterns (Hatch, 2002). When all interviews and transcriptions were completed, we reviewed the final transcripts first as individuals and then as a group, looking for (a) overall initial impressions and emerging big ideas, (b) patterns or repeated themes, and (c) the use of metaphor. We are teacher educators in early childhood education who teach the field's recommended practices to pre- and in-service practitioners, and because of this we were concerned about keeping our subjectivity in check and remaining objective throughout data collection and interpretation. Thus, we engaged in several recognized methods to do this and address trustworthiness, confirmability, and credibility, including triangulation, member checking, and peer debriefing (Lincoln & Guba, 1985).

Triangulation

Triangulation is an accepted method of ensuring trustworthiness in qualitative research in which the researchers use two or more sources of information to inform the central phenomenon (Creswell & Miller, 2000). We triangulated data by (a) utilizing multiple and varied forms of data, including individual and group interviews, forum group discussions, analysis of documents describing the program and related policies, and reflection on the lead researcher's past experience in the rooms observing caregivers' practices; (b) examining multiple perspectives represented among the different roles of the participants; and (c) utilizing a form of observer triangulation by comparing areas of agreement and disagreement among individual interpretations across the research team.

Member checking

Member checking is a valuable tool for ensuring trustworthiness in qualitative work (Lincoln & Guba, 1985). The lead researcher engaged in several e-mail and informal face-to-face exchanges with co-lead caregivers who were primary participants in the study; this was done to clarify and verify interpretations. In addition, the 90-min focus group acted as a means of member checking as it allowed us to discuss findings, preliminary interpretations, and potential implications with the participants.

Peer debriefing

Preliminary conclusions from this study were presented at several state and national conferences in the year following data collection. At those forums and at other professional meetings, the lead researcher spoke one on one with other researchers and leaders of professional organizations who have studied the practices featured in the study, soliciting thoughts and reactions to our initial interpretations.

Findings

Findings presented here are organized around eight dominant ideas that emerged from the data as features that describe the phenomenon of COC in the two well-established programs included in this study. These features are increased knowledge, stable relationships, family-type atmosphere, primary caregiving, family-centeredness, effective caregiver partnerships, the transition to preschool, and finally recommendations for improvement. Selected quotations, representative of participants' responses, allow their voices to tell the story of COC in the two stable infant toddler programs. It is important to note that although they are presented as distinct, there is overlap among the features, demonstrating an interconnectedness and mutual dependence among the ideas uncovered.

Feature 1: increased knowledge

Knowledge gained over time in the context of COC was a dominant theme cited explicitly and repeatedly by many respondents as the primary benefit of COC. Knowledge was conceptualized in two ways: increased understanding of child development in general and knowledge gained over time that helped caregivers understand individual children. Caregivers compared prior experiences in discontinuous care with COC, citing the ability to "watch" development "unfold" over time in individuals and in the group as key differences:

> The best thing about being a caregiver in continuity of care is watching the process, it's watching the developmental process from really, the beginning, and being able to see it through until children reach a completely different level, and being able to document that and talk it over with families, and I mean, there's so much discovery and growth that happens 0–3. It's AMAZING to get to be an observer and participant in that. (Caregiver Viviane, B-3 + P program)

Caregivers valued the length of time they had in the context of COC, indicating that it facilitated their understanding of the broader context of child development throughout the birth-to-3 period. Caregivers stated a belief that their increased knowledge of development in general and the ability to be with individual children over longer periods of time contributed to "smoother" or more "even" developmental progress of the infants and toddlers in COC in comparison to what they recalled from their experiences in discontinuous rooms. They described it as "less stopping and starting" and "less regression" and remarked that "no time is lost" as a child grows and develops in COC. It is important to note that caregivers highlighted how this increased knowledge resulted in them being able to anticipate next steps for children and make plans for individualizing care:

> I know these children so well since starting with them. When you get to know these children this well you can see where they're going. Just being able to know, literally just know, THAT child over there right now, I could put them to bed now, they've had a pacifier since they came to school, and know within a week that child is ready, right now to give that up and be 100% accurate. We're starting potty training, and again it's like, THIS child's ready, THAT child's not, right now we should start focusing on this from this angle. (Caregiver Jack, B-5 program)

Parents recognized and valued the in-depth knowledge that caregivers had about infants and toddlers in general and their individual children in particular. They especially appreciated caregivers' willingness to share this knowledge:

> We were just so, so impressed by the attention and the interest and the skill of both Viviane and Lucy. I mean, I've never seen anything like it. You know, the way that they would just day after day give us detailed reports about what was going on with her, they really knew so many things about her and it was genuine too. It wasn't just kind of a pro forma thing. (Father Demetri, B-3 + P program)

Caregivers reported feeling satisfaction with being able to use knowledge they gained over time to help groups and individual children to work, play, learn, and grow:

> To see them take off with what you are able to give them because you know where they are and what they're going towards at that moment. It's such a satisfaction for you to know that you just helped a child reach a major milestone. And to be able to see the joy in their eyes and to be able to offer that, they know that they just did something amazing too, and so they get such a satisfaction and they become even more secure and safe in knowing that they are really cared for and really taken care of. (Caregiver Jack, B-5 program)

Feature 2: stable relationships

Another feature that emerged from this study was the importance of the stability of relationships within the community. Caregivers and parents alike expressed that being in COC over a 3-year period decreased the "chaos" they felt in discontinuous situations:

> Well, in the traditional revolving door model you have to start over again and again so it kind of like getting a new family doctor, you know? You've got to tell him the whole history. This is what he likes, this is what he does, this is what you should know about what he doesn't like, don't make him do this, make him do that. Like you know, I feel like it is kind of starting over. Whereas this year ... there was no me getting to know them, no her getting to know them. So to not have to go through that every year is really brilliant. (Mother Monica, B-5 program)

Caregiver Lucy, who had many years of experience under both "revolving door" and continuity models, likened what she experienced in discontinuity to living through a divorce:

> I've seen what happens when children are transitioning into a new space, new caregivers, having to renegotiate relationships with new friends, caregivers; and to me it's just like being in a divorced family where you move, have to renegotiate your friends, and your school, and WHY? Why should you have to? (Caregiver Lucy, B-3 + P program)

All four co-lead caregivers noted that an increased sense of security as it relates to attachment was a potential benefit to the stability of relationships inherent in COC. Caregiver Lucy (B-3 + P program), said, "Attachment is definitely a main advantage ... and secondary attachments are really important ... Children come to us and we hope they have secure attachments, but not having to renegotiate relationships constantly, maintains that secure attachment."

Parents also emphasized that stability as it related and contributed to a sense of security important to them. They reported that COC was less "chaotic," "disruptive," and "stressful" than they had experienced in discontinuous care:

> The most beneficial thing for [son's name] is the sense of security because he knows his schedule and knows his friends in the classroom. They feel comfortable, secure, and predictable because they feel like, I just, I know what's going to happen, and I don't feel, I don't need to feel nervous or anxious when I'm going to school. (Mother Dao-Ming, B-3 + P and B-5 programs)

Feature 3: a family-type atmosphere

The metaphor of family and the roles within it dominated descriptions of the relationships between and among various members of caregiving teams and parents:

> I more or less think of everyone at the child care program as like an extended family. And the caregivers, I feel very comfortable talking to them about any concern I might have or expressing things that I like that they're doing or I want to make sure that, you know, I'm doing my part and whatever. And they love my kids. So it's a very much, uh, a family-type atmosphere. (Mother Meredith, B-5 program)

Parents spoke of how bonds of trust and open communication resulted within the "family-type atmosphere" facilitated by COC. In particular, parents appreciated caregivers' efforts to maintain consistency between home and child care in terms of the nature of caregiving interactions, reporting that this was "highly respectful" of their parenting values:

They actually mimicked my son's home life with them. The teachers worked so hard to keep things so consistent and so in line with home. I really felt like they tried to get to know us as parents and wanted to do things similar to how we would have done them at home, so there wasn't a huge difference between home and school. (Mother Debra, B-3 + P program)

In addition, parents drew comfort in seeing caregivers be openly affectionate with their children, replicating the kind of caring interactions their child would experience at home. They characterized this as caregivers "loving" their children:

Lilly Grace would talk about love with the kids and kiss and hug and just do all kinds of things. I actually think that there should be care and empathy and love present in the classroom. These kids need a kiss or a hug or love and I don't think that should be left at home. (Mother Maryanne, B-5 program)

From the caregivers' perspectives, loving infants and toddlers in care is both natural and essential. Caregiver Jack (B-5 program) said he "cannot imagine not loving the babies" and worried that being emotionally detached would be harmful to them. Lilly Grace spoke of her love of the babies as a "special calling":

I think we are in the nurturing profession. When we are with children, that's a special calling, we are called to, to love the babies, and it's something which is as natural as we breathe air around us, and it's only natural for us to love them and to take care of them, to form that bond with that baby because we know that love is what makes the world go round. (Caregiver Lilly Grace, B-5 program)

Caregivers created environments in which loving, caring interactions were reinforced among the children as well. Most referred to the infants and toddlers in care as "friends" and promoted prosocial caring interactions among the children. "Gentle, please; be gentle with your friends" was a refrain heard frequently. Having caregivers model and promote warm caring behaviors was important to parents, who reported a belief that it is important to children's growth as caring individuals:

I see a level of empathy and intimacy with my kids that I think, in part, is due to continuity of care. I think there's real depth in their relationships and in their ability to connect to other human beings. I think this kind of experience is fundamental for setting the stage for what their adult intimacy should look like. I think it's vital to have experience and exposure to peers, to be in a setting like this one, so that they get practice with conflict as well as friendship. (Mother Maryanne, B-5 program)

Feature 4: primary caregiving

Caregivers and parents provided important insight into the nature of primary caregiving within the context of COC. Caregivers spoke of how it was within the primary care relationship that they begin forming in-depth knowledge of children from the time they first enter the program. They stated the importance of this deep personal knowledge as necessary to the establishment of bonds of trust necessary in promoting security:

The child is learning to bond with that primary caregiver and the caregiver invests a lot of time, and energy and effort in that baby. And then the benefits are mutual. The caregiver, on the one hand, gets the satisfaction of interacting with the baby and watching the baby grow and blossom and develop into this young girl or boy. And the baby, on the other hand, is growing with so much security and trust which is the basis for all growth and development. And that child is going to be such a secure adult. (Caregiver Lilly Grace, B-5 program)

Not all parents could identify which of the two co-lead caregivers was the primary caregiver of their child when asked by the interviewer. However, all parents recognized and appreciated benefits arising from the practice:

I feel like she, Viviane, spent a little bit more extra time, extra attention to [son's name]. I don't know how to explain that feeling but when I was talking to her like every day at pick up or when I talk to her about how [son's name] was doing in the day, I can feel like she really watched him when [son's name] was doing something and she remembered what [son's name] was doing and she remembered what kind of progress he made. And I just feel like she spends some extra attention and time and she always rocked him to sleep during the nap time or told me she always sits by him and pats him on the back during the nap time. And I feel like he gets a little bit more extra care from Viviane. I feel very secure and I feel she is respected by us and she was trusted by us. (Mother Dao-Ming, B-3 + P and B-5 programs)

Even if parents did remember who their assigned primary caregiver was, over time, they began going to one or the other of the co-lead caregivers for different reasons at different times. As parents and caregivers came to know one another well, parents learned the caregivers' different strengths:

I think that they have different strengths and I call on them for different things. They're both very reassuring people. Viviane, I think, by her own admission likes babies more than some of the slightly older ones, so she's always happy around the babies. Lucy, I think, is sometimes a little bit more proactive in the room, like, she's a little bit more structured, perhaps. So I think I pull on them for different things. (Mother Dionne, B-3 + P program)

Caregivers spoke directly about how the primary roles changed over time as babies grew and developed and relationships with families entered new stages. Caregiver Lucy (B-3 + P program) characterized it as a change that occurs because of a "natural selection" or a "sorting" process that occurs over time. As babies, parents, and caregivers get to know one another better, they "select certain people that they feel that connection with." Viviane spoke of it in terms of children's choice—"these are the children who chose me"—and stressed the nonexclusivity of the primary care arrangement, noting the importance of both lead caregivers knowing all children and parents well:

In terms of communication with parents, a lot of times, I do more of the calling when my kids are sick and she'll do more calling when her kids are sick just because of their relationship with the child and maybe the parent's understanding of our relationship with the child too. But we both work very hard during the transition week ... not just bonding and forming a relationship with the children [in the primary group] but both of us forming a strong relationship with every set of parents so that they know that we're it. We're the people that you talk to when you have a concern. We're the people that you tell about their night. We're the people you tell about what they ate for breakfast or what color their poop was. We're those people; together, together. (Caregiver Viviane, B-3 + P program)

Feature 5: family-centeredness

Caregivers and parents expressed what we characterized as a mutual respect for one another, noting how they often used words such as "partnership," "colleagues," and "friendship" to describe how they worked together toward common goals:

We work very hard to create partnerships with all of our families. When we get them, we're getting them in some cases as new parents or at least new parents to that baby and they're giving us a great gift by sharing their child with us and we have an extreme amount of respect for that and want to do everything we can in our power to be a partner for them in making this amazing person. (Caregiver Viviane, B-3 + P)

The caregiver–parent partnership was identified as an "investment" by several participants, including parents and caregivers. The use of this word seemed to recognize both the importance of the relationship they were entering into as well as the amount of time they would be working together. Both programs entered into their partnerships with families using mindful, purposeful approaches that included weeks of part-time care of infants with a family member present and planned activities such as "parent–infant teas" and home visits:

That's an important thing to do to build that bond, you know, she'd, Lilly Grace, be willing to come over and spend some time in our home with him or meet him ... I really respected that she offered to do that and it made me feel like the relationship was at a deeper level than just "Oh, I teach your kid and it's great and wonderful but I'm, this is a job." (Mother Maryanne, B-5 program)

Parent empowerment emerged as an issue within the context of caregiver–parent relationships. Caregivers saw it as one of their responsibilities as professionals to help parents recognize themselves as experts on and advocates for their children, and they provided them encouragement to support them in their parenting role:

> It is not a 1-year relationship but they're [parents] going to interact with the caregiver over a period of three, three-and-a-half years or even more. Many parents tell me, "We trust you, you know the best." And I say, "You're the parents, you're the best teachers of the child. I'm here to help you ... I'm here to support you," because I want to validate what they do. (Caregiver Lilly Grace, B-5 program)

Viviane echoed Lilly Grace's sentiment about the importance of validating parents and added thoughts about the role of advocacy in empowering parents (i.e., caregivers as advocates of parents and parents as advocates for their children):

> We're always advocating for parents to be empowered, to always speak their minds about their children's educational experiences, about their children's social experience, about everything that goes on for their child. We tell them from the beginning that they're their child's first advocate. This is your child. Speak up for your child! Speak up for what you feel is right! If you see that something is going on and in your heart, you know that it should be different, don't be shy. (Caregiver Viviane, B-3 + P program)

Secondary participants, specifically preschool teachers, also spoke of empowerment, but they characterized it differently based on their program. In the B-5 program in which birth to 5-year-olds were all under one roof, families and their children were fairly well known by the teachers before they transitioned into preschool. These preschool teachers spoke of the families who transitioned from the COC infant toddler program in decidedly positive, admiring tones and expressed "how empowered" they were. Preschool teachers from the B-3 + P program, located in a separate building, literally up the hill from the infant toddler program, also spoke of parents as empowered. These teachers, who had little or no prior relationship with the children and families from the infant toddler program, used a different tone when speaking of parental empowerment, however—a tone that we found to be negative or complaining.

Being "under one roof" was mentioned by preschool teachers in the B-5 setting as a distinct advantage in building relationships with families and children and indeed coming to know and understand individual children before they entered their classrooms:

> One of the things I notice is that we preschool teachers get to see these faces as they start coming in. We get to see these kids as they're starting to walk down the sidewalk instead of being carried. So we get to celebrate little things with them before we have a professional relationship with them, so that's kind of neat. It's also nice that the parents get to see us preschool teachers. They get to see us teach a lot before they're ready to hand their children over to us which I think is more comforting because they know the kind of program that, you know, they know what's happening and where their child is going next. (Preschool teacher Tracy, B-5 program)

Finally, relationships formed between caregivers and parents and the empowerment of parents within the program as advocates for their children were seen as laying a foundation for future expectations for relationships and communication in educational settings:

> This place sort of set the bar for what the relationship should look like. So when [son's name] went to public school, I actually removed him ... because I felt like the bar was not high enough compared to what I got here. And this was my comparison point and so I went and looked in town and found a place where the communication was two ways, where they regarded my child in high esteem, where the emotional development of my child is important. So this has set the tone for me for my expectations for school, [kindergarten] through ... 12. (Mother Maryanne, B-5 program)

Feature 6: effective caregiver partnerships

Co-Lead Caregivers

In the group interview of administrators (secondary participants), the creation of the practice of hiring and staffing two co-lead professionals for child care rooms in the university system was discussed. Participants described it as, first, a matter of equity, righting a disparity they believed had existed between professional partners in their previous model (i.e., lead with assistant); and, second, a practice more responsive to the needs of families and children. The co-lead structure changed power and perception differentials and equalized salaries. Staffing schedules in this structure are arranged so that there is always a highly qualified lead caregiver present when the first parents arrive early in the morning and the last parents pick up their children in the evening.

The four co-lead infant toddler caregivers who were among the primary participants in this study had worked within the co-lead structure for a number of years. In their one-on-one interviews, they used family metaphors to describe their long-term partnerships. Three spoke of their working partnership as a marriage, and one described it as having a "mom and dad dynamic." They expressed a belief that the closeness of their partnerships was different than what they had experienced under the previous lead/subordinate model. Caregiver Lucy (B-3 + P program) said, "It's like a marriage. I feel like it would be devastating to have to divorce her, my co-teacher. But also like a marriage, you know we have those different personality styles and the children know that."

Caregivers spoke of how long it takes to develop an effective partnership, saying it takes a year or more before partners "really know" each other. They said "extended time" was critical for developing a "level of comfort and understanding" (Jack) in a partner's beliefs, styles, strengths, and preferences and achieving balance in daily caregiving tasks:

> Working with your co-teacher involves finding balance where you can really help support each other where you and they need supporting and then let the other one have some free reign where they're really good ... Really finding a good balance between the two teachers, how to make things work, what you like, what you don't like. (Caregiver Jack, B-5 program)

And like a marriage, or any long-term relationship, caregivers noted that creating effective partnerships takes work and investment in the relationship and often compromise:

> We have a good balance. In our classroom, I'm definitely more of the "dad" and she's more of the "mom" personality. We're both very nurturing, we're both very clear with the children about our expectations, but if the enforcer is called in, it's me! But I mean, we've got a lot in common and our ideas and our thought process about what children need and how our classroom runs best are definitely a compromise. We just worked it out. Division of labor-wise: I do paperwork because I love paperwork, she does a lot of the technology stuff because she loves technology stuff, and we work together on developmental profiles. It's a partnership. It's a lot of giving and taking and working together and you know, getting input from the other person and just looking at the other person and checking in. "We're with each on this, right?" And, definitely, we are. (Caregiver Viviane, B-3 + P program)

Feature 7: the transition to preschool

The transition of 3-year-olds from the infant toddler COC program into preschool was handled thoughtfully and carefully. Yet it brought with it challenges for most of the adults involved, including members of the infant toddler caregiving team. Caregiver Viviane described it as a time "mixed with joy and sadness." Indeed, all of the caregivers and aides in the study shared how hard it was to say goodbye to children and parents they had grown attached to over the course of 3 years. In addition to this emotional component, caregivers noted that making the transition from working with big 3-year-olds and starting over with a new group of very young infants and their families was daunting physically (e.g., setting up their rooms, a return to lifting and carrying nonmobile children) as well as cognitively (e.g., adjusting notions of what children are, what they "like," and what "they need"). One caregiver characterized this process as "gearing up." Despite the difficulties, caregivers expressed strong commitment to COC as "the best," and they approached the transition with a spirit of hope that the children would develop and thrive within their new relationships with their new teachers:

> A lot of what has helped me in coming to terms with "the big transition" is knowing that for whatever reasons I love this child, that teacher, their new teacher, is going to have a whole different set of reasons for loving them. They're going to make the time to form the relationship, and they're going to get their own reasons for loving them, and it's going to happen. Whether I give them all seven of their developmental profiles full of pictures telling them everything I have known about this child for their entire life or not is almost irrelevant because

they need to know that child for who they are from the moment they walk in their door. (Caregiver Viviane, B-3 + P program)

All of the caregivers in the study had experience in both continuous and discontinuous care settings. In their view, COC was superior in that it established a firm foundation, in a way inoculating the children against disruption or stress in future transitions:

> Continuity of care really builds an emotional platform, stability, a foundation that those children can use when it comes time to transition [to preschool]. When children are passed along continuously, they are always being passed into different arms, just passing off, time after time after time, and the child doesn't really ever have a sense of belonging and feeling absolutely safe and secure. So I think that when they have that secure foundation that's built through continuity of care, I think that when that transition comes, and again it's a little bit sad and may be a little scary for them, but at the same point, they're excited and ready for it, they want it. (Caregiver Jack, B-5 program)

Preschool teachers were asked directly whether they noticed any differences between 3-year-olds and the families who joined the multiage preschool classrooms from COC and those coming from either home or non-COC infant toddler programs. There was agreement that in general the COC children were better able to "hit the ground running":

> She knows to trust the teacher. That's something that she learned from continuity of care, I believe, that the teacher is there for her and that she can expect a certain degree of respect and support from her teacher where a kid coming from outside that kind of environment, it might take them a little bit longer to bond with the teacher. (Preschool teacher Paul, B-3 + P program)

Tatsu, a preschool teacher in the B-5 program, credited the success children had in transitioning to trust built from strong attachment relationships in the COC program: "They're confident they can make the same quality of attachment with the new teachers and new peers once they move to the preschool room." Preschool teachers as a group noted that the children who transitioned from COC were generally more self-confident and ready to engage in the play and routines in the new classroom in general. Pavla, a preschool teacher in the B-3 + P program, said, "They [those from COC] are more confident children ... when they come here, you know, they look already ready to just continue playing the same way what was going on over there; to be a respected child."

Parents from both the B-3 + P and B-5 programs expressed gratitude for the extensive preparation they and their children had as they transitioned to preschool:

> ... they start visiting, they'll take small groups or the whole class over into the classroom so the kids can play with the toys, meet the kids, meet the teachers ... they start off with small amounts of time then increase the time. They will increase to allow snacks in the preschool room or naps in the preschool room so again they're just getting more and more familiar with doing the different activities in that room. (Mother Dionne, B-3 + P program)

Despite the careful planning on the part of program staff for the preschool transition, some parents admitted to having initial difficulty moving from the COC infant toddler program into preschool. This was true even when it was in the same building, as in the case of the B-5 program. Parents saw this transition as a challenge that they could work on together with caregivers and teachers:

> It was pretty rough at first. I kind of anticipated it because I had a friend who told me that Tatsu and Tammy, who are [daughter's name] teachers now, are very different from the infant toddler teachers. They very much are ... you know, where I think Lilly Grace and Jack are half teacher half nurturers/caretakers, the preschool teachers are more teachers than anything, more than they are caretakers or nurturers, not that they don't, that, but they really, they clearly place emphasis on teaching independence, which I couldn't be more happy about, but that was a challenge for [daughter's name]. So she, for the first couple of months, you know, had a hard time with me leaving. She was very quiet and shy in the class. I mean that was one of the things that we worked on together. (Mother Madeline, B-5 program)

Parents in the study identified transitions as a "big adjustment" in general and attributed this to new caretaking styles and an increased emphasis on "education" over "nurturing" and "care."

However, parents in general seemed to view the difficulties of transition as simply "part of life" and did not appear particularly concerned:

> So it was a big adjustment, but this year, you know, she's been great, and honestly, if she [daughter's name] didn't have a hard time adjusting, I kind of almost think that would be weird, you know what I mean? So I mean I want her to have to go through an adjustment period because that's what, you know, life is, it's like one adjustment after another; so yeah, it was an adjustment. (Mother Madeline, B-5 program)

Feature 8: recommendations for improvement

Respondents tended to focus on features of COC that could be considered benefits and appeared reluctant to consider challenges, even when pushed to do so by interviewers and the facilitator of the forum group. When encouraged for a response, two caregivers and a parent indicated that although it had not been a problem for them, they worried about parents who "did not like" the caregiving team and might feel "stuck." This issue was subsequently brought up in the forum discussion. The consensus was that this had not been a problem in the past, and they doubted it would be in the future for two reasons. First, they said, parents "know what they are getting into" when they come to one of their programs. Second, because COC involves long-term commitment, parents and caregivers "invest" in building and maintaining relationships from the very beginning. One caregiver said everyone "worked harder" to relate to one another than they might "if we just had to be together 9 months or so."

When parents were asked "What could be done to improve the program?" they offered no substantive challenges to COC as a practice. Parents did, however, contribute suggestions about the program overall, such as "stay open later" and "maybe hold more social functions for families." Some complained about the expense of the program. Largely, however, parents responded by praising their child's program and highlighting aspects of COC they particularly liked. When Debra was asked what could be improved in the infant toddler program, she said the following:

> If they kept them until they were 5! [laughter] I can't think of any, I can't think of anything else. I mean I think the class size was appropriate, I thought their leadership was excellent; it's expensive, but that's a whole other discussion about the cost of child care. I mean that's just the reality of it, but for me if they would have, I wish he could have stayed longer. (Mother Debra, B-3 + P program)

One parent, who described herself as "critical," was instead full of praise for the program, commenting on how much she valued the caregivers' knowledge of children:

> They sent out a survey recently asking me [about improvements] and I'm an educator who's really critical and always has suggestions, and I looked at Abby, who's the director there, and said, "I got nothing for you." I love it ... I really love what they do. It's bizarre for me to say I don't have any suggestions. But they beat me to the punch ... they just are so good at what they do I feel like they know children so well and so much better than me that they really are on it. (Mother Monica, B-5 program)

Finally, this father's response to the question of what could be done to improve the infant toddler program provides a positive way to end the presentation of findings: "I can't think of anything. Really. I mean, it exceeded, it exceeded my expectations by leaps and bounds. I can't think of any ways to improve it. Frankly, everything about it is good!" (Father Demetri, B-3 + P program).

Discussion

In this study, we examined the perspectives of adults who experienced infant toddler COC in two programs in which COC had been the norm for several years. Findings both support and extend prior research about COC and have implications for scholars, policymakers, those engaged in pre-and in-service professional development, and practitioners and administrators considering implementing COC in infant toddler programs. The study's guiding questions are used to organize the discussion: (a) What does COC look like in infant toddler programs in which COC is a well-established, long-running practice? (b) What do adults who experience well-established COC in infant toddler programs say about its benefits and challenges? (c) What is the nature of primary caregiving and family-centered care in well-established, long-running infant toddler COC? and (d) What happens when the children from COC in these groups turn 3 and transition to preschool?

What COC looks like

The first question in this study concerned the very nature of COC, or what it looks like when fully implemented as recommended. We elected to address this in programs with caregivers with several years of COC experience. Although each of the sections here contributes to an understanding of the nature of COC in these settings, we highlight several important ideas from the findings to create a general overall description.

COC in a well-run, well-established program provides caregivers with time to come to know individual children and their families very well. As they work with each new group of children in a 3-year continuity looping cycle, their knowledge and understanding of children and how they develop and the implications of this for practice continue to grow. Because they will be together for such a long period of time, caregivers and parents invest time and energy in developing and nurturing their relationships with one another. Caregivers make the effort from the very beginning to get to know, and then follow practices with each baby that align with, parents' values and what is done in the home. This solid beginning and the strong, positive relationships that form over time contribute to a culture of mutual respect and trust that grows and then defines the community of children, parents, and caregivers. The stability that exists in the absence of frequent breaking and reforming of relationships keeps stress levels down and creates a calm emotional climate. In addition, caregivers watch their children progress smoothly in all areas of development, noting how different this is compared to the periodic regressions in behavior and development they experienced before COC was implemented. In partnership with families, caregivers encourage parents to feel empowered as advocates for their children, a disposition that lasts over time and carries over into future educational settings. When children transition to preschool, they hit the ground running in their new settings. This period of time, however, is mixed with joy and sadness for caregivers, who must say goodbye to children and families for whom they have developed tremendous fondness.

Perceived benefits and challenges

The second question in this study concerned participants' perceived benefits and challenges of COC. Benefits discussed include caregivers' increased knowledge of child development and of individual children, the stability of relationships occurring in COC, and parental empowerment fostered within the positive caregiver–parent relationships. Three challenges are discussed: difficulties caregivers face navigating children's transition to preschool, the length of time needed for caregivers to form effective partnerships (continuity of caregiving team), and difficulties that may occur when the infant toddler and preschool programs are disconnected from one another (continuity of B-5 program).

Benefits

We conclude that in general the benefits revealed in this study confirm those suggested by earlier work, both scholarly and practice based, such as Raikes and Edwards (2009) and Lally and Mangione (2008). However, this study adds some detail to existing studies about how particular benefits may be achieved.

Knowledge of children. Findings indicate that caregivers' knowledge of children in terms of their understanding of growth and development in children overall and of individual children in particular is facilitated within COC. Caregivers perceived that knowledge gained over time made them more responsive to each of the children under their care and that this in turn facilitated the security of the children's attachment. Caregiver knowledge built over time is a contributor to the type of sensitive, individualized responsiveness that builds the trust necessary for secure attachment, as suggested by other researchers, including Howes and Hamilton (1992) and Raikes (1996). Furthermore, caregiver knowledge was highly valued by parents in the study, who appreciated how well caregivers knew their children as well as how knowledgeable they were about child development and early childhood education.

Stability of relationships and environments. A stability attributed to not having to endure the chaos of multiple transitions existing within the revolving door model of infant toddler care was valued among families and professionals alike. Stability was believed to contribute to lower stress overall across the community of children, caregivers, and families. This confirms numerous earlier studies, such as Cryer et al. (2005), de Schipper et al. (2004), Hegde and Cassidy (2004), and Howes and Hamilton (1993). What is new in the current study is the perception of caregivers that the stability inherent to COC contributed to smoother, more even forward progress and less regression in children's development.

Parent empowerment. In this study, supportive bonds were formed between and among caregivers and parents that were mutually supportive and respectful. Parents clearly indicated that they valued the knowledge and expertise of the caregivers and appreciated caregivers' attempts to follow parents' lead in their individual care responses with their children. The strong working caregiver–parent partnerships formed suggest a commitment to family-centeredness on the part of the program (Gonzalez-Mena, 2012; Keyser, 2006; Pianta et al., 2012).

The COC caregivers in this study, however, went beyond what has previously been thought of as family-centered practices. Not only did they form strong partnerships with parents, but the caregivers saw it as part of their role to encourage parents to be strong advocates for their children. This advocacy was apparent to preschool teachers, who noted differences between how empowered the parents from COC were compared to those coming from discontinuous programs or without prior experience with child care. This finding suggests to us that parent development and empowerment can occur in COC.

Challenges

Challenges to COC suggested by earlier literature (e.g., it is too difficult to implement, caregivers will not like it, parents might feel stuck with the same caregivers over time; Aguillard et al., 2005; Hegde & Cassidy, 2004) were not present in this study. This makes sense because this study was conducted in programs in which COC was a well-established practice and the accepted norm. Most of the caregivers in the programs had been present during the transition to COC and in fact were instrumental in encouraging administrators to adopt COC. Those caregivers more recently hired knew that looping through the first 3 years with infants and toddlers was the expectation of the position, and parents understood when they enrolled in these programs that COC was the model followed. When reflecting on the potential challenge to COC of parents feeling stuck, caregivers said that it does not happen in their programs, and they credited this to the investment made by caregivers and families to establish and maintain positive relationships for the long term.

Because this study examined COC in well-established programs, we were able to examine challenges not anticipated from prior research. The potential difficulties uncovered and discussed here do not provide compelling reasons to reject COC but rather demonstrate its complexity and the importance of thoughtful planning before and during implementation. The challenges discussed include gearing up to transition to preschool, continuity in the caregiving team, and continuity in programming from birth to age 5.

Gearing up. One unanticipated challenge occurred for infant toddler caregivers related to the transitioning of their children to preschool, a period of time one caregiver referred to as "gearing up." As presented in the findings, navigating this transition was fraught with emotional, cognitive, and physical challenges for caregivers. The caregivers in this study reported that they come to love the babies they work with over the 3 years of a looping cycle, and they grow fond of the families with whom they have worked as partners. While mourning the loss of these important relational ties they have much work to do in anticipation of a new group of babies and parents and little time to grieve.

Continuity of the primary caregiver team. Findings from this study support the importance of continuity of the lead caregivers, specifically keeping co-leads (or lead and assistant) together over a continuity cycle. The relationship between partnering lead caregivers in this study was an important aspect of positive feelings about COC expressed by caregivers and parents alike. Parents appreciated having time to get to know and trust the caregivers and to learn the balance of strengths represented in the team. Caregivers were in general agreement that it takes about a year of working with a partner for them to learn how to balance their talents and capabilities with those of the other person, to come to rely on each other as working partners and confidants, and to develop a seamless rhythm in the flow of their days. Existing research does not directly address the importance of long-term caregiving relationships or the formation and maintenance of continuous partnerships or its role in COC.

Continuity across birth to 5. Differences found when comparing the B-3 + P and B-5 programs suggest that there may be advantages to housing infant toddler and preschool programs together. Caregivers in the B-5 program believed it was very important to be able to see the full range of development, birth to 5, so they could understand what comes next and so that the preschool teachers could understand what came before. In addition, the B-5 caregivers had daily opportunities to interact and exchange ideas with their preschool colleagues, which both infant toddler caregivers and the preschool teachers valued. All of the professionals in that setting deemed this important, particularly when it came to easing the transition from infant toddler COC into the preschool rooms.

Although the under-one-roof finding is not supported explicitly within the existing research literature, its implications are supported by those who study transitions. Prevalent in early childhood special education scholarship are cautions about keeping the number of disruptions in care at a minimum to ensure continuity in services for the welfare of both the children and the families (Hebbeler et al., 2007; Shotts, Rosenkoetter, Streufert, & Rosenkoetter, 1994; Wolery, 1989).

Primary caregiving and family-centered practices in COC

The third question addressed in this study concerned the nature of primary caregiving and family-centered care practices in the two COC programs. These two practices, considered relationship-based practices in child care, are discussed here.

Primary caregiving

Primary caregiving as a practice was appreciated by parents and caregivers in this study and credited with contributing to the depth of knowledge about children acquired by caregivers, as discussed earlier. This is as might be expected from the literature (Bernhardt, 2000; Howes, 1999; Lally et al., 1995). Primary caregiving was seen as a positive practice in the two programs; for example, it helped caregivers gain knowledge of individual children within a small group, it helped them form initial relationships with families, and it reduced the overall amount of paperwork and record-keeping each caregiver needed to do. These findings support prior research (Bernhardt, 2000; Elfer et al., 2003; Lally & Mangione, 2008; Zero to Three, 2008).

What was not expected, however, was the shifting and blurring of roles and responsibilities that occurred between primary caregivers over the extended time the groups were together in the COC settings in this study. Over time, children and parents began to choose their own primary as they came to know individual caregivers, or they relied on both lead caregivers for different reasons after learning who to go to for what based on experience. Reflecting on this, we conclude that this was a natural, logical outgrowth of the relationships that form among group members who come to see themselves as family.

Continuity between home and program: family-centeredness
COC was credited with creating a *family-like atmosphere* in which warmth and affection abounded, and this positive emotional climate was valued by parents and caregivers. The use of family metaphors when discussing their relationships with one another (e.g., marriage, family, divorce, and mom and dad) was taken as evidence of family-centeredness practices by us. Likewise, reports from parents that caregivers were willing to do things like they would at home were seen as indicating family-centeredness. These findings appear clearly related to family-centered practices, which are firmly based on the notion of mutual respect between caregivers and parents about the expertise each brings to the caregiving relationship (Gonzalez-Mena, 2012; Keyser, 2006; Pianta et al., 2012). Although continuity between home and child care and the creation of a family-like atmosphere do not explicitly appear in the existing literature on family-centeredness, the importance of consistency between home and child care in terms of expectations, physical environment, and emotional factors is supported by Stephen, Dunlop, and Trevarthen (2003).

The transition to preschool
The final question addressed in this study was about what happens when children transition from the COC programs to preschool. The gearing up of caregivers discussed earlier as a potential challenge to COC in part addresses this question. Another important finding related to this question emerged, however. Preschool teachers identified what they perceived as differences among 3-year-olds who transition to preschool from COC and those who come from home or discontinuous settings. They said that at least initially, during the first days and weeks, COC children are more social, are more advanced in self-help skills, and understand better how to relate to their teachers to get their needs met. This finding challenges Recchia's (2012) conclusion that the very nature of COC may make it more difficult for 3-year-olds to adapt to preschool.

Implications and limitations

Numerous implications are implicit in the work presented and discussed here, and other implications for features of COC that are particularly interesting are highlighted and considered in this section. For instance, when considering the findings of the present study alongside Recchia's (2012), we conclude that much more research is needed to understand the nature of children's transition to preschool from COC. For instance, does COC build a strong foundation in children, making transitions and problems in general easier to deal with, as suggested by the study reported here? Or does the stability make the transition more jarring, the move to new caregivers painful and upsetting?

Another area of interest arising from this study is that three types of continuities within COC emerged in the discussion: continuity of the primary caregiver team and continuity across birth to age 5 that were discussed as potential challenges, and continuity between home and program discussed as a benefit. We recommend that both scholars and program administrators come to understand more fully the nature of continuity—or various continuities—as they relate to long-term versus short-term relationships in child care. Do these continuities optimize positive outcomes for babies?

Findings around effective partnerships that lead to the conclusion about the importance of caregiver continuity suggest that administrators should carefully consider staffing patterns . The implication from this study is that it is beneficial to keep as many of the adults on the infant toddler caregiving team as consistent as possible over time, particularly the pair of co-lead caregivers (or lead and assistant), but also aide(s), part-time hourly assistants, volunteers, and substitute caregivers. This requires attentiveness to the resources and support provided to caregivers to keep them in the setting and decrease turnover, which was notably low in these programs.

A broader policy recommendation emerges when we consider the potential advantages uncovered related to caring for children birth to age 5 years in one unified physical setting. Infant toddler caregivers were able to meet regularly to discuss issues of practice with preschool teacher colleagues, facilitating effective partnerships and helping all early childhood practitioners better understand the developing child, birth to 5. Being in the same facility for infant toddler COC and preschool was seen as facilitating the transition to preschool: Children and families became familiar with preschool staff long before the transition, the physical transition process was aided by being in the same building, and the infant toddler caregivers and children benefitted from ongoing contact following the transition to preschool.

Another interesting finding with important implications about how we understand it is how primary caregiving seemed to evolve and change over time within COC. In these settings, this was based on parents and children learning what different caregivers had to offer. The findings in this study do not diminish the importance of assigning primary caregivers to children as a practice or as an ideal in infant toddler group care. We suggest that the nature of important relationships may be different, or may perhaps evolve over the long term of COC, but we caution that this finding should be considered in terms of context and time. The fluidity of primary caregiving roles in this study began several months after a continuity cycle had begun, not at the beginning; it was within highly resourced, well-established programs with many years of experience with COC. More research is needed on the nature of primary caregiving within COC.

Finally, we recommend that programs wishing to implement COC work first to identify relational care as a core philosophical value. They need to create an atmosphere that supports relationships between and among children, professional practitioners, parents, and administration. We came to see COC as sufficiently complex that it should not be the first step in a quality improvement plan but rather be considered added value to a program already engaging in other important practices, such as supporting sensitive and responsive caring behaviors, engaging in family-centered care, and practicing primary caregiving.

Possible limitations of the study

This study took place in university-affiliated child care programs situated on a large research university campus in a socially and politically conservative midwestern state in the United States. Despite its conservative leanings, the state is fairly progressive in some of its considerations of young children in child care. For example, it is one of 21 states currently requiring primary caregiving for infants and toddlers in child care programs. In addition, in this state caregivers and child care programs must "demonstrate a reasonable effort to achieve continuity of care" (Schmit & Matthews, 2013, p. 6). The requirements for primary caregiving and COC compel early childhood professionals in this state to invest time, energy, and other resources toward developing, implementing, and assessing COC practices.

The predispositions of the participants in this study and us to support COC suggest limitations to this study in terms of objectivity. For primary and secondary participants, COC was the norm and had been for many years; thus, the expectation was that participants would be generally supportive of the model. We addressed our own biases toward support for COC by using a qualitative descriptive study design so that the words of the participants would tell the story. In all likelihood, however, study participants' biases impacted the way this story unfolded, as did the fact that participants were all well educated, middle income, majority White, and living in a stable community. What a similar study might reveal with a different sample is a question for future study.

Another potential limitation relates to parents, in that the selection of the parent participants in the study was based on recommendation by participating lead infant toddler caregivers. It is possible that these parents may have been recommended because they were highly supportive of COC, which the caregivers hoped to promote.

Finally, only one form of COC was practiced in the settings examined in this study, a method commonly referred to as *looping*. Another way to address continuity is through multiage groupings of infants and toddlers. It is unclear whether or how the perspectives of participants may have differed within a multiage program.

Final thoughts

Elicker et al. (2014) suggested that "one possible hindrance to the widespread implementation of continuity of care is that research evidence for its benefits is scarce" (p. 141). This study adds to the relatively small yet growing number of works specifically addressing COC as well as to the research literature across the multiple fields of study that address infants and toddlers in general. Not only did this study confirm benefits cited in earlier research, but it also uncovered new benefits and unique challenges that need to be considered when implementing COC. Note that this study provides support to infant toddler professionals seeking to adopt COC as well as the professionals who support them through policy, administration of programs, pre- and in-service professional development, and ongoing research.

References

Ackerman, D. J. (2008). Continuity of care, professional community, and the policy context: Potential benefits for infant and toddler teachers' professional development. *Early Education & Development, 19,* 753–772. doi:10.1080/10409280801960505

Aguillard, A. E., Pierce, S. H., Benedict, J. H., & Burts, D. C. (2005). Barriers to the implementation of continuity of care practices in child care centers. *Early Childhood Research Quarterly, 20,* 329–344. doi:10.1016/j.ecresq.2005.07.004

Ainsworth, M. D. S., Blehar, M. C., Waters, E., & Wall, S. (1978). *Patterns of attachment: A psychological study of the strange situation.* Hillsdale, NJ: Erlbaum.

Bary, R. (2010). It's all about relationships: Infant and toddler pedagogy. *In the First Years/Nga Tau Tautahi, 12*(2), 15–18.

Bernhardt, J. L. (2000). A primary caregiving system for infants and toddlers: Best for everyone involved. *Young Children, 55*(2), 74–80.

Bowlby, J. (1969). *Attachment and loss: Vol. 1. Attachment.* New York, NY: Basic Books.

Bowlby, J. (1988). *A secure base: Parent-child attachment and healthy human development.* London, England: Basic Books.

Bowlby, R. (2007). Babies and toddlers in non-parental daycare can avoid stress and anxiety if they develop a lasting secondary attachment bond with one carer who is consistently accessible to them. *Attachment & Human Development, 9,* 307–319. doi:10.1080/14616730701711516

Bronfenbrenner, U., & Morris, P. A. (2006). The bioecological model of human development. In W. Damon & R. M. Lerner (Eds.), *Handbook of child psychology: Vol 1. Theoretical models of human development* (6th ed., pp. 793–828). New York, NY: Wiley.

Center for Law and Social Policy. (2015). *Charting progress for babies in childcare.* Retrieved from http://www.clasp.org/babiesinchildcare/recommendations

Charmaz, K. (2000). Grounded theory: Objectivist and constructivist methods. In N. K. Denzin & Y. S. Lincoln (Eds.), *Handbook of qualitative research* (pp. 509–536). Thousand Oaks, CA: Sage.

Childcare Aware of America. (2015). *Resources: Partnerships.* Retrieved from the National Association for Child Care Resource and Referral Agencies website: http://naccrra.org/early-head-start-child-care-partnerships/resources

Copple, C., Bredekamp, S., Koraleck, D., & Charner, K. (Eds.). (2013). *Developmentally appropriate practice: Focus on infants and toddlers.* Washington, DC: National Association for the Education of Young Children.

Creswell, J. W., & Miller, D. L. (2000). Determining validity in qualitative inquiry. *Theory Into Practice, 39*(3), 124–130. doi:10.1207/s15430421tip3903_2

Cryer, D., Hurwitz, S., & Wolery, M. (2000). Continuity of caregiver for infants and toddlers in center-based child care: Report on a survey of center practices. *Early Childhood Research Quarterly, 15,* 497–514. doi:10.1016/S0885-2006(01)00069-2

Cryer, D., Wagner-Moore, L., Burchinal, M., Yazejian, N., Hurwitz, S., & Wolery, M. (2005). Effects of transitions to new child care classes on infant/toddler distress and behavior. *Early Childhood Research Quarterly, 20,* 37–56. doi:10.1016/j.ecresq.2005.01.005

Cummings, E. M., & Davies, P. (1996). Emotional security as a regulatory process in normal development and the development of psychopathology. *Development and Psychopathology, 8,* 123–139. doi:10.1017/S0954579400007008

de Schipper, J. C., Van Ijzendoorn, M. H., & Tavecchio, L. W. C. (2004). Stability in center day care: Relations with children's well-being and problem behavior in day care. *Social Development, 13,* 531–550. doi:10.1111/j.1467-9507.2004.00282.x

Ebbeck, M., & Yim, H. Y. (2008). Fostering relationships between infants, toddlers and their primary caregivers in child care centres in Australia. In M. Jalongo (Ed.), *Enduring bonds: The significance of interpersonal relationships in young children's lives* (pp. 159–177). London, England: Springer.

EDUCARE. (2015). *Research and results: Continuity of care.* Retrieved from http://www.educareschools.org/results/continuity-of-care.php

Eisenberg, N. (1992). *The caring child.* Boston, MA: Harvard University Press.

Elfer, P., Goldschmied, E., & Selleck, D. (2003). *Key persons in the nursery: Building relationships for quality provision.* London, England: David Fulton.

Elicker, J., & Fortner, C. (1995). Adult-child relationships in early childhood programs. *Young Children, 57*(4), 10–17.

Elicker, J., Ruprecht, K. M., & Anderson, T. (2014). Observing infants' and toddlers' relationships and interactions in group care. In L. J. Harrison & J. Sumsion (Eds.), *International perspectives on early childhood education and development: Vol. 11. Lived spaces of infant-toddler education and care: Exploring diverse perspectives on theory, research, and practice* (pp. 131–145). London, England: Springer.

Essa, E. L., Favre, K., Thweatt, G., & Waugh, S. (1999). Continuity of care for infants and toddlers. *Early Child Development and Care, 148,* 11–19. doi:10.1080/0300443991480102

Goldstein, A., Hamm, K., & Schumacher, R. (2007). *Supporting growth and development of babies in child care: What does the research say?* Retrieved from the Zero to Three website: http://main.zerotothree.org/site/DocServer/ChildcareResearchBrief.pdf?docID=3542

Gonzalez-Mena, J. (2012). *Child, family, and community: Family-centered early care and education* (6th ed.). Upper Saddle River, NJ: Pearson.

Goossens, F. A., & van Ijzendoorn, M. H. (1990). Quality of infants' attachments to professional caregivers: Relation to infant-parent attachment and day-care characteristics. *Child Development, 61,* 832–837. doi:10.2307/1130967

Grodsky, E., & Gamoran, A. (2003). The relationship between professional development and professional community in American schools. *School Effectiveness & School Improvement, 14,* 1–29. doi:10.1076/sesi.14.1.1.13866

Hatch, J. A. (2002). *Doing qualitative research in education settings.* Albany: State University of New York Press.

Hebbeler, K., Spiker, D., Bailey, D., Scarborough, A., Mallik, S., Simeonsson, R., & Singer, M. (2007). *Early intervention for infants and toddlers with disabilities and their families: Participants, services, and outcomes. Final report of the National Early Intervention Longitudinal Study (NEILS).* Retrieved from the SRI International website: http://www.sri.com/work/publications/national-early-intervention-longitudinal-study-neils-final-report

Hegde, A. V., & Cassidy, D. J. (2004). Teacher and parent perspectives on looping. *Early Childhood Education Journal, 32,* 133–138. doi:10.1007/s10643-004-1080-x

Honig, A. S. (2002). *Secure relationships: Nurturing infant/toddler attachment in early care settings.* Washington, DC: National Association for the Education of Young Children.

Honig, A. S. (2010). Keys to quality infant care: Nurturing every baby's life journey. *Young Children, 65*(5), 40–47.

Horm, D. M., Goble, C. B., & Branscomb, K. R. (2011). Infant toddler curriculum: Review, reflection, and revolution. In N. File, J. J. Mueller, & D. B. Wisneski (Eds.), *Curriculum in early childhood education: Re-examined, rediscovered, renewed* (pp. 105–119). New York, NY: Routledge.

Howes, C. (1999). Attachment relationships in the context of multiple caregivers. In J. Cassidy & S. P. Phillips (Eds.), *Handbook of attachment theory, research and clinical applications* (pp. 671–687). New York, NY: Guilford Press.

Howes, C., & Hamilton, C. E. (1992). Children's relationships with caregivers: Mothers and child care teachers. *Child Development, 63,* 859–866. doi:10.2307/1131238

Howes, C., & Hamilton, C. E. (1993). The changing experience of child care: Changes in teachers and in teacher-child relationships and children's social competence with peers. *Early Childhood Research Quarterly, 8,* 15–32. doi:10.1016/S0885-2006(05)80096-1

Institute of Medicine & National Research Council. (2012). *From neurons to neighborhoods: An update: Workshop summary.* Washington, DC: National Academies Press.

Keyser, J. (2006). *From parents to partners: Building a family-centered early childhood program.* St. Paul, MN: Redleaf Press.

Lally, J. R., Griffin, A., Fenichel, E., Segal, M., Szanton, E., & Weissbourd, B. (1995). *Caring for infants and toddlers in groups: Developmentally appropriate practice.* Washington, DC: Zero to Three.

Lally, J. R., & Mangione, P. L. (2008). The Program for Infant Toddler Care. In J. P. Roopnarine & J. E. Johnson (Eds.), *Approaches to early childhood education* (5th ed., pp. 25–47). Englewood Cliffs, NJ: Prentice Hall.

Lincoln, Y., & Guba, E. (1985). *Naturalistic inquiry.* Beverly Hills, CA: Sage.

Louis, K. S., & Marks, H. M. (1998). Does professional community affect the classroom? Teachers' work and student experiences in restructuring schools. *American Journal of Education, 106,* 532–575. doi:10.1086/444197

Mann, M. B., & Carney, R. N. (2008). Building positive relationships in the lives of infants and toddlers in child care. In M. R. Jalongo (Ed.), *Enduring bonds: The significance of interpersonal relationships in young children's lives* (pp. 147–157). New York, NY: Springer.

McMullen, M. B., Addleman, J., Fulford, A. M., Mooney, S., Moore, S., Sisk, S., & Zachariah, J. (2009). Learning to be *me* while coming to understand *we*: Encouraging prosocial babies in group settings. *Young Children, 64*, 20–28.

McMullen, M. B., & Lash, M. (2012). Babies on campus: Considering service to infants and families among other competing forces in university-affiliated programs. *Early Childhood Research & Practice, 14*. Retrieved from http://ecrpauth.crc.uiuc.edu/v14n2/mcmullen

Moustakas, C. (1994). *Phenomenological research methods.* Thousand Oaks, CA: Sage.

National Head Start Association. (2014). *Early Head Start-child care partnership project.* Retrieved from http://www2.nhsa.org/archive/201403

National Institute of Child Health and Human Development. (1996). Characteristics of infant child care: Factors contributing to positive caregiving. *Early Childhood Research Quarterly, 11*, 269–306. doi:10.1016/S0885-2006(96)90009-5

National Scientific Council on the Developing Child. (2004). *Young children develop in an environment of relationships* (Working Paper No. 1). Cambridge, MA: Center for the Developing Child.

Norris, D. (2010). Raising the educational requirements for teachers in infant-toddler classrooms: Implications for institutions of higher education. *Journal of Early Childhood Teacher Education, 31*(2), 146–158. doi:10.1080/10901021003781221

Ounce of Prevention Fund. (2015). *Early brain development.* Retrieved from http://www.theounce.org/who-we-are/early-brain-development

Owen, M. T., Klausli, J. F., Mata-Otero, A., & Caughy, M. O. (2008). Relationship-focused child care practices: Quality of care and child outcomes for children in poverty. *Early Education & Development, 19*, 302–329. doi:10.1080/10409280801964010

Phillips, D. A., & Lowenstein, A. E. (2011). Early care, education, and child development. *Annual Review of Psychology, 62*, 483–500. doi:10.1146/annurev.psych.031809.130707

Pianta, R. C., Barnett, W. S., & Justice, L. M. (Eds.). (2012). *Handbook on early childhood education.* New York, NY: Guilford Press.

Program for Infant Toddler Care. (2015). *Mission statement: The Program for Infant Toddler Care.* Retrieved from https://www.pitc.org/pub/pitc_docs/about.html

Raikes, H. (1993). Relationship duration in infant care: Time with a high-ability teacher and infant-teacher attachment. *Early Childhood Research Quarterly, 8*, 309–325. doi:10.1016/S0885-2006(05)80070-5

Raikes, H. (1996). A secure base for babies: Applying attachment theory concepts to the infant care setting. *Young Children, 51*(5), 59–67.

Raikes, H., & Edwards, C. (2009). *Extending the dance in infant and toddler caregiving: Enhancing attachment and relationships.* Baltimore, MD: Brookes.

Recchia, S. L. (2012). Caregiver–child relationships as a context for continuity in child care. *Early Years, 32*, 143–157. doi:10.1080/09575146.2012.693908

Riley, D., San Juan, R., Klinkner, J., & Ramminger, A. (2008). *Social and emotional development: Connecting science and practice in early childhood settings.* St. Paul, MN: Redleaf Press.

Ruprecht, K., Elicker, J., & Choi, J. (in press). Continuity of care, caregiver-child interactions, and toddler social competence.

Sandelowski, M. (2010). What's in a name? Qualitative description revisited. *Research in Nursing & Health, 33*, 77–84.

Schmit, S., & Matthews, H. (2013). *Better for babies: A study of state infant and toddler child care policies.* Washington, DC: Center for Law and Social Policy.

Schumacher, R., Hamm, K., Goldstein, A., & Lombardi, J. (2006). *Starting off right: Promoting child development from birth in state early care and education initiatives.* Retrieved from the Center for Law and Social Policy website: http://www.clasp.org/admin/site/publications/files/0519.pdf

Schumacher, R., & Hoffmann, E. (2008). *Continuity of care: Charting progress for babies in child care—Research based rationale.* Retrieved from the Center for Law and Social Policy website: http://research.policyarchive.org/13791.pdf

Shotts, C. K., Rosenkoetter, S. E., Streufert, C. A., & Rosenkoetter, L. I. (1994). Transition policy and issues: A view from the states. *Topics in Early Childhood Special Education, 14*, 395–411. doi:10.1177/027112149401400308

Snyder, C. (2011). *Infants and toddlers: Continuity of care—"It's good to see you again!"* Retrieved from the High/Scope website: http://www.highscope.org/file/NewsandInformation/ReSourceReprints/Spring2011/It'sGoodToSeeYou_72.pdf

Stephen, C., Dunlop, A., & Trevarthen, C. (2003). *Meeting the needs of children from birth to three: Research evidence and implications for out-of-home provision.* Retrieved from the Scottish Executive Education Department website: http://www.gov.scot/Resource/Doc/47102/0025583.pdf

Theilheimer, R. (2006). Molding to the children: Primary caregiving and continuity of care. *Zero to Three, 26*(3), 50–54.

Tobin, R. (2010). Descriptive case study. In A. J. Mills, G. Durepos, & E. Wiebe (Eds.), *Encyclopedia of case study research* (pp. 289–290). Thousand Oaks, CA: Sage.

Vandell, D. L., Belsky, J., Burchinal, M., Steinberg, L., Vandergrift, N., & NICHD Early Child Care Research Network. (2010). Do effects of early child care extend to age 15 years? Results from the NICHD Study of Early Child Care and Youth Development. *Child Development, 81,* 737–756. doi:10.1111/cdev.2010.81.issue-3

Waters, E., Weinfield, N. S., & Hamilton, C. E. (2000). The stability of attachment security from infancy to adolescence and early adulthood: General discussion. *Child Development, 71*(3), 703–706. doi:10.1111/cdev.2000.71.issue-3

Whitaker, R., Orzol, S., & Kahn, R. (2006). Maternal mental health, substance use, and domestic violence in the year after delivery and subsequent behavior problems in children at age 3 years. *Archives of General Psychiatry, 63*(5), 551–560. doi:10.1001/archpsyc.63.5.551

Wolery, M. (1989). Transitions in early childhood special education: Issues and procedures. *Focus on Exceptional Children, 22*(2), 1–16.

Yin, R. K. (2012). *Applications of case study research.* Thousand Oaks, CA: Sage.

Zero to Three. (2008). *Caring for infants and toddlers in groups: Developmentally appropriate practice* (2nd ed.). Washington, DC: Author.

Appendix
Interview guide

All one-on-one and group interviews began with a discussion of the general goals of the study and a collection of demographic information from participants. Below are questions that guided each discussion.

Caregiving team (one-on-one interviews)

- Tell me about your program. How is it different from others in which you have worked?
- Please describe your experience with continuity of care with birth to 3-year-olds. When did it begin? How was it decided to adopt this practice? Who participated in that decision? How were families included or informed about the decision, and how did they respond? How did you personally feel about the change, and how did other members of the program staff respond to this decision?
- What would you say are the main advantages of continuity of care in your program versus the prior practices? Any disadvantages, unexpected surprises, difficulties arise?
- Do you engage in primary caregiving? Why or why not? Tell me how this works.
- Let's talk about relationships in the group in general: among the children, co-lead caregiver, director, colleagues from other rooms, part-timers, hourlies and the aides, and families.
- How do you include parents in your program? What do you see as their role in the decisions you make? How often do you talk to them? Meet formally? etc.
- What is your preferred title—caregiver, teacher, practitioner, or something else—and why? Have families or colleagues ever treated you like or called you a babysitter?
- Talk about the transition from the infant toddler program to the preschool room. How is this different than before you implemented continuity of care? How is this BIG transition for you personally? How do you begin a new infant group? How do you prepare families and transition children into the setting in the very beginning, starting a new infant group?
- What would you say you like best about your experience with continuity of care? What could still be improved?
- Is there anything else you would like to tell me? Anything I should have asked?

Parents (one-on-one interviews)

- What has been your experience with continuity of care at [this setting] ?
- What is your perspective on having your child in a program with the same teachers and their peers for an extended period of time, up to 3 years?
- Do you know who your child's primary caregiver is? Do/did you feel closer to one caregiver over another? (If so, why might that be?) What about your child's relationship with the caregivers? Was he/she closer to one than the other? (If yes, why do you think this was?)

- How about your child's relationships with other children in the class? Was he/she close to anyone in particular? Did he/she form friendships?
- Were the relationships you and your child formed important to you in terms of how you felt about being in the program?
- Have you been in other programs in which children were moved to other classrooms more frequently or had more transitions among the teachers? How did these experiences influence your child's relationship with the teachers and the other children in the classroom? What about your relationship with the teachers and the program?
- If applicable: What was your experience with transitioning from the infant toddler program to the preschool program? How was your child prepared for this big transition? What, if anything, is different in your relationship with the teachers in the preschool program?
- Or, if applicable: Do you have any concerns about transitioning from the infant toddler program to preschool? What is your major concern?
- What would you say you like best about your experience with continuity of care? What could still be improved?

Preschool teachers (group interviews)

- Please describe the transition process for three-year-olds and their families entering your program.
- What, if anything, do you notice about the transition or adjustment to your classroom for 3-year-olds from the continuity of care program as compared to 3-year-olds who come to your room from another child care program or with no group care experience?
- What about the parents or families from the birth-to-3 continuity programs? Is there anything different about these parents than others that you notice?
- Is there anything else you would like to tell me? Anything else you think I should have asked?

Administrators (group interview)

- Tell me about the decision in the two programs serving birth to 3 to implement continuity of care. How was it decided to adopt this practice? Who participated in the decision? How were families included in the decision, and how did they respond? How did you personally feel about the change, and how did other members of the program respond?
- What do you see as beneficial, positive in the birth-to-3 programs as implemented now, with continuity of care, and on the flipside what have been the challenges?
- Tell me about how transitions are handled in the programs, including the transition of families with new infants, transition of new toddlers into the intact groups when group size changes, transition to the preschool classroom, transition of caregivers back to infant care after children move on to preschool.
- How is communication facilitated between infant toddler program staff and preschool staff?
- What do you look for when you hire new caregivers for the infant toddler program? Is this different from hiring a preschool teacher, and if so, how?
- Is there anything else you would like to tell me? Anything else you think I should have asked?

Continuity of Care, Caregiver–Child Interactions, and Toddler Social Competence and Problem Behaviors

Karen Ruprecht, James Elicker, and Ji Young Choi

ABSTRACT

Research Findings: Continuity of care is a recommended practice in child care intended to promote secure and supportive relationships between infants and toddlers and their caregivers. Toddlers ($N = 115$) between 12 and 24 months were observed in 30 continuity and 29 noncontinuity classrooms. The average duration of care for toddlers with caregivers was 14 months in the continuity rooms and 5 months in noncontinuity rooms. Toddlers observed in continuity rooms experienced higher levels of interactive involvement with their caregivers and were rated by their caregivers as having fewer problem behaviors compared with the toddlers in noncontinuity rooms. Toddlers in rooms with higher staff–child ratios also experienced more involved caregiving. We did not find evidence that the level of involved caregiving mediated the association between continuity of care and toddlers' social competence or problem behaviors. *Practice or Policy*: Continuity of care may be a promising practice for programs that strive to provide high-quality care for infants and toddlers.

An emerging trend in infant–toddler care and education is the use of relationship-based practices to promote positive developmental outcomes (Edwards & Raikes, 2002; McMullen & Dixon, 2009; Owen, Klausli, Mata-Otero, & O'Brien-Caughy, 2008). One important and frequently recommended relationship-based practice in child care centers is continuity of care, in which a caregiver is assigned a small number of infants over an extended period of time, up to 3 years (Cryer et al., 2005; Schumacher & Hoffman, 2008). This is in contrast to the more common practice of changing caregivers and rooms as infants reach developmental milestones, sometimes as often as every 6 months (Cryer, Hurwitz, & Wolery, 2000). However, though widely recommended, continuity of care has not been systematically studied in terms of its effects on caregiver–toddler interactions or toddler behavior in child care. This article describes common approaches for implementing continuity of care for toddlers, reviews existing evidence regarding the practice and its effects on caregivers and children, and presents new data from a quasi-experimental study comparing continuity versus noncontinuity toddler classrooms in child care centers.

Programs implement continuity of care in a variety of ways. The most frequently recommended way is to keep children and caregivers together for the first 3 years (Lally & Tsao, 2004). Programs can do this by implementing a looping strategy, in which two caregivers start with a primary care group of infants and move with those children to different classrooms until age 3, when the caregivers loop back to the infant room and begin to care for a new group of children (Hegde & Cassidy, 2004). Children in these types of classrooms are typically similar in age, making it possible for the entire group to move to a new classroom. Another method involves child care centers offering mixed-age grouping, in which infants and toddlers are grouped in the same classroom and stay with their teachers until they reach the age of 3 (Theilheimer, 2006). Other options for offering continuity of care involve variations of the mixed-age classroom and looping approaches. For example, child care centers may offer continuity of care by placing similar-age children in the same classroom (instead of mixed-age children) and change the classroom environment so that as the children develop, the room is adapted to fit their developmental needs (Cryer et al., 2000). Other programs may choose to implement continuity with one caregiver and his or her primary care group within a larger group setting. When children in the primary care group are ready to transition to the next classroom, the teacher follows them, while the other teacher and younger primary care group transition at a later time, typically when all of the children are old enough or have reached certain developmental milestones (Cryer et al., 2000, 2005). Although this method is a form of looping and attempts to keep children and caregivers together, it does present some challenges because a small group of children move with one teacher instead of all of the children in the classroom moving together with two teachers to the next classroom. Despite the fact that programs implement continuity of care in a variety of ways, the main requirement is that children remain with their caregivers over time (Cryer et al., 2000; Lally & Tsao, 2004). Therefore, this article defines continuity of care based on the length of time centers keep young children and teachers together rather than the method of implementation.

Theoretical, empirical, and practitioner support

One conceptual basis for practicing continuity of care is attachment theory, primarily the principle that positive, sensitive care with a stable, responsive, and consistent caregiver over time will result in a secure attachment relationship. Secure attachments in turn provide a foundation for positive developmental outcomes for children (Bowlby, 1969/1982; Howes, 1999). These relationships provide a secure emotional base for the infant to explore the world and support cognitive and emotional development, well-being, and social competence (Ahnert, Pinquart, & Lamb, 2006; Elicker, Englund, & Sroufe, 1992; van IJzendoorn, Vereijken, Bakermans-Kranenburg, & Riksen-Walraven, 2004).

Previous research on both maternal and nonparental caregiver attachment has shown that infants who experience stable, consistent, sensitive, responsive care from their primary caregivers develop more secure attachment relationships (Ahnert et al., 2006; Barnas & Cummings, 1994; Cassidy & Shaver, 1999; Howes, Hamilton, & Philipsen, 1998; Howes & Smith, 1995; Raikes, 1993). Sensitive, responsive interactions with a consistent caregiver over time may help diminish the distress that may result from frequent caregiver changes, particularly for children between 18 and 24 months (Cryer et al., 2005; Howes & Hamilton, 1992). It is assumed that fewer changes in caregivers will result in better care and outcomes for young children (Howes & Hamilton, 1992, 1993; Raikes, 1993). Although the duration of the adult–infant relationship provides an obvious kind of continuity, those who recommend continuity of care as a child care practice often assume that sensitivity, responsiveness, and involvement will *increase* over time as the caregiver and child get to know each other better (Owen et al., 2008; Raikes, 1993; Ritchie & Howes, 2003).

Some studies have linked attachment security to caregiver–toddler interactive involvement and have found that caregivers who had secure attachments with children also displayed more interactive involvement with them (Elicker, Fortner-Wood, & Noppe, 1999; Howes & Smith, 1995) Caregiver–toddler interactive involvement is the quality and intensity of the interactions between the caregiver and the child. However, the effects of continuity of care practices on caregiver–toddler interactive involvement have not been directly studied.

Published studies focused on the practice of continuity of care in child care settings have been few in number to date, and results have been mixed. One study found that children in child care programs that promote more stable, consistent caregiving relationships have teachers who are more responsive and are more engaged with the children (Raikes, 1993). Other studies have provided evidence of benefits of continuity of care for some children but not for others, and usually preschool-age children are studied rather than infants and toddlers (Owen et al., 2008; Ritchie & Howes, 2003).

Some research has shown no evidence for associations between continuity of care and children's behavior or other developmental outcomes (Cryer, 2007; Cryer et al., 2005). To date, there have been no published reports of research directly comparing the interactions and outcomes of children younger than 3 years of age in classrooms using continuity of care practices with those of children in classrooms that did not use continuity of care. Furthermore, published studies on the practice of continuity of care demonstrate wide variability in the amount of time that caregivers and children are grouped together, from about 3 months to 3 years (Barnas & Cummings, 1994; Howes & Hamilton, 1992; Raikes, 1993). This wide variability suggests a lack of an agreed-on duration of time necessary to meet the definition of continuity of care from the empirical literature, despite the recommendation from the early childhood field to keep children and caregivers together for the first 3 years (Lally & Tsao, 2004; Program for Infant Toddler Care, n.d.).

Despite limited empirical support for continuity of care, the early childhood education field strongly promotes continuity of care as a best practice. Professional organizations, including the National Association for the Education of Young Children (Copple & Bredekamp, 2009), Early Head Start (Early Head Start Performance Standards, n.d.), and Zero to Three (Theilheimer, 2006), have encouraged or required continuity of care, relying primarily on the theoretical rationale for these practices rather than rigorous research evidence. The widely used Program for Infant Toddler Care caregiver training program also promotes continuity of care as a practice that can strengthen relationships between primary caregivers and children (Program for Infant Toddler Care, n.d.).

Continuity of care and stability

A central component of continuity of care as a child care programming strategy involves increasing the amount of time caregivers and children are together so that caregivers have the opportunity to develop sustained relationships with the children in their care. Although the practice of continuity of care per se has limited empirical support, there is evidence in the research literature that stability in the teacher–child relationship over time may increase the level of caregiver–child interactive involvement, increase children's social competence, and reduce problem behaviors.

Studies have examined the relationship between attachment security and the amount of time child care providers and infants and toddlers spend together. Raikes (1993) studied 61 provider–infant dyads between the ages of 10 and 38 months in one center-based care site that kept caregivers and children together until the age of 3. Those children who spent consistent time in the care of one high-ability caregiver displayed higher attachment security. After 6 months with the same caregiver, the secure attachment rate was 50%; after 9 months, it increased to 67%; and of children who had been with the same caregiver for 1 year, 91% had secure attachments with their primary caregivers. In another study Elicker et al. (1999) found that infants who entered family child care at a younger age and had longer durations in care had higher levels of interactive involvement and attachment security with those caregivers.

Additional studies have found that caregiving continuity or stability is associated with young children's development and well-being. Howes and Hamilton (1992) followed a sample of 72 children in child care from the toddler to the preschool years. Completing observations every 6 months, they found that when caregivers remained the same, attachment security was stable over time. However, when caregivers changed, children were observed to be less secure with their caregivers at 24 and 30 months. After 30 months, attachment security remained more stable, even when caregivers changed.

Temporal stability with caregivers may impact young children's interactions with their caregivers in both stressful and nonstressful situations. Barnas and Cummings (1994) examined experimentally the responses of infants and toddlers ranging from 11 to 27 months to stable versus nonstable caregivers. Stable caregivers were classified as those who had been at the child care center for more than 3 months; nonstable caregivers were those who had been at the center less than 3 months. Toddlers, when distressed, initiated more proximity and comfort-seeking behaviors toward more stable caregivers. Furthermore, stable caregivers were more successful in soothing the toddlers. Even without immediate distress, toddlers more often sought out the more stable caregivers, suggesting that they were using them as a secure base.

Taken together, these findings suggest that infants and toddlers enrolled in out-of-home care who experience more changes in nonparental caregivers, in either the short or long term, may be vulnerable to having less positive or engaging interactions with their caregivers. Based on these findings, we hypothesized that toddlers who experienced continuity of care in their child care arrangements would experience higher levels of interactive involvement from their child care teachers.

Continuity of care, positive caregiving, and toddlers' social competence and problem behaviors

An important dimension of infant–toddler child care shown to predict later social competence is how caregivers interact with the children in their care (deSchipper, Tavecchio, & van IJzendoorn, 2008; Howes & Hamilton, 1992; van IJzendoorn et al., 2004). Involved, sensitive-responsive caregiving, labeled *positive caregiving* in some studies, includes dimensions such as responding promptly, consistently, and supportively to an infant's social gestures and signals; responding helpfully to distress cues; expressing positive feelings toward the infant; and stimulating the infant's cognitive development (National Institute of Child Health and Human Development [NICHD] Early Child Care Research Network, 1996).

Researchers in the NICHD Early Child Care Research Network (Clarke-Stewart, Vandell, Burchinal, O'Brien, & McCartney, 2002) found that when caregivers were more positive and responsive, children displayed fewer behavioral problems at home and were more cooperative in both the home and child care environments. The NICHD Early Child Care Research Network (2001) also assessed children's peer interactions later at 24 and 36 months. When family and child characteristics were controlled, findings indicated that more positive early caregiving in child care was associated later with more positive play with other children. In other research, children who were 2 to 5 years old who experienced more involved, sensitive, responsive caregiving interacted more positively with peers and displayed fewer internalizing behavior problems and less aggressive behavior than children receiving less responsive care (deSchipper, van Ijzendoorn, & Tavecchio, 2004; Howes & Hamilton, 1993; NICHD Early Child Care Research Network, 2001; Tran & Weinraub, 2006).

Young children's developing social competence may be related to continuity in care arrangements. Howes and Hamilton (1993) followed children from ages 1 to 4 years in child care centers. By age 4, children who had experienced more changes in child care teachers were rated by current child care providers as lower in gregarious behaviors and higher in social withdrawal and aggression. Children who had changed primary teachers before 24 months of age were more aggressive later, regardless of the relationship quality. This finding supports the rationale for continuity of care, as more changes in teachers were associated with negative impacts on younger children. Ritchie and Howes (2003) found that preschool children who were placed in programs that used the practice of keeping children and caregivers together for at least 1 year, and those whose primary caregivers interacted responsively and sensitively with them, were more likely to have secure attachment relationships with the caregiver. Children between 1 and 15 months who changed from family care to out-of-home child care experienced more internalizing and externalizing problems than those who remained at home (Tran & Weinraub, 2006). Cryer et al. (2005) found that infants experienced distress when they transitioned to new child care caregivers and classrooms. Based on this evidence, we hypothesized that positive, interactive involvement would be associated with lower rates of children's problem behaviors. Furthermore, we also hypothesized that child–caregiver interactions may mediate the association between continuity of care practices and toddlers' social competence and problem behaviors. For example, children in continuity classrooms may have higher rated levels of social competence and fewer reported problem behaviors because child–caregiver interactions are generally more positive and supportive in these rooms compared to noncontinuity rooms. Previous research has demonstrated that there is a link between attachment security and providers who are more sensitive in their caregiving, suggesting that caregivers who are more involved and interactive with the children in their care may be able to better assess and support social competence or ameliorate problem behaviors in young children (Ahnert et al., 2006; van IJzendoorn et al., 2004). However, because of the limited research, it is not known whether child–caregiver interactions mediate the relationship between continuity of care and toddlers' behavior. Finally, certain child characteristics, such as gender and temperament, have been linked to toddler social competence and problem behaviors, and so these variables must be considered or controlled in studies of continuity of care (Else-Quest, Hyde, Goldsmith, & Van Hulle, 2006; Putnam, Gartstein, & Rothbart, 2006).

Considering the limited empirical evidence, it is important to rigorously examine continuity of care as it is being implemented in child care programs. The following research questions were explored:

(1) Are toddlers who experience continuity of care for at least 9 months receiving more involved, responsive caregiving compared with toddlers who are not in continuity of care classrooms?
(2) Do toddlers in continuity of care classrooms exhibit higher levels of social competence and fewer problem behaviors compared with toddlers in classrooms that are not implementing continuity of care?
(3) Does the quality of caregiving mediate the association between continuity of care and toddler social competence and behavior problems?

Method

Design

A quasi-experimental research design was used because of the practical and ethical issues involved in randomly assigning providers or children to a continuity of care treatment group and noncontinuity of care control condition (Shadish, Cook, & Campbell, 2002). Despite strong recommendations to implement such care, the number of child care programs that have fully implemented continuity of care for infants and toddlers has been found to be quite limited (Cryer et al., 2000). Within the state where the study was conducted, 27 child care centers were identified as fully implementing continuity of care in line with recommended practice. Therefore, a sample matching strategy was used so that centers and classrooms in the noncontinuity of care group would have similar characteristics to the continuity centers and classrooms.

Participants

Centers and classrooms

A purposeful sampling method using an intensity strategy was used to recruit centers that were substantially implementing continuity of care. Purposeful sampling allows for grouping participants according to preselected criteria relevant to a particular research question. Intensity sampling is a form of purposeful sampling that identifies information-rich cases that manifest the construct of interest, in this case continuity of care (Patton, 2002). Because child care regulations defining and guiding continuity of care were not precise and sometimes were not rigorously enforced, it was necessary to construct the sample so two distinctive groups of providers with respect to continuity of care could be compared while attempting to control for other potential important influencing factors. To the extent possible, the continuity and noncontinuity groups were matched for equivalence based on type of program, demographics of families served, geographic location, and state Quality Rating and Improvement System levels.

Interviews were conducted with 11 infant/toddler specialists working in the state's child care resource and referral agencies to identify both continuity and noncontinuity centers. The specialists provided names of programs that had policies in which infants and toddlers remained with the same caregivers for at least 1 year. The specialists also provided names of centers that moved infants and toddlers to new classrooms more frequently. This process produced a list of 50 potential centers for the study—27 that were implementing continuity of care and 23 that were not implementing continuity of care. Recruitment letters were sent to all of these centers.

In the next phase of recruitment, telephone calls were made to each center. Directors were interviewed about how they managed placements for children in the 12- to 24-month age range to verify implementation of continuity of care. The interviews also provided information about how long the caregivers currently in toddler classroom(s) had been with the children. If caregivers in the continuity toddler rooms had been with the children for at least 9 months, the classrooms were eligible for the study.

Ultimately, one to four classrooms serving 12- to 24-month-old children in each center eligible for the study were selected. A total of 11 continuity centers (including 33 classrooms) and 14 noncontinuity centers (including 29 classrooms) were recruited. Three continuity classrooms in two of the centers declined to participate. Therefore, the final sample included 30 continuity classrooms within nine centers and 29 noncontinuity classrooms within 14 centers.

Children
A total of 119 children ages 12–24 months enrolled full time in the selected classrooms were eligible for the study, and 115 children were invited to participate. A maximum of four children per classroom were selected to participate. Two classrooms had six returned consent forms, and four children were randomly selected to participate from both of these classrooms. The number of children observed per classroom ranged from one to four depending on the number of returned parental consent forms and the availability of the children on the day of the observation.

Of these 115 children, 57 children were enrolled in the continuity classrooms and 58 children were enrolled in the noncontinuity classrooms. Only typically developing children were included in the sample because children with disabilities may create unique differences in caregivers' interactions unrelated to continuity of care practices.

Caregivers
A total of 59 lead caregivers were observed in the continuity and noncontinuity classrooms. There were 30 caregivers in the continuity rooms and 29 in the noncontinuity rooms. There were no differences in education levels between caregivers in the continuity and noncontinuity classrooms. More than one third (38%) of caregivers in both continuity and noncontinuity classrooms had earned at least an associate's degree.

Procedure

Observations
Child care observations occurred on a single typical day, defined by the child care director, so that a normal range of activities and experiences was captured. When necessary, observations were scheduled around mealtime and naptime; observations were conducted in either the morning or the afternoon and lasted approximately 3 to 3½ hr. Afternoon observations were conducted only if a child arrived late or when there were several children to observe in one classroom and it was not possible to complete all of the child observations in the morning. A total of 22 of the 115 observations were completed in the afternoon, equally split between the continuity and noncontinuity classrooms.

The observer distributed the child temperament and social competence questionnaires to the primary caregivers or lead teachers and asked them to complete both questionnaires for the observed child(ren). In addition, the observer asked the child care teachers several structured questions regarding their training and education and the number of providers each focal child interacted with during the day. The observer verified information the child care director provided over the phone regarding how continuity of care was implemented in the classroom by asking a standard set of continuity screening questions (see the Appendix). Group size and adult–child ratio were observed and documented throughout the data collection visit.

Data collector training and reliability

All observations were completed by two trained observers who had significant experience in collecting child care observational data. Interrater reliability was established on the Adult Interaction Scale by practicing coding first in taped segments and then in live segments. Data collectors established reliability by collecting live data in two noncontinuity child care classrooms and one continuity classroom. Interrater reliability (Kappa) was .84 ($p < .0.001$). One additional reliability check was performed via training tapes at the midpoint of data collection in which the observers rated children independently. The interrater reliability (Kappa) for the raters at the midpoint of the data collection period was .85 ($p < .0.001$).

Measures

Continuity of care

A measure of the degree of implementation of continuity of care was created for this study to ensure that the classrooms sampled had distinctive continuity and noncontinuity characteristics (see the Appendix). The scale was used as a screening tool to help determine which sites were implementing continuity of care. Child care directors and infant–toddler caregivers were asked five questions regarding how children were grouped and cared for daily. Questions focused on how children typically transitioned from classroom to classroom, whether the caregiver transitioned with the children to a new classroom, and the number of caregivers involved in the care of the focal child each day. In addition, observers noted the adult–child ratio in each classroom and observed the practices of primary caregiving. Each question was rated on a scale from 0 to 2, with 2 indicating full implementation. The continuity scale was scored by summing scores for the five indicators. A maximum score of 10 was possible, and a classroom had to score a minimum of 6 points in order to be considered a continuity of care classroom. The average score for the continuity classrooms was 8 (range = 6–10), and for the noncontinuity classrooms the average score was 4 (range = 1–5). Directors' and caregivers' responses were confirmed during the observation by asking both the same questions regarding transition policies and practices. If there was disagreement, the data collector scored the item based on observed practices and a review of center policies, if needed. Items such as group size, ratio, primary caregiving tasks, and daily stability were scored based on observation.

Caregiver education and state-rated quality

To control for structural quality level, caregivers completed a brief survey regarding their educational attainment and the hours of training they had received in the past year. Data collectors also confirmed the state-rated quality level of each center by asking the director and checking the state child care database that tracks the quality level of each licensed child care facility. The state's Quality Rating and Improvement System assigns programs to one of four levels. Level 1 centers met basic health and safety requirements, Level 2 centers met all Level 1 requirements plus had incorporated learning environments for young children into their practice, Level 3 centers met all previous requirements and had a curriculum, and Level 4 centers were nationally accredited by one of five state-recognized accrediting agencies (Family and Social Services Administration, n.d.).

Toddler social competence and problem behaviors

The Brief Infant-Toddler Social Emotional Assessment (Briggs-Gowan & Carter, 2002) was used to measure toddlers' social emotional competence and problem behaviors. The Brief Infant-Toddler Social Emotional Assessment consists of 60 items selected from the Infant-Toddler Social Emotional Assessment, and each item is scaled as follows: 0 = not true/rarely, 1 = somewhat true/sometimes, 2 = very true/often, or N = no opportunity. Child care teachers responded to items based on behaviors observed in child care. The measure contains two subscales: problem behaviors (49 items) and social competence (11 items). Mean scores for social competence and behavior problems (0–2) were computed and used in the analysis. Internal consistency of the scales in the sample data was .92 for the social competence subscale and .76 for the problem behaviors subscale ($N = 115$).

Caregiver–child interactive involvement

Caregiver interactive involvement with the child was assessed by trained observers using the Adult Interaction Scale (Rubenstein & Howes, 1979), which was developed to assess the level of involvement of adults with individual children between the ages of 11 and 30 months. This measure has been used in several large-scale studies, such as the Cost, Quality, and Outcomes Study (Peisner-Feinberg et al., 2000) and the National Child Care Staffing Study (Whitebrook, Sakai, Gerber, & Howes, 2001). Observed interactions were rated on a 6-point scale. Interactions are rated as follows: absent (0) if the adult is not present in the room or not visible to the child; ignores (1) if the adult ignores the child; routine (2) if the caregiver touches the child for changing or other routine care needs but makes no verbal responses to the child; minimal (3) if the caregiver touches the child only for necessary discipline, to move a child away from another, to answer direct requests for help, or to give verbal directives with no reply encouraged; simple social (4) if the caregiver answers the child's verbal bids but does not elaborate or use some unnecessary positive physical contact; elaborated (5) if the caregiver engages in some positive physical gestures, maintains a close proximity to the child, acknowledges the child's statements and responds but does not restate the child's statement, sits with the child during play, or suggests play materials; and intense (6) if the caregiver hugs or holds the child, restates the child's statements, engages the child in conversation, plays interactively with the child, or sits and eats with the child, providing a social atmosphere. The observers live coded caregiver–child interactions for each child in four equally spaced 15-min segments over a 3-hr time period using 20-s coding intervals. The mean level of interactive involvement (range = 0–6) over all intervals was calculated, and this mean score was used in the analyses.

Child temperament

The Infant Characteristics Questionnaire (Bates, Freeland, & Lounsbury, 1979) was used to assess each child's temperament as perceived by the child care teacher, to control for the possible effect of temperament on either caregiver–child interactive involvement or toddler social competence/behavior problems. The Infant Characteristics Questionnaire consists of 32 Likert-type items including a general key item asking directly for the overall degree of difficulty the child presents for the caregiver. Caregivers score children on a 7-point scale, with a score of 1 representing the least difficult temperament behaviors, a score of 4 representing average behaviors of the child, and a score of 7 representing difficulties or inconsistencies the child may exhibit in his or her behaviors and routines. A high score on the scale indicates that the child has a more difficult temperament. The mean score for this scale (range = 0–7) was computed and used in the analysis. Cronbach's alpha was .92 for this sample.

Covariates

Child gender (1 = male), child age, household income, parent education (1 = bachelor's degree or higher), and caregiver:child ratio (1 = 1:4) were included as covariates in the analyses. Household income was composed of four categories: less than $25,000, $25,000–$55,000, $55,001–$85,000, and $85,001–$100,000+. Parent education was measured using three categories of educational attainment: high school diploma/general equivalency diploma, associate's degree/certificate/some college, or 4-year college degree or higher. Caregiver:child ratio was observed and coded as 1 = 1:4 or 0 = higher than 1:4.

Results

Preliminary analyses

Comparison analyses between the continuity of care and noncontinuity of care groups were used for all variables to determine whether the data met assumptions for inferential statistical tests and to assess the equivalence of the continuity and noncontinuity sample groups. Descriptive statistics for variables for each group (i.e., continuity of care vs. noncontinuity of care) are presented in Table 1.

Group equivalence

Independent-samples t tests and chi-square tests were used to determine whether continuity and noncontinuity groups were equivalent, or well-matched, based on child, family, caregiver, and classroom demographic characteristics. There were no significant group differences in level of difficulties in child temperament, household income, parental education level, or caregiver education/training between the continuity and noncontinuity groups.

As expected and planned, there was a significant group difference in the length of time the child had been with the caregiver, with children in continuity classrooms having been with their caregivers for longer periods of time, $t(113) = 13.34$, $p < .001$. There was a significant difference in the mean age of children in the continuity and noncontinuity groups, with children in the continuity group slightly older than the children in the noncontinuity group, $t(113) = -2.20$, $p < .001$. There were more boys in the continuity versus noncontinuity group, $\chi^2(1, N = 115) = 4.60$, $p < .05$. More classrooms in the continuity group were rated at the highest level of the state's quality rating system than classrooms in noncontinuity sites, $\chi^2(3, N = 115) = 8.72$, $p < .05$. Classrooms in the continuity group also had higher staff:child ratios (1:4 vs. 1:5 and 1:6) compared to classrooms in the

Table 1. Comparisons Between Continuity of Care and Noncontinuity of Care Groups ($N = 115$).

t Test	Continuity of Care (n = 57) M (SD)	Noncontinuity of Care (n = 58) M (SD)	t	df
Interactive involvement	2.46 (0.08)	2.05 (0.07)	3.94***	113
Social competence	1.43 (0.05)	1.32 (0.05)	1.58	113
Problem behaviors	0.36 (0.05)	0.55 (0.03)	−3.05**	113
Length of time with caregiver	13.96 (4.03)	5.07 (0.40)	13.34***	113
Child age (months)	20.07 (0.48)	18.47 (0.55)	2.20*	113
Child temperament (ICQ)	3.35 (0.10)	3.30 (0.10)	0.34	113
Chi-Square Test	%	%	χ^2	df
Child gender (male)	59.65	39.66	4.60*	1
Parent education (at least BA)	46.55	53.45	0.08	1
Household income			0.48	3
Less than $25,000	22.41	24.56		
$25,000–$55,000	21.05	21.05		
$55,001–$85,000	19.30	19.30		
$85,001–$100,000+	35.09	35.09		
State quality rating level			8.72*	3
Level 1	0	3.45		
Level 2	22.81	32.76		
Level 3	12.28	24.14		
Level 4	64.91	39.66		
Caregiver education (at least AA)	34.48	42.12	0.71	1
Caregiver:child ratio (higher than 1:4)	40.35	63.79	6.33*	1

Note. ICQ = Infant Characteristics Questionnaire; BA = bachelor's degree; AA = associate's degree.
*$p \leq .05$. **$p \leq .01$. ***$p \leq .001$.

noncontinuity group, $\chi^2(1, N = 115) = 6.33, p < .05$. Age, gender, ratio, and the state quality rating were controlled for in the final analyses.

Mean differences in caregiver–child interactive involvement and toddler social competence and problem behaviors

A preliminary examination of the response variables in continuity versus noncontinuity groups revealed that observed caregiver–child interactive involvement was rated significantly higher and caregivers' reports of toddlers' behavior problems were significantly lower for children in the continuity group compared to the noncontinuity group: observed caregiver–child interactive involvement, $t(113) = 3.94, p < .001$; toddlers' behavior problems, $t(113) = -3.05, p < .01$. Observed toddler social competence was not significantly different between children in the continuity versus noncontinuity groups, $t(113) = 1.58, p > .05$.

Primary analyses

Hierarchical linear modeling (HLM) was used to analyze the data structure in which children (Level 1) were nested within classrooms (Level 2) that were either continuity of care or noncontinuity of care. This nested structure violates the assumption that observations are independent. Children in the same classroom are likely to share similar characteristics (e.g., family background) to one another than to children in other classrooms. HLM accounts for the resultant correlation in error terms and allows for more explicit examination of higher level relationships (Raudenbush & Bryk, 2002). In addition, HLM allows examination of cross-level associations. As noted earlier, of specific interest were the cross-level associations between children's exposure to a continuity of care classroom (Level 2 variable) and (a) their level of interactive involvement with caregivers (Level 1 criterion variable) and (b) their social competence and behavior problems (Level 1 response variable).

In order to justify the use of HLM, we ran an unconditional model (a model only with outcome variables) for each outcome variable, and intraclass correlation coefficients (ICCs) were calculated from the model. Results showed an ICC of .47 for problem behaviors, indicating that 47% of the variance in children's problem behaviors was at the caregiver/class level (Level 2) and 53% of the variance in children's problem behaviors was at the child level (Level 1). For social competence, the ICC was .18, indicating that 18% of the variance in children's social competence was at the caregiver/class level and 82% of the variance in children's social competence was at the child level. The ICC for caregiver–child interactions was .48, indicating that 48% of the variance in caregiver–child interactions was at the caregiver/class level and 52% of the variance in child–caregiver interactions was at the child level. A relatively high ICC justifies the use of HLM (Lee, 2000).

After justifying the use of HLM, we ran random-intercept models for each outcome variable to examine whether continuity of care status predicted caregiver–child interactive involvement, child social competence, and child problem behaviors (see Table 2). Covariates in the model included gender, age, temperament, staff–child ratio, household income, parent education, caregiver education, and the state-rated quality level.

Continuity of care and caregiver–child interactive involvement

As shown in Table 2, a significant association between continuity of care and caregiver–child interactive involvement ($b = .29, p \leq .05$) was found. This result suggests that caregivers in continuity classrooms generally had higher levels of interactive involvement with their children. Our results further showed that one covariate, caregiver–child ratio, was also significant ($b = .44, p \leq .01$). Controlling for continuity of care status, we found that toddlers in classrooms with higher staff:child ratios of 1:4 had higher levels of interactive involvement with their caregivers compared with toddlers in classrooms with lower staff:child ratios (1:5).

Table 2. Intercept as Outcome Model.

	Interactive Involvement		Social Competence		Problem Behaviors	
Factor	b	SE	b	SE	b	SE
Child/family factors						
Gender (1 = male)	−.02	.10	−.06	.07	<−.01	.06
Child age	.02	.02	.03**	.01	−.01	.01
Child temperament	.05	.07	−.13**	.05	.11**	.04
Household income						
$25,000–$55,000	.21	.15	.10	.10	.02	.09
$55,001–$85,000	.31	.20	−.08	.13	.06	.11
$85,001–$100,000+	.34	.18	−.08	.12	.02	.10
Parent education[a]	−.09	.13	.09	.09	−.02	.08
Caregiver/classroom factors						
Continuity of care (1 = yes)	.29*	.13	.09	.07	−.16*	.08
State quality rating level						
Level 2	<−.01	.46	<.01	.26	.38	.28
Level 3	−.05	.47	.07	.27	.28	.29
Level 4	.04	.45	.04	.26	.34	.28
Caregiver education[b]	−.16	.13	.05	.07	.12	.08
Caregiver:child ratio[c]	.44**	.14	−.03	.08	−.13	.09
Intercept	1.19*	.47	1.17***	.27	.06	.29
Random Effects	Estimate	SE	Estimate	SE	Estimate	SE
Level 2 effects (U_{0j})	.27	.09	<.001	<.001	.19	.04
Level 1 effects (r_{ij})	.44	.05	.33	.02	.24	.02

[a]Parent education: 1 = bachelor's degree or higher. [b]Caregiver education: 1 = at least an associate's degree. [c]Caregiver:child ratio: 1 = 1:4 versus 0 = higher than 1:4.
*$p \leq .05$. **$p \leq .01$. ***$p \leq .001$.

Continuity of care and toddlers' social competence and problem behaviors

Our results showed no association between continuity of care status and toddler social competence (see Table 2). Results from the covariates showed that older children were more likely to exhibit higher social competence than younger children ($b = .03$, $p \leq .01$), and children with more difficult temperaments tended to display lower social competence ($b = −.13$, $p \leq .01$).

As shown in Table 2, there was a significant association between continuity of care and children's problem behaviors ($b = −.16$, $p \leq .05$), indicating that caregivers rated children in continuity classrooms as having fewer problem behaviors compared with children in noncontinuity classrooms. One covariate, children's temperament ($b = .11$, $p \leq .01$), was also significant. The result indicates that children with more difficult temperaments exhibited more problem behaviors than children with less difficult temperaments.

Caregiver–child interactive involvement as a mediator between continuity of care and toddler problem behavior

The final research question explored whether caregiver–child interactive involvement mediated the association between continuity of care and toddler problem behaviors. In order to examine this question, we conducted a series of Sobel tests. A 2-1-1 mediational model approach was used because of its flexibly in allowing for testing of mediated effects when the data structure is nested (Krull & MacKinnon, 2001). The current data had a nested structure because a group/classroom-level predictor (i.e., continuity of care) was hypothesized to affect an individual/child-level outcome (i.e., toddler problem behavior) through an individual/child-level mediator (i.e., interactive involvement).

In the previous models, continuity of care was significantly related to toddlers' problem behaviors but not social competence. Thus, the mediation examination was conducted only with problem behaviors as an outcome. In order to identify (a) whether caregiver–child interactive involvement was significantly related to toddlers' problem behaviors and (b) whether the association between continuity of care and toddlers' problem behaviors became weaker when caregiver–child interactive involvement (mediator) was controlled, we included both continuity of care and caregiver–child

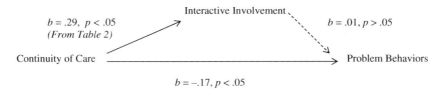

Figure 1. Mediational model of continuity of care and problem behaviors.

interactive involvement in the model as predictors of toddlers' problem behavior. As shown in Figure 1, no significant association was found between child–caregiver interactive involvement and toddlers' problem behaviors ($b = .01$, $p > .05$). Thus, no mediation effect of child–caregiver interactions on the association between continuity of care and toddlers' problem behaviors was found in the current study.

Discussion

The practice of continuity in infant–toddler child care is meant to establish continuous relationships between caregivers and the children in their care. Continuity of care draws on developmental processes described in attachment theory (Cryer et al., 2000; Owen et al., 2008). Time with a stable, consistent caregiver is expected to promote familiarity and increase involvement and sensitive-responsiveness from the caregiver and thus have positive impacts on children's development (Elicker et al., 1999; Raikes, 1993).

The findings from this quasi-experimental comparison of child–caregiver interactive involvement and toddlers' social competence and problem behaviors in continuity and noncontinuity child care rooms showed that toddlers between the ages of 12 and 24 months in continuity of care classrooms experienced significantly more interactive involvement with their caregivers compared with toddlers who were in noncontinuity of care classrooms. Caregivers in continuity of care classrooms also reported that toddlers had fewer problem behaviors compared with toddlers in noncontinuity of care classrooms. Finally, although child–caregiver interactive involvement was higher in the continuity rooms and problem behaviors were lower, we did not find evidence that caregiver–child interactive involvement mediated the relationship between continuity of care and toddler social competence and problem behaviors.

Caregiving in continuity of care child care rooms

These findings provide new evidence that maintaining a continuous placement between toddlers and their caregivers for a year or more is associated with higher levels of interactive involvement in caregiving (Elicker et al., 1999; Howes & Hamilton, 1992; Owen et al., 2008; Raikes, 1993; Ritchie & Howes, 2003). Toddlers in continuity of care classrooms received more interactive caregiving than toddlers in noncontinuity of care classrooms.

These findings also replicate a substantial body of research that shows that positive aspects of caregiving are greater when staff–child ratios are higher (NICHD Early Child Care Research Network, 1996, 2000). Continuity of care practices as recommended often also emphasize higher staff–child ratios, and previous research has identified staff–child ratios as a strong predictor of quality caregiving (e.g., NICHD Early Child Care Research Network, 2000). So quite apart from the issue of continuity of care, these results add evidence that implementing higher staff–child ratios in toddler classrooms in child care centers can result in higher levels of interactive and quality caregiving.

Programs that implement continuity of care as a practice provide more time and opportunities for caregivers and toddlers to develop stable and positive relationships and for the caregiver to get to know and understand each child's needs and signals. Implicit in the discussion of continuity in caregiving is the idea that relationships between caregivers and children take time to develop. According to attachment theory, time with a responsive, sensitive caregiver is a key factor in developing a secure emotional bond with that caregiver (De Wolff & Ijzendoorn, 1997; Howes, 1999).

When caregivers have the opportunity to establish longer term relationships with the children in their care, they may be more likely to make a commitment and take the time to learn more about the children in their care, including their signals and cues and their likes and dislikes, because the program supports continuous relationships. Hegde and Cassidy (2004) found in a small qualitative study that caregivers in continuity rooms felt they could better anticipate the children's needs and how to comfort the children in their care. Caregivers also felt that having the gift of time allowed them more of an opportunity to bond with the children by providing more responsive and sensitive care.

Continuity of care and social competence

Although this research did not find the hypothesized statistically significant difference in reported toddler social competence in the continuity versus noncontinuity rooms, we did find that toddlers in the continuity rooms exhibited fewer behavior problems and also that the child's age and temperament, as rated by the child care teacher, was associated with children's social competence. Older toddlers displayed higher levels of social competence, and children with more difficult temperaments displayed lower levels of social competence. The continuity or noncontinuity practices did not account for significant additional variance in children's social competence, and we did not find evidence that caregiver–child interactive involvement mediated the relationship between continuity of care practices and toddler social competence. Perhaps the link between continuity of care and toddler social competence is more complex than our original hypothesis suggests, with other variables, such as parental/family influences or the quality of peer interactions in the classroom, playing a role in the development of social competence. Because social competence is highly variable among children at this age, it may be that other influences, either within or outside of the child care environment, are stronger influences on developing social competence. For example, attachment security with caregivers, mothers, and fathers was not assessed in this study, and early attachment security is an established predictor of early childhood social competence (e.g., Elicker et al., 1992). Given these possibilities, future research might include an assessment of attachment security in both child care and home relationships and document toddlers' history of care both in and out of the home. Future researchers may also want to investigate the role peers may play in developing social competence in young children. Some research has suggested that peer relations may be an important factor in young children's social competence development (Williams, Ontai, & Mastergeorge, 2007; Wittmer, 2012).

Continuity of care and problem behaviors

Toddlers in continuity of care classrooms were more likely to be rated by their caregivers as having fewer problem behaviors compared with toddlers in noncontinuity classrooms, even after we controlled for toddler age and temperament. This finding adds to previous research findings that when children in child care centers had more daily continuity in staffing, peers, and program structure, they displayed more advanced and less problematic social development (e.g., deSchipper, Tavecchio, van Ijzendoorn, & Van Zeijl, 2004; deSchipper et al., 2004). Previous research has also found that children who experience transitions in their nonparental caregiver before 24 months of age are more likely to be rated as aggressive (Howes & Hamilton, 1993). Thus, continuity of care classrooms may ease children's problem behaviors by providing more security, stability, and predictability within the child care environment, thus leading to lower ratings of problem behaviors by the caregivers in those rooms.

Another possibility is that caregivers' perceptions and judgments about toddlers' behavior may deepen and become more positive given additional time with each child. With a deeper and more individualized understanding, caregivers may perceive and report fewer problem behaviors in the child. This hypothesis should be studied in future research.

Temperamental variation clearly played a role in toddler problem behavior in this sample, although continuity of care was a stronger correlate of problem behaviors. Therefore, the processes involved in the association of continuity of care with toddler problem behaviors may warrant further investigation. Attachment security with the caregiver is an obvious process we did not observe in this study, but there are other possible intervening variables that might be explored, including family factors, limit setting and behavior management by the caregiver, and support for positive peer interactions in the toddler room.

Implications for policy and practice

These findings suggest several important issues for practitioners and policymakers. First, child care providers should consider adopting policies in which caregivers and children can spend more time together in the child care environment. Instead of moving young children to new classrooms and teachers based on age or the achievement of developmental milestones, providers should consider arrangements in which younger children spend a longer amount of time with their teachers rather than moving them as often as every 6 months to a new classroom (Cryer et al., 2000). Second, the practice of continuity of care may help teachers view children's behavior as typical for that individual rather than problematic. It is possible that having more time to build a relationship with each child allows teachers a broader and more accepting view of the child's development, leading to more effective guidance.

Finally, another related issue for providers and policymakers to consider is higher caregiver–child ratios in infant–toddler care settings. Although there is an economic reason to enroll as many children in a classroom as state licensing allows, this research provides further evidence that higher caregiver–child ratios predict higher levels of interactive caregiving. Higher caregiver–child ratios are an important structural feature of child care that provides the setting for higher caregiver–child interactive involvement to occur. Studies have found that higher caregiver–child ratios are associated with important quality features that can lead to better developmental outcomes for children. One study found that higher caregiver–child ratios were related to higher quality infant–toddler care (Phillipsen, Burchinal, Howes, & Cryer, 1997). Another study found higher caregiver–child ratios were one of the strongest predictors of positive infant caregiving (NICHD Early Child Care Research Network, 1996). Thus, providing environments with higher caregiver–child ratios, coupled with strategies to increase temporal continuity of care, is an important factor in providing relationship-based care for infants and toddlers, supporting higher quality caregiver–child interactions and more optimal toddler social development.

Limitations of the study and conclusion

This study provides the most focused evidence to date in the literature regarding the potential impact of a continuity of care practice on caregiver–child interactions and toddler social behaviors. There are limitations with the current study in addition to those already discussed. There were variations in the ways in which programs implemented continuity of care across the child care centers participating in the study. Some centers had mixed-age groups of children from 0 to 3 years, some centers kept children and caregivers together for 24 or 36 months, some caregivers changed classrooms with the children, whereas others adapted the classroom environment in place as the children got older. However, the continuity and noncontinuity samples were systematically assessed and found to be distinctly different, although the continuity of care classrooms observed were somewhat heterogeneous. It is possible that some continuity of care practices contribute more to responsive caregiving and children's development than others.

Future research could be designed to examine whether the different implementation strategies of continuity of care are related to different child or teacher outcomes. Furthermore, other practices within continuity of care classrooms, such as the amount of time caregivers and children are together, limiting caregiver transitions, daily stability of the caregiver, and primary caregiving, may be related to interactive involvement and children's development. These individual factors could also be explored in future studies.

Another limitation of the study is that it was not possible for the observers to be uninformed about which classrooms were practicing continuity of care and which classrooms were not. Future studies could account for these factors, if possible, by finding ways to mask observers from the continuity of care policies in the centers they are observing.

Another limitation of the study involves the self-selection of the programs that implemented continuity of care. There may well have been unmeasured differences between centers that agreed to participate and those that chose not to participate. It is possible that centers that implement continuity of care have other features that were not measured that contributed to the results. For example, centers that implement continuity of care may attract teaching staff who are skilled in relationship building or considered high-ability teachers (Raikes, 1993).

Finally, in a quasi-experimental group comparison study, causality cannot be determined, and it is impossible for us to conclude definitively that the differences in caregiver–child interactions and problem behaviors were caused by differences in continuity of care. A limitation of using a quasi-experimental design is that there are no assurances that groups were equivalent on a wide range of variables, and the groups may have differed in important ways that were not measured (Shadish et al., 2002). The strongest research design is a true experimental design in which child care providers would have been randomly selected and children within those classrooms would have been randomly assigned to a continuity or noncontinuity classroom. However, because of ethical and practical considerations inherent in the field of early care and education and strong ethical principles about parental choice and control in child care decisions, it was not possible to randomize, particularly because of the limited number of providers implementing continuity of care in the study area and nationwide and because parents quite rightly wish to maintain control of their infants' child care placements.

Despite these potential limitations, this research adds to a small yet growing body of evidence that suggests that continuity of care is a promising practice for programs that strive to provide high-quality care for infants and toddlers. Positive, involved, responsive caregiving is the heart of relationship-based child care practices. In this study, toddlers in continuity of care rooms engaged in more interaction and more intense involvement with their caregivers than did toddlers in noncontinuity of care classrooms. In addition, toddlers in continuity of care rooms presented fewer behavioral problems as perceived by their caregivers compared to their counterparts in the noncontinuity rooms. The practice of continuity of care may serve as a foundation for higher quality caregiver–child interactions and provide stronger support for preventing or reducing toddlers' behavioral problems.

ORCID

Karen Ruprecht http://orcid.org/0000-0002-0572-6279

References

Ahnert, L., Pinquart, M., & Lamb, M. E. (2006). Security of children's relationships with nonparental care providers: A meta-analysis. *Child Development, 77*, 664–679. doi:10.1111/j.1467-8624.2006.00896.x

Barnas, M. V., & Cummings, E. M. (1994). Caregiver stability and toddlers' attachment related behavior towards caregivers in day care. *Infant Behavior and Development, 17*, 141–147. doi:10.1016/0163-6383(94)90049-3

Bates, J. E., Freeland, C. A. B., & Lounsbury, M. L. (1979). Measurement of infant difficultness. *Child Development, 50*, 794–803. doi:10.2307/1128946

Bowlby, J. (1982). *Attachment and loss: Vol. 1. Attachment.* London, England: Hogarth. (Original work published 1969)

Briggs-Gowan, M. J., & Carter, A. S. (2002). *Brief Infant-Toddler Social and Emotional Assessment (BITSEA) manual, version 2.0.* New Haven, CT: Yale University.

Cassidy, J., & Shaver, P. R. (Eds.). (1999). *Handbook of attachment: Theory, research, and clinical applications.* New York, NY: Guilford Press.

Clarke-Stewart, A., Vandell, D. L., Burchinal, M., O'Brien, M., & McCartney, K. (2002). Do regulable features of child care homes affect children's development? *Early Childhood Research Quarterly, 17,* 52–86. doi:10.1016/S0885-2006(02)00133-3

Copple, C., & Bredekamp, S. (Eds.). (2009). *Developmentally appropriate practice in early childhood programs serving children birth through age 8* (3rd ed.). Washington, DC: National Association for the Education of Young Children.

Cryer, D. (2007). *The study to evaluate the effects of continuity of caregivers in infants and toddlers in child care.* Unpublished manuscript, University of North Carolina–Chapel Hill.

Cryer, D., Hurwitz, S., & Wolery, M. (2000). Continuity of caregiver for infants and toddlers in center-based child care: Report on a survey of center practices. *Early Childhood Research Quarterly, 15,* 497–514. doi:10.1016/S0885-2006(01)00069-2

Cryer, D., Wagner-Moore, L., Burchinal, M., Yazejian, N., Hurwitz, S., & Wolery, M. (2005). Effects of transitions to new child care classes on infant/toddler distress and behavior. *Early Childhood Research Quarterly, 20,* 37–56. doi:10.1016/j.ecresq.2005.01.005

De Wolff, M. S., & Ijzendoorn, M. H. (1997). Sensitivity and attachment: A meta-analysis on parental antecedents of infant attachment. *Child Development, 68,* 571–591. doi:10.1111/cdev.1997.68.issue-4

deSchipper, J., Tavecchio, L., & van IJzendoorn, M. (2008). Children's attachment relationships with day care providers: Associations with positive caregiving and child's temperament. *Social Development, 17,* 444–470. doi:10.1111/j.1467-9507.2007.00448.x

deSchipper, J., Tavecchio, L., van Ijzendoorn, M., & Van Zeijl, J. (2004). Goodness of fit in center day care: Relations of temperament, stability, and quality of care with the child's adjustment. *Early Childhood Research Quarterly, 19,* 257–272. doi:10.1016/j.ecresq.2004.04.004

deSchipper, J., van Ijzendoorn, M., & Tavecchio, L. (2004). Stability in center day care: Relations with children's well-being and problem behavior in day care. *Social Development, 13,* 531–550. doi:10.1111/j.1467-9507.2004.00282.x

Early Head Start Performance Standards. (n.d.). *Education and early childhood development.* Retrieved from http://eclkc.ohs.acf.hhs.gov/hslc/standards/hspps/1304/1304.21%20Education%20and%0early%20childhood%20development.htm

Edwards, C. P., & Raikes, H. (2002). Extending the dance: Relationship-based approaches to infant/toddler care and education. *Young Children, 57*(4), 10–17.

Elicker, J., Englund, M., & Sroufe, L. (1992). Predicting peer competence and peer relationships in childhood from early parent-child relationships. In R. D. Parke & G. W. Ladd (Eds.), *Family-peer relationships: Modes of linkage* (pp. 77–106). Hillsdale, NJ: Erlbaum.

Elicker, J., Fortner-Wood, C., & Noppe, I. (1999). The context of infant attachment in family child care. *Journal of Applied Developmental Psychology, 20,* 319–336. doi:10.1016/S0193-3973(99)00019-2

Else-Quest, N., Hyde, J., Goldsmith, H., & Van Hulle, C. (2006). Gender differences in temperament: A meta analysis. *Psychological Bulletin, 132,* 33–72. doi:10.1037/00332909.132.1.33

Family and Social Services Administration. (n.d.). *Levels of quality.* Retrieved from http://www.in.gov/fssa/pathstoquality/3731.htm

Hegde, A., & Cassidy, D. (2004). Teacher and parent perspectives on looping. *Early Childhood Education Journal, 32,* 133–138. doi:10.1007/s10643-004-1080-x

Howes, C. (1999). Attachment relationships in the context of multiple caregivers. In J. Cassidy & P. R. Shaver (Eds.), *Handbook of attachment theory and research* (pp. 671–687). New York, NY: Guilford Press.

Howes, C., & Hamilton, C. (1992). Children's relationships with child care teachers: Stability and concordance with parental attachments. *Child Development, 63,* 867–878. doi:10.2307/1131239

Howes, C., & Hamilton, C. (1993). The changing experience of child care: Changes in teachers and in teacher-child relationships and children's social competence with peers. *Early Childhood Research Quarterly, 8,* 15–32. doi:10.1016/S0885-2006(05)80096-1

Howes, C., Hamilton, C., & Philipsen, L. (1998). Stability and continuity of child-caregiver and child-peer relationships. *Child Development, 69,* 418–426. doi:10.1111/j.1467-8624.1998.tb06199.x

Howes, C., & Smith, E. (1995). Relations among child care quality, teacher, behavior, children's play activities, emotional security and cognitive activity in child care. *Early Childhood Research Quarterly, 10,* 381–404. doi:10.1016/0885-2006(95)90013-6

Krull, J., & MacKinnon, D. (2001). Multilevel modeling of individual and group level mediated effects. *Multivariate Behavioral Research, 36,* 249–277. doi:10.1207/S15327906MBR3602_06

Lally, J. R., & Tsao, C. (2004). *Continuity of care: Handout from Module II, exploring primary caregiving and continuity of care training session*. Unpublished document, Program for Infant Toddler Care, Sausalito, CA.

Lee, V. E. (2000). Using hierarchical linear modeling to study social contexts: The case of school effects. *Educational Psychologist, 35*, 125–141. doi:10.1207/S15326985EP3502_6

McMullen, M. B., & Dixon, S. (2009). In support of a relationship-based approach to practice with infants and toddlers in the United States. In J. Brownlee (Ed.), *Participatory learning and the early years* (pp. 109–128). London, England: Routledge.

National Institute of Child Health and Human Development Early Child Care Research Network. (1996). Characteristics of infant child care: Factors contributing to positive caregiving. *Early Childhood Research Quarterly, 11*, 269–306. doi:10.1016/S0885-2006(96)90009-5

National Institute of Child Health and Human Development Early Child Care Research Network. (2000). Characteristics and quality of child care for toddlers and preschoolers. *Applied Developmental Science, 4*, 116–135. doi:10.1207/S1532480XADS0403_2

National Institute of Child Health and Human Development Early Child Care Research Network. (2001). Child-care and family predictors of preschool attachment and stability from infancy. *Developmental Psychology, 37*, 847–862. doi:10.1037/0012-1649.37.6.847

Owen, M. T., Klausli, J., Mata-Otero, A., & O'Brien-Caughy, M. (2008). Relationship focused child care practices: Quality of care and child outcomes for children in poverty. *Early Education & Development, 19*, 302–329. doi:10.1080/10409280801964010

Patton, M. (2002). *Qualitative research and evaluation methods* (3rd ed.). Thousand Oaks, CA: Sage.

Peisner-Feinberg, E. S., Burchinal, M. R., Clifford, R. M., Culkin, M. L., Howes, C., Kagan, S. L., & Yazejian, N. (2000). *The children of the Cost, Quality, and Outcomes Study go to school: Technical report*. Chapel Hill: University of North Carolina at Chapel Hill, Frank Porter Graham Child Development Center.

Phillipsen, L. C., Burchinal, M. R., Howes, C., & Cryer, D. (1997). The prediction of process quality from structural features of child care. *Early Childhood Research Quarterly, 12*, 281–303. doi:10.1016/S0885-2006(97)90004-1

Program for Infant Toddler Care. (n.d.). *PITC's six program policies*. Retrieved from http://www.pitc.org/pub/pitc_docs/138?x-r=disp

Putnam, S., Gartstein, M., & Rothbart, M. (2006). Measurement of fine-grained aspects of toddler temperament: The early childhood behavior questionnaire. *Infant Behavior and Development, 29*, 386–401. doi:10.1016/j.infbeh.2006.01.004

Raikes, H. (1993). Relationship duration in infant care: Time with a high-ability teacher and infant-teacher attachment. *Early Childhood Research Quarterly, 8*, 309–325. doi:10.1016/S0885-2006(05)80070-5

Raudenbush, S., & Bryk, A. (2002). *Hierarchical linear models: Applications and data analysis methods*. Newbury Park, CA: Sage.

Ritchie, S., & Howes, C. (2003). Program practices, caregiver stability, and child-caregiver relationships. *Journal of Applied Developmental Psychology, 24*, 497–516. doi:10.1016/S01933973(03)00028-5

Rubenstein, J., & Howes, C. (1979). Caregiving and infant behavior in day care and in homes. *Developmental Psychology, 15*, 1–24. doi:10.1037/0012-1649.15.1.1

Schumacher, R., & Hoffman, E. (2008). *Continuity of care: Charting progress for babies in child care*. Retrieved from the Center for Law and Social Policy website: http://www.clasp.org/publications/cp_rationale3.pdf

Shadish, W. R., Cook, T. D., & Campbell, D. T. (2002). *Experimental and quasi-experimental designs for generalized causal inference*. Boston, MA: Houghton-Mifflin.

Theilheimer, R. (2006). Molding to the children: Primary caregiving and continuity of care. *Zero to Three, 26*(3), 50–54.

Tran, H., & Weinraub, M. (2006). Child care effects in context: Quality, stability, and multiplicity in nonmaternal child care arrangements during the first 15 months of life. *Developmental Psychology, 42*, 566–582. doi:10.1037/0012-1649.42.3.566

van IJzendoorn, M., Vereijken, C., Bakermans-Kranenburg, M., & Riksen-Walraven, J. (2004). Assessing attachment security with the Attachment Q-sort: Meta analytic evidence for the validity of the observer AQS. *Child Development, 75*, 1188–1213. doi:10.1111/j.14678624.2004.00733.x

Whitebrook, M., Sakai, L., Gerber, E., & Howes, C. (2001). *Then and now: Changes in child care staffing, 1994-2000. technical report*. Washington, DC: Center for the Child Care Workforce.

Williams, S., Ontai, L., & Mastergeorge, A. (2007). Reformulating infant and toddler social competence with peers. *Infant Behavior and Development, 30*, 353–365. doi:10.1016/j.infbeh.2006.10.008

Wittmer, D. (2012). The wonder and complexity of infant and toddler peer relationships. *Young Children, 67*(4), 16–25.

Appendix

Continuity of Care Scale

Length of time between child and caregiver	
Of the children that are currently in the classroom, how many have been with the same teacher for at least nine months?	Child 1: _____ Time with CG: _____ Child 2: _____ Time with CG: _____ Child 3: _____ Time with CG: _____ Child 4: _____ Time with CG: _____ Child 5: _____ Time with CG: _____ Child 6: _____ Time with CG: _____ Child 7: _____ Time with CG: _____ Child 8: _____ Time with CG: _____
Transitions	
Can you describe how your center typically moves children ages 12-24 months to new classrooms and caregivers?	____0 points: Children moved to a different caregiver every 6 months or less ____1 point: Children and caregivers together between 6-9 months ____2 points: Children and caregivers together for over 9 months
Caregiver-Child Continuity	
How do you handle transitions for children between the ages of 12-24 months?	____0 points: Provider uses intentional transitions (child visits new room/caregiver prior to moving; child does not have opportunity to stay with same caregiver) ____1 point: Provider has policy of maintaining teacher-child continuity from the time the child enrolls in child care until the child is 12-18 months old ____2 points: Provider has a clear policy of maintaining teacher-child continuity from the time the child enrolls in child care up until the time the child is between the ages of 19-36 months
Group Size/Ratio	
How many teachers and children are currently enrolled in the classroom? ____Teachers ____Children	____0 points: Ratio is 1 teacher to 6 children ____1 point: Ratio is 1 teacher to 5 children ____2 points: Ratio is 1 teacher to 4 children
Primary Caregiving	
What tasks does the primary caregiver perform in the classroom? If the classroom meets half of these criteria (4 checks), assign a score of 1; if they meet 75% of the criteria (6 checks) assign a score of 2. This will also be assessed and verified at the observation by the data collector. ____Teacher assigned to a small group of children ____Primary caregiver sits with primary caregroup during snack/meals ____Primary caregiver is responsible for diaper changes for caregroup at least 75% of the time ____Primary caregiver soothes children in primary caregroup to sleep	____0 points: No clear primary caregiving system exists (both caregivers equally take care of the children) ____1 point: Primary caregiver responsible for some of the care of the focal child (some sharing of caregiving responsibilities) ____2 points: Primary caregiver responsible for a majority of the care of the focal child

____Primary caregiver interacts with children in primary caregroup via book reading, play time, etc. ____Primary caregiver takes the lead on documenting daily activities for child (fills out daily activity sheets for children) ____Parents have the opportunity to talk to the primary caregiver on a daily basis at either drop off or pick up times ____Primary caregiver provides information on children's development (i.e., completes developmental checklists, makes recommendations to parents about their child, points out achievement of developmental milestones to parents)	
Daily Stability	
How many caregivers do children typically experience in a day?	____0 points: Child has more than 4 caregivers throughout the day ____1 point: Child has 3-4 caregivers throughout the day ____2 points: Child has 2 primary caregivers throughout the day

The Four Roles of a Master Toddler Teacher

Jill Uhlenberg

ABSTRACT
Research Findings: This case study of an experienced toddler teacher resulted in the identification of 4 roles that the teacher played in mediating a culture of respect and participation in the classroom. These 4 roles contrast the roles discussed in Leavitt's (1994) ethnographic study *Power and Emotion in Infant-Toddler Day Care*. I used a series of data collection methods, including field observations, reflective collaboration with the teacher, and interviews with an assistant teacher, to discover the themes that emerged: (a) Liberator, (b) Curriculum Organizer, (c) Chief Historian, and (d) Learner. The role of Liberator was by far the most substantial of the themes that emerged from the data. The other 3 roles overlapped with the Liberator role, although each demonstrated some distinct characteristics. *Practice or Policy*: The findings of this study cannot be applied directly to other classrooms because of the limitations of the specific culture, history, and lived experiences of the participants. However, examining the lived experiences of the toddlers and their interactions with this teacher may provide reflective, effective, and productive content for the professional development activities of other caregivers. In addition, research cited expresses a need for multiple ways of knowing how very young children grow, develop, learn, communicate, and participate.

Over the past decade, more and more very young children, children from birth to 3, have experienced group child care in some type of out-of-home setting. With the number of children younger than 5 years old in the United States whose mothers are working currently approaching 11 million (Child Care Aware, 2014), the welfare of these children in child care settings is in question. The Cost, Quality and Child Outcomes Study Team (1995) affirmed that 90% of infant/toddler child care center settings were of mediocre to poor quality. More recently, Hyson and Tomlinson (2014) reported, "On the whole, child care quality is poor, and it is poorest in programs serving children under age 3" (p. 21). Hall and Rudkin (2011) reported that these very young children are not visible to much of the world, have no voice in how they wish to be treated, or have few opportunities for meaningful involvement in social events outside their families. Research shows that caregivers of children younger than 3 are often transient members of the field of child care and have had no professional development on how to intentionally guide the learning of very young children (Degotardi, 2010; Goouch & Powell, 2012; Hallam, Fouts, Bargreen, & Caudle, 2009; National Association for the Education of Young Children, 2009). Infant and toddler caregivers are often isolated in classrooms that lack opportunities for professional development, including even the time to engage with others caring for a similar age group (Goouch & Powell, 2012). Yet these caregivers are the most important part of the toddler classroom as they develop relationships with children as well as facilitate learning with materials and opportunities.

Purpose of the study

The purpose of this case study was to examine the strategies a master teacher of 2-year-olds demonstrated in providing high-quality toddler child care. These strategies were identified through the interactions between the teacher and toddlers during the routines and activities that were planned and implemented in the classroom. The study explored how the teacher shared power with the toddlers.

Daily experiences in toddler care

Research on the daily experiences of very young children has been mostly top down (Hallam et al., 2009)—that is, reporting data from teachers', parents', or other adults' viewpoints and examining caregiver qualifications as they relate to the quality of caregiving (Brownlee & Berthelsen, 2009; Recchia, Lee, & Shin, 2015; U.S. Administration for Children and Families, 2015). This is in contrast to research on child care from the bottom up, which is designed to provide the perspective of the child on what he or she experiences in child care. However, even some bottom-up studies have reported a more global view of these lived experiences rather than focusing on the events and practices that affect individual children in their daily lives in child care (Hallam et al., 2009; Penn, 2009). In addition, Johansson and Emilson (2010) cautioned that researchers are limited in terms of toddlers' abilities and competence in participating in research, as these children are young and often preverbal.

Studies often focus on the routines of the daily schedule because a substantial amount of time in toddler classrooms is spent in routine caregiving activities such as diapering, eating, napping, and hand washing. Despite the opportunities to converse, these activities are often carried out without conversation between the caregiver and child, and they are frequently carried out as interruptions of child-selected activities (Degotardi, 2010; Goouch & Powell, 2012; Hallam et al., 2009; Penn, 2009). In the Goouch and Powell (2012) study, when caregivers spoke to children, they were mostly directive and terse, telling children what to do. Although interactions appeared to increase during unstructured times of the daily schedule, the routine times lacked conversation and were done *to* the child rather than done *with* (Goouch & Powell, 2012). Toddlers learn through this lack of conversation how the classroom culture works and their roles within it (Elliot, 2009); that is, they are recipients of the actions but not really participants. This lack of a *serve-and-return* (Center on the Developing Child, 2011) approach to adult–child interaction threatens healthy brain development in toddlers and also prevents caregivers from receiving and understanding the children's perspectives.

Leavitt's (1994) research, an ethnographic account of common procedures and activities in infant and toddler child care settings, demonstrated the low level of quality care provided to these children from a bottom-up perspective. This account included clear examples of the lack of a serve-and-return approach. Through anecdotes of specific interactions between an adult caregiver and individual young children, Leavitt reported power struggles, lack of sensitivity toward young children's feelings and emotions, and inappropriate programming that she and her college students observed over 20 years of fieldwork.

The lived experiences of these children included caregivers' complete and total power over every aspect of the children's day. The culture of child care as described in Leavitt's (1994) research places all power in the adults and the routines they establish in the caregiving process, at least in their work with children.

Shared power

A call for including young children as competent learners who participate in all aspects of their learning is evident in recent research (Berthelsen, 2009; Brownlee & Berthelsen, 2009; Duncan, 2009; Elliot, 2009; Göncü, Main, & Abel, 2009; Hall & Rudkin, 2011; Penn, 2009; Recchia et al., 2015). In order for children to fully participate in a classroom culture, teachers must establish a culture that focuses on the social nature of learning and that includes a wide variety of activities that provide participation for all involved, including conflict resolution, so that all children's voices will have efficacy (Göncü et al., 2009). This can happen only when teachers or caregivers are willing to build relationships that provide a context for learning and that value toddlers as agents of their own learning (Berthelsen, 2009).

Berthelsen charges toddler teachers to think in new ways that do not limit views of children's learning capacities to age-related norms. Rather teachers are to provoke learning through engaging children with materials and experiences that challenge them to problem-solve and think in new ways. Starting with materials that offer the child opportunities for control may be easier for teachers to do (Duncan, 2009). Allowing toddlers to become autonomous in other aspects of the classroom offers greater challenges for teachers, as Leavitt (1994) described.

The lack of shared power between teachers and children was evident in Leavitt's (1994) research. She documented teachers as controllers of classroom space and materials as well as controllers of time spent in routines and planned and unstructured activities. In addition, she suggested that teachers performed as objectifiers of the toddlers, treating them more as objects to be manipulated than as individual persons to respect as learners who could initiate their own learning and participate in a shared culture.

Hyson and Tomlinson (2014) noted that low-quality infant and toddler care is still in place in terms of routinization of daily life in the child care center as well as in the lack of choice for children. Ongoing research continues to report the low quality of care described by Leavitt (1994; Degotardi, 2010; Goouch & Powell, 2012; Hallam et al., 2009) in terms of giving directives without listening to children's questions or responses. Perceptions of toddlers' abilities and expectations for their behavior remain embedded in the culture of the caregiver. That is, caregivers who believe that toddlers cannot learn because they are too young or are nonverbal will perpetuate that approach through the culture of the classroom, in planning the curriculum, and in interactions with the children. Duncan (2009) encouraged caregivers to challenge themselves in regard to what they perceive as toddlers' capabilities or potential for learning.

Methods

Setting and program

This classroom was situated on a university campus in a Midwestern state. The study site was designated as a toddler classroom in which full-day child care was provided for children 18–36 months old. The program served faculty, staff, and university student families. The university offered a teacher preparation program in early childhood education, so the campus children's center was considered both a service to university parents and a field site for students seeking a teaching license in early childhood education. Thus, students constituted both part-time employees in the center and observers and participants in daily programming for coursework.

The program was well supported by the university, with teachers receiving a fair salary and good fringe benefits, in sharp contrast to most child care programs across the United States (Mauzy, 2014). These factors led to low staff turnover in the research site, again in contrast to other child care programs. The families represented diversity in socioeconomic status given that university students are at least temporarily low income in most cases. However, despite the economic differences, the student and faculty parents all participated in a culture that valued higher education.

Participants

The participants in the study were the classroom teacher, Alyssa, and her class of nine children. Other classroom assistants, mostly student employees who worked part time, were present at different times during field observations, but only one student's comments were recorded, and only in reference to Alyssa's comments and behaviors. The focus of the field observations was the classroom teacher and her interactions with the toddlers.

Lead teacher

Alyssa, the lead teacher, was Caucasian and was married but had no children at the time of the study. She had earned a bachelor's degree in early childhood education from a different university and had been employed in the program for 8 years prior to the study. During that time, Alyssa had been lead teacher in each of the three different classrooms—infant, toddler, and preschool. She had been the full-time teacher in the infant classroom during the 2 years prior to this study. Although the child care program did not implement a continuity of care program, Alyssa had opted to change classrooms the month that the main study began, moving from the infant room to the toddler room. This experience provided her with intimate knowledge of most of the children in the toddler classroom. This situation also provided the toddlers with a basic understanding of the classroom culture that Alyssa fostered as well as provided Alyssa with a clear knowledge of the children as they moved into toddlerhood.

Children

Nine toddlers, ages 18–36 months, were members of this class. Six of the children had been enrolled in the infant room during the previous year, whereas three new toddlers joined the group in the fall when the study began. Two of the toddlers were African American and one was Asian. The remaining four toddlers were Caucasian. Four of the children were girls and five were boys.

Student staff

One student employee was interviewed regarding her perceptions of Alyssa's role in the classroom. Monica (a pseudonym) was a veteran student staff member who had worked at the center for all 4 years of her college education, then returned as a graduate student. During this time, she had worked in the toddler room for 2 years with other lead teachers and 2 years with Alyssa. Other student staff were not interviewed because they were newer to the center or classroom or they had not been employed there long enough to understand clearly what Alyssa was trying to accomplish with the toddlers. In addition, many of the student staff had worked in child care settings that were less developmentally appropriate, and therefore they were less familiar with the child-centered approach that Alyssa provided.

Data and procedures

The summer prior to the current study, a pilot study focused on relationships between and among Alyssa and her children was conducted. Utilizing field observations of Alyssa and the older infants, this 6-week pilot study provided the initial themes around power and the sharing of power that were used as the framework for analyzing events and conversations (Leavitt, 1994). A collaborative reflection process was implemented that included Alyssa and me. Each day I typed handwritten field notes in a journal of interactions, adding comments and questions. Alyssa reviewed this journal at the end of each day during her planning time and added her own comments as well as responded to questions posed by me. Alyssa and I together identified themes that emerged from these observations and reflections. Those themes from the pilot study were expanded and refined in the collaborative reflection process. The refined themes became the framework for recording field notes during the main study, which began in August with the new school year.

Several types of data were used in this study, including observations, field notes, an electronic journal, and interviews. Functioning as a participant observer, I observed in the classroom for approximately 9 hr, in 3-hr blocks, each week for 4 months. The 3 hr spent in the classroom were generally between breakfast and outdoor playtime in the mornings and encompassed at least an hour each day spent in learning centers of the children's choice. The primary focus of the pilot study observations was the adult–child interactions that occurred during routine and unstructured times of the day. While Alyssa was engaged in all activities in the classroom, assistants often performed the routine events, such as diapering, hand washing, food preparation, and calming children at naptime. Thus, the current study focused on Alyssa's interactions with children during the less routine times of the daily schedule. During each daily observation, field notes were recorded of the children's words and actions as well as Alyssa's responses, questions, and conversations.

I functioned as a *nonparticipant*, or *participant as observer* (Creswell, 2013, p. 167), visiting the classroom for approximately 9 hr, in 3-hr blocks, each week for 4 months. My presence in the classroom potentially made me a participant, as the toddlers were able to see and engage with me at any time. However, the site frequently served as an observation site for university students, which had conditioned the toddlers to accept an adult into their space without feeling the need to include him or her in their activities. Although I did not discourage interactions that the toddlers initiated, neither did I respond openly or encourage the continuation of any such interactions. On one occasion a toddler stood nearby and watched me write field notes, at one point taking the pencil from me and marking the paper. After that event, the toddlers ignored my presence.

Each day after observing in the classroom, I typed the field notes into the computer, generating an electronic journal that was made available to Alyssa through an e-mail attachment. During her planning time each afternoon, she read and responded to the journal entries in writing, using a different font, returning the document to me by attachment. At the end of each week, Alyssa and I discussed the week's field observation notes and Alyssa's written responses. I asked questions during this discussion, including why she had chosen to act in a certain way, provided specific materials, or demonstrated a strategy to the classroom assistants. I recorded and transcribed these conversations and then added the comments and explanations to the electronic journal for later analysis by Alyssa. This cycle of cooperative reflection provided Alyssa an opportunity to correct any subjective perceptions or inaccuracies in the electronic journal.

The student staff interview was focused on the events involving Alyssa and the children that were recorded in field notes. I interviewed Monica twice, once after approximately 2 months had elapsed and then at the end of the classroom observations. I recorded and transcribed these interview notes and then offered Monica the opportunity to review the notes, which Monica declined. Alyssa read the interview notes and added reflective comments to further explain her actions or conversations. This second insider perspective from Monica added triangulation to the data, although in a more superficial way because Monica had not engaged in reviewing and reflecting on her own comments, nor had she been privy to Alyssa's reflections.

Data analysis

Initial coding from the pilot study was related to the themes of power that Leavitt (1994) described: (a) Time Controller, (b) Space Controller, and (c) Objectifier. These themes described the adults and their views on how to provide care for infants and toddlers. Observation notes from the pilot study provided, in the initial analysis, opposite themes from the ones Leavitt described. That is, Alyssa allowed the older infants flexibility in planning and implementing the daily schedule. She allowed the children to freely explore space and materials within the classroom and outside in play areas. And she gave each child individual attention that indicated that she valued each as a learner in the classroom.

Observations and reflections from the main study expanded on these themes. I initially made copies of field notes and cut the paper copies into pieces, then physically sorted the observations into the initial set of themes. As more observations were completed, the classifications became less general and specifically related to emerging themes that more clearly defined Alyssa's actions and interactions.

The theme of Liberator was identified in the pilot study and was carried forward in the main study. It seemed to be the overriding theme because so much of Leavitt's (1994) report involved adult dominance over the toddlers at all times and in all events. Alyssa's liberation countered that theme of dominance throughout both the pilot study and the main study. At first liberation seemed to be the only theme that emerged, as all codes could be collapsed into that one. However, when I returned to the classification process with specific observation notes, subthemes began to emerge based on the frequency of codes. These subthemes, although all related to the theme of Liberator, became more obvious as distinct themes. This led me to be more observant of these themes in succeeding observation periods. Reviewing the themes with Alyssa provided me with encouragement to continue, as she added personal anecdotes and reflections that supported my description of emerging themes.

The Curriculum Organizer theme was most clearly observed from within the Liberator theme. Much of Alyssa's work involved preparing the classroom, the materials, and the staff to carry out planned activities each day. With the overriding theme of liberation, these events and activities occurred through a lens of flexibility of time and location, as well as flexibility in the adults' perceptions of how children would use the materials and spaces in the classroom.

Further analysis teased out the theme of Chief Historian . With every routine and every transition in the daily schedule, Alyssa was constructing a history with the toddlers that gave them a foundation of expectation as well as a sense that all had lived through the activities together. Although the sense of history among Leavitt's (1994) toddlers was less positive, they certainly had experienced a shared history. In Alyssa's classroom, this history was a succession of positive experiences for both the children and the adults.

The final emerging theme of Learner was one that Alyssa suggested herself based on the final week's review of observation notes. She reflected that she had learned much about herself and her teaching in the study, and she acknowledged that for her, personal learning was an ongoing goal—that is, she wanted to learn about each child in her classroom as an individual, as well as learning more about toddlers as a group. Each year of teaching a new group provided her with new opportunities to learn more, which she relished. I recognized this theme as existing throughout the pilot study and the main study and also acknowledged that, while being a learner herself, Alyssa also focused on others' learning around her, including that of both staff and children.

As these four themes emerged through the journal and succeeding discussions, Alyssa weekly reviewed emerging themes, validating or disagreeing with my perceptions and conclusions. Taken as a whole, the roles Alyssa played in the classroom provided a portrait of the culture that she and the children had constructed and that included both Alyssa's *emic* and my *etic* perspectives (Creswell, 2013).

Findings and discussion

Based on an analysis of field notes, journal entries, reflective collaboration between researcher and teacher, and interviews of the assistant teacher, Alyssa demonstrated four roles as the teacher in this toddler classroom. Those roles were (a) Liberator, (b) Curriculum Organizer, (c) Chief Historian, and (d) Learner. The role of Liberator was by far the most substantial of the themes that emerged from the data because of its connection to the sharing of power. The other three roles overlapped with the Liberator role while demonstrating some distinct characteristics.

Liberator

A *liberator* is defined as someone who "makes free, releases from subjugation … or injustices" ("Liberator," 2014). This role is immersed in the concept of power sharing. The children in Leavitt's (1994) study experienced power as recipients rather than as wielders of power, through lived experiences in near dictatorship, in which the caregivers kept control of the time and schedule as well as the materials and space that the children could use. In contrast, the lived experiences in Alyssa's classroom engaged toddlers in practicing how to use power. But they received this power only because Alyssa chose to share it.

Alyssa offered freedom to toddlers in many forms and during many events of the day. She freed them from the traditional structure of adult-imposed scheduling and curriculum. She freed the toddlers from adult intervention as much as possible. This represented Alyssa's conscious decision to allow children to make choices that could be made by the teacher (Brownlee & Berthelsen, 2009; Degotardi, 2010; Hall & Rudkin, 2011) and in fact were made by the teachers described in Leavitt (1994). By making this choice, she freed the toddlers to construct their own way of learning about things in which they were deeply interested. The toddlers could participate in an activity or not, as they chose. The only activities that were not negotiable were diapering, hand washing, and naptime, although children still could choose whether they actually fell asleep or stayed awake.

First and foremost, Alyssa established a classroom designed to offer choices (Brownlee & Berthelsen, 2009; Center on the Developing Child, 2011; Duncan, 2009). The toddlers could move about freely, selecting the toys or activities that interested them. The daily schedule provided structure but Alyssa chose to adjust it freely depending on the children's interests. New materials or objects regularly appeared on a table or in a play space, and the toddlers gravitated to that place. An example of this is the following anecdote.

One day, Alyssa began to tape a large piece of construction paper onto the table surface with masking tape. Two toddlers joined her at the table, but one left almost immediately. Vic stayed and watched. Although he did not reach for the tape, Alyssa offered him a piece, which he placed on the paper. Alyssa handed him another piece and allowed Vic to place it on the paper wherever he wanted. They continued until Vic was satisfied and stopped asking for pieces of tape. Alyssa later wrote that she had wanted to tape the paper down quickly so that the toddlers could paint on it, but she could not miss an opportunity to involve Vic with an experience with a new material (Duncan, 2009).

This anecdote demonstrates how Alyssa liberated Vic by giving him the power to explore a material that is often considered off limits to very young children, especially in a tape dispenser with a sharp surface to cut the tape. She safely scaffolded his exploration by remaining engaged with him until he was satisfied (Hall & Rudkin, 2011; McMullen & Dixon, 2009).

A second example of liberation for the toddlers involves Alyssa's strategy of *more rather than less*, which leads to another view of power sharing. Leavitt's (1994) descriptions of teachers controlling which toys could be used at any particular time, such as allowing a child only one marker for drawing, demonstrate how caregivers exert their power over children, negating the idea that "from an early age, [children] are agents of their own learning and active makers of meaning" (Berthelsen, 2009, p. 2). The principle of more rather than less emerged frequently in Alyssa's comments about how she mediated teaching and learning in the toddler room. She frequently adjusted her plans by adding new utensils to pique the toddlers' interest further, and in the process she defused struggles over materials ownership and reduced boredom by extending activities to promote longer engagement. In so doing, she used a more child-centered approach as she liberated the children to engage in more opportunities to practice their power over materials and activities (Degotardi, 2010; Duncan, 2009; Hall & Rudkin, 2011).

Outside, Xena, 18 months, and Vic, 22 months old, dashed into the storage shed as soon as the door opened. Xena emerged with a green ball nearly 24 inches in diameter. She yelled "Ballllllllllll!" and threw the ball across the cement. Then she returned to the shed for new conquests. When Alyssa read this entry, she described it as typically toddler:

> As toddlers go, Xena was momentarily interested in the ball. She also wanted to explore the rest of the contents in the shed. It follows the *pull and dump* type of play that toddlers do, except that instead of a container to empty, it was the shed. They love to see what's inside something and get it all out if they can! (Emphasis added)

She remarked that toddlers do this often, with no intention of playing with materials once they are dumped.

In this event, Alyssa recognized the toddler preference for more rather than less in selecting their play materials. The pull-and-dump approach is common among toddlers and is often frustrating to caregivers because it leads to messes (Duncan, 2009). Alyssa supported the practice as a way to keep toddlers engaged and learning—pulling and dumping *is* the activity rather than playing with a ball or some other toy, which adults might expect. According to Leavitt (1994), "The exercise of control often operates to the children's detriment as they are ... repressed in the expression and development of their personal autonomy" (p. 42). Here Alyssa expanded the toddlers' opportunities to develop personal autonomy, liberating them from the practice of limiting materials (Elliot, 2009).

Although toddler play is most often carried out as an individual play experience, the toddlers in the group sometimes discovered a way to play with one another. By supporting this freedom of choice, Alyssa kept them engaged, extending their play by allowing access to additional paints and paper, and included learning new social skills and negotiating the shared use of materials (Göncü et al., 2009).

New paints at the double easel brought four toddlers to engage in painting. After they painted individually for a time, they stepped from one side of the easel to the other, adding new colors to others' paintings and switching paint cups back and forth. This easel *dance* lasted for nearly 10 min. When Vic joined the group, Alyssa pulled a large sheet of paper out and placed it on the table to expand the available painting space, adding two more paint cups and brushes to the table.

Whereas Leavitt (1994) described the dominance of teachers as the focus of power and importance, Alyssa demonstrated to staff how to offer more opportunities for the toddlers to explore and gain experience (Duncan, 2009; Göncü et al., 2009). In other words, Alyssa recommended making the classroom more toddler oriented and less teacher oriented. Indeed, Alyssa's reflection about this event indicated her willingness to share power with the toddlers. She wrote,

> I originally put the paint on both sides of the easel in an attempt to spread out the colors and cut down on conflict. The children eventually find their own way of organizing themselves so that everyone is happy, at least for a short time.

Alyssa rarely stopped a child from participating in his or her choice of activity. Rather, she continually mediated activities to facilitate the toddlers tolerating one another. When she did stop a child, it was always to prevent the toddler from breaking a toy or upsetting or injuring another child. Rather than stopping or redirecting the toddlers if they began to use materials in a new way that she had not planned, Alyssa immediately recognized the potential for new learning (Duncan, 2009; Elliot, 2009). Sometimes she anticipated the need for new materials or utensils and supplied them almost as quickly as the toddlers could use them. At other times Alyssa stepped back and watched the toddlers' experiments.

Shortly after the easel dance occurred, Xena began to brush red paint on the paper Alyssa had taped down on the table. Xena continued painting in one area of the paper until she painted a hole through the paper and was actually painting on the tabletop. Monica, a veteran student staff member, suggested to Xena that she move to a different spot on the paper. Xena complied, but after a few strokes she returned to the same painted hole, and Monica allowed her to continue. For more than 10 min, Xena painted the same spot on the paper. The hole grew larger until it was approximately 8 inches in diameter. Xena occasionally tried a different color of paint but always returned to red as her favorite. Alyssa and Monica both encouraged Xena's experimentation by not intervening (Elliot, 2009). Alyssa repeatedly wrote in her responses to field notes that as long as a toddler was causing no harm to anyone or anything, he or she should continue to experiment. "It's OK for toddlers to do things, make a mess ... I tend to bring out more stuff if there is a stressful situation—offer more things rather than take privileges away."

This selective intervention was another of Alyssa's strategies to share power with the toddlers. Allowing toddlers to be messy as a learning experience outweighed the value of compliance with perceived rules, such as paint only on the paper and not on the table (Hallam et al., 2009).

In many toddler classrooms, the adults' need for control intrudes on children's activities through keeping to the schedule (Hallam et al., 2009; Leavitt, 1994; Recchia et al., 2015). Alyssa wrote,

> I don't want to disrupt children who are engrossed with their activities and force them to stop what they're doing just to join me in a different activity. Toddlers are perceived to generally have short attention spans and will leave a current activity for something new just because someone announces the new activity. They may have stayed with the first activity much longer without the intrusion of the adult's announcement.

For example, when Monica told Reese that it would be snack time soon, Reese rushed to the table. He waited for the food to be served and began to eat as the other children joined him. While he was chewing his first cracker, another adult remarked that after snack they would be going outside. Reese immediately cleared his snack remains, including two untouched crackers, and hurried to put on his jacket.

Alyssa wrote,

> As toddlers go, if something more appealing comes along, they quickly change their plan. Sometimes I try to keep the transitions low key to not distract those who are still involved in something else, but this can get difficult. If at all possible, it works best to not announce events too soon in advance. Toddlers don't have a concept of time yet and telling them that something will occur later or pretty soon doesn't necessarily make sense to them.

Adults in this case unwittingly contributed to the short attention span for which toddlers are quite famous. This informal and potentially unconscious use of power can be mediated to allow for toddlers to move at a more leisurely pace that encourages social activities or deeper engagement with materials, such as chatting over snack, rather than attending to the social convention of following the schedule precisely (Duncan, 2009; Göncü et al., 2009; Hallam et al., 2009; Leavitt, 1994).

Early in the school year, Alyssa would ask the toddlers if they wanted some specific toy or materials. The toddlers responded with mostly nonverbal gestures or facial expressions or sometimes with sign language. As the year progressed, the power continuum shifted to toddlers asking specifically for the materials they wanted. The toddlers took on the larger role of selecting activities rather than waiting for an adult to offer materials (Brownlee & Berthelsen, 2009). They also learned they could refuse materials the adults selected. Leavitt's (1994) report suggested that such resistance to adult control of every component of the day would be considered problematic: "Insofar as children's expressions of their physical and emotional needs and inclinations are subordinate to the adult-imposed schedule, they are silenced" (p. 41). As toddler caregivers face children who are taking more initiative and expressing more intentionality, the adults' sense of losing control over the classroom and children likely increases, potentially causing teachers to provide even greater control (Elliot, 2009; Hallam et al., 2009).

The aforementioned examples illustrate how Alyssa allowed the children to select and use materials, or adjust the timing of activities, in contrast to controlling materials and time as described in Leavitt (1994). The next section describes how Alyssa developed curriculum.

Curriculum organizer

Planning and organizing the environment and curriculum are part of every teacher's work. Organizing the classroom into an interesting and useable space is the first step. For many teachers it may also be the last, and their curriculum is finished (Duncan, 2009). Or as described in Leavitt (1994), teachers planned and prepared minimal curriculum, providing limited materials on a whim or expecting children to just use what they could find in the classroom without consideration for children's interests or abilities. Learning was not perceived as a goal in these classrooms, so routines became the bulk of the day's curriculum (Degotardi, 2010; Goouch & Powell, 2012; Hallam et al., 2009).

The research site used theme-based curriculum, and Alyssa wrote plans based on these themes. However, the themes provided creative incentive for her more than a specific curriculum for the toddlers. Alyssa reported that she followed the children's lead in developing curriculum:

> Observation of their daily actions helps you recognize what their interests are—getting to know your group. Then you just bring in materials with the expectation that they'll explore rather than use things as an older child would do. Toddlers don't *get* the [curriculum] themes, but staff can be more original in planning with a theme. (Emphasis added)

An example of how Alyssa planned and adapted curriculum occurred when she observed the toddlers shaking their *sippy cups* at snack time. Sippy cups are small cups with a lid that is fitted with a spout for toddlers to suck or drink from. By shaking these cups, the toddlers could sprinkle milk over the table, crackers, napkins, and one another. In response to this event, Alyssa explained, "I give them similar containers in the water table or shaker bottles that they can dribble powder or liquid from to give them the opportunity to explore in this way." Her adaptations provided appropriate opportunities to experience the same cause-and-effect activities that some adults may consider inappropriate at the snack table (Duncan, 2009; Hallam et al., 2009).

Alyssa planned curriculum to give the toddlers what they were interested in doing, thereby acting as both a guide and supporter of their learning. She explained that she "threw in things that they don't necessarily have experience with to see if they are interested in that." Alyssa was willing to adjust her curriculum in deference to the toddlers' needs and interests because she consistently and continually evaluated what was happening, what the children were learning, and how they were developing:

> If the adult still wants a cooking project to be a muffin, you take away the batter to cook it. But knowing they like to stir, I will get out other materials to allow them to stir—water and spoons and bowls, or dry materials in the sensory table.

All of these actions defined Alyssa as the teacher that Dewey (1902) clamored for—one who makes content part of the experience in ways that are developmentally useful to the learners and who supports toddlers in their learning through the creative use of materials that meet their needs (Degotardi, 2010; Duncan, 2009; Elliot, 2009).

As the staff and children spent time together, they began to build a common history. The next section describes some ways in which Alyssa served as Chief Historian for the toddler classroom.

Chief historian

Developing a mutual history requires accumulating interactions with others so that those past experiences can be a basis for future interactions (Berthelsen, 2009). The Objectifier role described in Leavitt (1994) demonstrated how adults limited their interactions with the children to adult-defined, narrow-focused, and systematic events in which actions were directed toward the children rather than with them—that is, viewed the children as objects that needed some interactions to control them. This view treats young children as only recipients of interactions rather than reciprocal participants.

"Relationships are formed when two partners accumulate a history of interactions that bring expectancies from past experiences into their future interactions with each other" (Berthelsen, 2009, p. 2). History, to a toddler, is not long ago. Communal events that imprint in toddlers' memories must be either often repeated or memorable for some special reason. In order to support the toddlers in this classroom as Chief Historian, Alyssa established enough structure to make life predictable, which is essential for toddlers, as well as provided those more memorable events. This was accomplished partly through the classroom routines, activities that all toddlers experienced in approximately the same time frame. Routines became much of the shared history among the toddlers (Degotardi, 2010; Goouch & Powell, 2012; Hallam et al., 2009; Leavitt, 1994).

Alyssa remarked, "Some toddlers would fall apart if you didn't do them [routines] the same or similar each time, like snack or diapers." Toddlers need routines and a predictable environment as a foundation for growth and development (Elliot, 2009; McMullen & Dixon, 2009). This predictability establishes toddlers' trust in adults, knowing that some things will be the same from one day to the next. The toddlers demonstrated their understanding of the routines established in this classroom in a variety of ways.

One day, lunch had arrived early. The toddlers did not appear to like the food catered from campus food service on this particular day, so they did not eat much, and they left the tables nearly 20 min before their usual naptime. Alyssa suggested that the staff wait to place cots, allowing the children to play for a while. However, the toddlers refused to play. Instead, each toddler took his or her sleeping toy from its storage place, looked around the classroom, and then moved to the place where his or her cot was normally placed. They each lay down on the floor in *their spot* as if the cots had been put out.

The toddlers were able to develop their own history, which they shared with one another and Alyssa. Such relationships support the accumulation of a history of interactions that occur in the local cultural context of a particular classroom (Berthelsen, 2009) and that view toddlers as active participants (Elliot, 2009). This could not happen without Alyssa's conscious choice to function as Chief Historian in a setting that provided toddlers with a sense of agency and power.

The toddlers sometimes shared more history with Alyssa and one another than they shared with the students who were part-time workers. An example of this lack of shared history occurred one morning after Alyssa had put water in the pretend play kitchen so that it would drip into the miniature coffee pot.

Winnie, at 21 months old, had been *making coffee* with every available container in the play kitchen. She carried one pot across the room and showed it to a student staff person there. The adult told Winnie that the water belonged in the water table, on the opposite end of the classroom from the play kitchen. Winnie considered this comment. She took the coffee pot to the water table and dropped pot and all into the water, then looked for a new activity.

Alyssa's comments on this story reflected that everyone in the classroom was a learner, that some of the staff were not aware of what the children were or were not permitted to do. They simply functioned from their personal histories from elsewhere (Degotardi, 2010). The adult did not share the history that Winnie had developed with Alyssa and the materials in the classroom. Facilitating the blending of the social histories that each person brought to the classroom was part of Alyssa's role as Chief Historian, and she used such anecdotes for professional development of the student staff. Just as the group members worked on establishing community, they worked together on building a shared history from the individual histories of the participants. Together they built a collective culture (Elliot, 2009; Göncü et al., 2009) through social and affective engagement with one another.

The toddlers also developed working relationships with one another as they built a group history. Alyssa reported, "They figure each other out—personality traits and social or emotional features, who likes to do X [activity], set up their own patterns, a way of life" in the classroom. They also learned who among them was most likely to prevail during a confrontation, with those shared experiences with conflicts becoming part of the classroom history.

Two older toddlers, Kim and Lance, both 30 months old, often played together. One day, during outdoor play, Lance occupied a clear plastic tub, approximately 18 × 24", on the sidewalk outside the center. A loud, one-sided conversation took place that was unintelligible to the adults watching. Kim yelled at Lance, so he climbed out of the tub without speaking, taking a towel with him. Kim yelled again and Lance considered the scene, then returned the towel to her. He watched Kim arrange the towel inside the tub; then he climbed in and lay down, pretending to sleep. Kim picked up a second towel and covered Lance with it.

Throughout the interaction, Lance remained silent, but obviously he understood what his role was in this relationship with Kim. Alyssa's explanation of this event demonstrated just how well she knew each toddler. She wrote,

> Kim often used the tub this way. We were putting water in it for those who didn't like the big pool but she found her own way to use it. Lance was one who often seemed to be involved in a variety of situations. He is a very curious and social child and just loved verbal interaction. This scene strikes me as funny but not surprising. Lance was often involved in verbal exchanges with a couple of children, some of which we could understand and some we couldn't. Kim, who was also strong personalitied [sic], obviously got her message across to Lance who chose to comply.

The conversation between the toddlers clearly involved mutuality; that is, both understood what was happening and how to proceed. They had built a history through previous interactions. Negotiation that leads to such shared understandings builds the group's history and encourages ongoing participation (Göncü et al., 2009).

Part of the emerging theme of Chief Historian included celebrations. Among the toddlers, these generally were frequent, brief, spontaneous, and simple. Adults' cheering for a toddler's accomplishment was common, even for the simplest of tasks, such as placing a puzzle piece or walking in adult-size shoes without falling. Progressing toileting skills were greeted with great enthusiasm. Sometimes the children initiated the cheers and applause, and sometimes it was the adults.

Reese watched as Alyssa left the classroom and walked down the hall. When she returned in a few minutes, he asked "Potty?" Alyssa responded that yes, she had used the potty. Reese then shouted "Yay!" and smiled as he clapped his hands.

Other celebrations evolved from the announcement that snack was ready or that the group could ride tricycles in the hallway outside the classroom. Opening the bubble-making equipment, moving into the hallway to play, or the end of a favorite song were all causes for celebration in the toddler room. The fact that all participants celebrated together demonstrates the existence of strong relationships within the classroom (McMullen & Dixon, 2009). The toddlers actively contributed to the collective knowledge or group history. Alyssa's work as Chief Historian was to blend the social histories that each person brought to the classroom into a mutual group history. This could not happen without Alyssa's conscious choice to function as a cultural mediator and to specifically choose the culture to mediate (Berthelsen, 2009).

The final role that emerged in this study was that of Learner. Alyssa viewed that role as vital for all of the classroom staff as well as the children.

Learner

Alyssa's role as Learner manifested itself throughout the other three roles she played. Her observations of the children's activities prompted her to develop her curriculum further, demonstrating another means of sharing power. She was an active learner in the classroom along with the toddlers, learning more about toddlers in general and her group in particular with each activity that she offered (Duncan, 2009; McMullen & Dixon, 2009). In contrast, Leavitt's (1994) caregiver descriptions depicted adults who saw children as objects and therefore not worthy of study. When children are objectified by adults in this way, they are considered only recipients of the adults' labor. That is, adults act on the children rather than sharing interactive relationships with them. These caregivers needed only to understand the time frame, routines to be accomplished, and how to control children within those experiences through the management of materials and space. From that perspective, there was nothing new to learn. For Alyssa to function as both a teacher and a learner in the classroom, that interactive relationship had to be present (Goouch & Powell, 2012).

Alyssa's active learning about others demonstrated to the toddlers, the student staff, and the field experience students that learning occurs all the time. Her role as a cultural mediator of that learning affected everyone in the classroom. This role extended to the parents as well, as Alyssa ensured that children felt safe and secure in this classroom. Communicating with parents "becomes especially critical when schools serve children from diverse backgrounds" (Göncü et al., 2009, p. 190). This perspective of diversity also then provides opportunities for more learning.

By valuing the toddlers' inventiveness in exploring materials and relationships, Alyssa demonstrated that she was an active participant in the learning. She knew enough about toddlers to have clear expectations for their behaviors. This prior knowledge guided her planning and development of the child-centered curriculum. Alyssa knew that toddlers would not choose the conventional way of doing many activities in her classroom, and she actually encouraged this diversion from conventional expectations (Berthelsen, 2009; Duncan, 2009; Elliot, 2009).

In the process of observing the toddlers' invented behaviors, Alyssa was constantly learning more about toddlers in general and her individual toddlers specifically. Each toddler participated in the teaching and learning with Alyssa, so that they reciprocally mediated each other's learning. This perspective of the toddlers as "agents of their own learning and active makers of meaning" (Berthelsen, 2009, p. 2) is in sharp contrast to caregivers' perspectives in Leavitt (1994)—that the toddlers were more objects to be managed.

Summary

The toddlers in this fledgling community had one role—to learn about everything around them, during every waking hour. This included exploring their environment as well as the people around them (Hallam et al., 2009). However, the toddlers needed both freedom and structure to mediate this learning. Both of these components were supported by Alyssa's philosophy of cultural mediation as she offered them a physically and emotionally safe environment within which they were free to investigate materials and construct learning (Berthelsen, 2009; Goouch & Powell, 2012; McMullen & Dixon, 2009).

Adults' conventional values, as described by Leavitt (1994), led to adult planning, rules, and schedules and, at the extreme end of that continuum, marginalization of the children as minimal participants in their learning. Toddlers' invented behaviors were not only allowed but encouraged by Alyssa as she worked to establish the children's interests and abilities as the foundation for each day's events.

Traditional classroom activities for young children involve many large group events, and for preschool and older children these can be appropriate. Toddlers are more egocentric than group oriented (Piaget, 1954), and often keeping the toddlers together in a group is a greater focus in child care than any learning that might occur (Hallam et al., 2009). In any group caregiving setting, conventional behaviors are expected through organization, and rules and routines may appear necessary to keep that group running smoothly. Some teachers resort to setting up perpendicular shelving in the corner of the classroom in an effort to keep the toddlers *penned up* for group time. However, these conventional behaviors are more adult oriented than child oriented and considered less important in Alyssa's classroom than elsewhere (Duncan, 2009; Leavitt, 1994).

Center staff or field experience students who act in the belief that their work with toddlers should be group oriented are often new to this classroom. An adult who has worked in other child care settings, experienced more adult-oriented philosophies, or has not experienced toddlers in groups often chooses the group convention over the individual toddler's way of learning. Where Alyssa allowed a child to make a mess, a less experienced adult in the classroom may have stopped the child's exploration through attempts to control time and space or materials. Alyssa chose to establish personal freedom as a priority and served as a Liberator for that freedom (Berthelsen, 2009).

Although the toddlers sought routines to guide their behavior to a certain extent, they also sought the frontiers of acceptable behavior, more commonly described as *testing limits*. Limit testing was part of the learning that occurred in the classroom, as well as in other settings. Toddlers tested limits by learning about their classroom's physical environment as well as testing issues of authority, power, and communication. Defining the extent of the classroom's rules (such as how far to throw a toy), leaving the classroom at will without adult supervision, or repeating acts that try an adult's patience all are examples of the kinds of limits a toddler might test. How caregivers responded to this testing was often a clear demonstration of the philosophical stance of the adults (Elliot, 2009; Leavitt, 1994).

Some toddlers were more energetic at this task than others. Other toddlers served as an audience to the front runners, gaining their knowledge of the limits more vicariously. Within Alyssa's environment of shared power, the toddlers used power in the many venues in which it was offered to them by the adults, including learning how much power they were allotted (Berthelsen, 2009). In Leavitt's (1994) classrooms, that power was nearly nonexistent. In Alyssa's classroom, it was pervasive.

Alyssa's respect for toddlers as learners was an integral part of the developing community. An atmosphere of respect extended throughout her classroom and touched adults and children alike Degotardi, 2010). Staff and toddlers were actually treated similarly. When Alyssa discussed the staff's role with the toddlers, the conversation turned to her supervision role. She defined her leadership style, stating that she led by "giving them [staff] lots of freedom and expecting them to do well." This mirrors the descriptions of how Alyssa interacted with the children. This parallel use of strategies added to Alyssa's learning about both the staff and the toddlers.

Leavitt's (1994) implied roles of toddler caregivers included Time Controller, Space Controller, and Objectifier. These roles demonstrated the philosophical view that young children were objects to be managed rather than thinking, questioning, emotional, and exploring individuals. In contrast, the roles that emerged in this study depicted Alyssa as Liberator, Curriculum Organizer, Chief Historian, and Learner, demonstrating her view that toddlers deserved responsive caregiving that empowered them to participate in the culture in their classroom (Berthelsen, 2009; McMullen & Dixon, 2009).

Limitations

The findings of this study cannot be applied directly to other classrooms because of the limitations of the specific culture, history, and lived experiences of the participants and the interpretive nature of the teacher's and my analyses of the data. The selection of events for reflective analysis was the result of my cultural experiences and was socially constructed collaboratively with the teacher (Creswell, 2013). Critical analyses, however, of both this study and Leavitt's (1994) research may provide opportunities for readers to analyze and evaluate their own practices in caring for young children.

Although diverse in terms of socioeconomic background and cultural differences, the toddlers' parents clearly valued education. The majority of parents were students enrolled in undergraduate and graduate programs at the university. Approximately one third of families consisted of parents who were faculty members. This parental value spilled over to the center in expectations for the children's programming, which may not be the case in non-campus-based child care programs.

I was familiar with the culture of the child care program, having served as a coteacher with Alyssa previously, and had observed in this classroom as a member of the university faculty. My additional experience in national accreditation provided a context for acting as a participant observer in a somewhat objective manner. These facts contribute to the trustworthiness of the study.

At the time of the data collection, I was the director of the program and Alyssa was the assistant director and one of six full-time teachers. Alyssa had worked extensively in planning and developing the program as it grew from one classroom to three during the 8 years she had been employed there. Staff had frequently observed one another teaching, as well as being observed by field experience students or visiting teachers, because the program served as a demonstration site for students and community child care providers. Within this toddler group, however, I was neither well known to the children nor familiar with the lived experiences of the group. On occasion, one or two children would invite an interaction with me while I was recording field notes, but I tried to limit interactions as much as possible. This status may provide additional trustworthiness to the findings (Creswell, 2013).

The relationship between Alyssa and me may have affected her behavior in the classroom. If this was the case, it was not obvious, as over time her interactions with outside observers, parents, adult student assistants, and the children appeared to be consistent between both pilot and research study observations. The need to continually check for potential bias was clear. The process for Alyssa to reflect on the field notes, as well as my perception of emerging themes, was an attempt to clearly understand her motives and philosophy and to dispel research biases as much as possible. This is in contrast to Leavitt's (1994) admission of the lack of the caregivers' voices in her findings.

The long-term construction of the program's culture is another contribution to the trustworthiness of the study. Regardless, it is important to remember that the patterns that emerged from field notes were the result of inferences from the words and actions of all of the participants, but mainly from Alyssa.

It is significant that toddlers behave in this campus-based classroom just as they do in other classrooms, constantly exploring, asking for things, wanting what others have, and seldom sitting still (Leavitt, 1994). The difference is that in Alyssa's classroom, the struggle for autonomy, controlling their own learning, and experiencing everything around them to the fullest is both permitted and encouraged. Adults respect toddlers' right to share power in this classroom community (Penn, 2009). The toddlers are expected and encouraged to test the limits of their learning.

Implications for practice and research

Professional development needs

Duncan (2009) charged that

> as early childhood practitioners our own *constant vigilance* in reflecting on, and challenging our daily practices, as well as supporting our colleagues to do the same, will be a key for the best possible early childhood education provisions for the very young child. (p. 181)

She reminded that time is vital for teachers, to consider what they are doing, reflect repeatedly, and then try again. This effort will be important for the long-term professional development needs of early childhood teachers, especially those in infant and toddler classrooms. In other words, teachers need ongoing mentoring, coaching, and shared reflections with colleagues to truly improve their teaching. Sheridan, Edwards, Marvin, and Knoche (2009) also called for more opportunities for caregivers to access high-quality coaching and consultation, as well as other effective professional development strategies that are accessible and effective. One such strategy would be caregivers examining their own understandings of what toddlers' abilities are and what that means for planning curriculum and classroom experiences (Duncan, 2009). Another professional development strategy would be developing the ability to reflect on where the power lies within their practice in order to support their ability to share that power with toddlers (Hall & Rudkin, 2011). Finally, professional development that helps caregivers to meet others working in the field to compare experiences and ideas for improving practice would address caregivers' feelings of isolation and low self-efficacy (Goouch & Powell, 2012).

The profile of master toddler teacher that Alyssa presents indicates that mediating a toddler classroom is very hard work. A toddler teacher first must understand and value toddlers at their level and for their characteristics, both generically and individually, including the external culture the child brings to the group. This knowledge gives Alyssa the means to plan and implement appropriate curriculum and classroom organization that enhances the growth and development of all of the children. But this understanding of toddlers is only the first step and one that is attained by many toddler teachers in high-quality child care settings. Indeed, as McMullen and Lash (2012) reported, understanding development is only one component of quality in child care.

The second choice that Alyssa consciously makes is to share the power in her classroom. This choice is more difficult for many toddler teachers because, logically, it gives the toddlers more power. If toddlers are seen as unable to use this power to the enhancement of the group, or in the facility of rules and routines, then adults may not be willing to allow the shift of power to occur. Teachers must be willing to allow time for toddlers to practice using their power, to be prepared for messy environments, and to accept the toddler decisions that result from access to power. Sharing power is not simply giving it away. Rather, toddler teachers must learn how to scaffold children's developing abilities to use power appropriately with others who are also learning how to use power. Professional development on the development of executive function that is designed to engage caregivers in this discussion, along with examples of successful power sharing, are both needed (Center on the Developing Child, 2011).

Third, the teacher becomes the cultural icon for his or her classroom and affects all of the learning or lack of learning that occurs there; that is, teachers make the difference. Leavitt (1994) described teachers who also culturally mediate the learning that occurs in their classrooms, but with very different results from Alyssa's. These teachers make the difference in their classrooms because they choose the culture that dominates the setting, a culture of adults maintaining power over all. Distinct differences exist between Alyssa and Leavitt's teachers in terms of sharing power, maintaining dynamic tensions among and between the individual and the group, and building relationships. Alyssa emphasizes the individual toddler first and the group second, and the adults in the classroom receive the lowest priority. Leavitt described adults who establish themselves as the priority in the classroom, with the group emphasized second and individual toddlers last. Caregivers and teachers of young children need professional development in understanding cultural differences and ways to enhance understanding of each other's perspectives and how they play out in classrooms that support children's learning.

The current recommendation for infant and toddler caregivers is to implement a relationship-based program. Raikes and Edwards (2009) compared this to a *dance* between the adults and child in the care setting and between the caregivers and parents of the child. McMullen and Dixon (2009) suggested that in order for relationships to be at the heart of best practice, three critical elements must be implemented: (a) mindful practice, through being responsive to infants and toddlers, relying on continuity, familiarity, and predictability; (b) reflective practice, including "thinking before, during, and after our actions and interactions," both as individuals and in collaboration with parents and other adults (p. 119); and (c) respectful practice, demonstrating that caregivers see every person within the sphere of interactions as being competent and of value to the community of the care center.

Elliot (2009) defined the issue for many toddler caregivers:

> Too often, our early childhood programs are defined in technical terms of practice ... Curricula focused on limited outcomes prescribe and describe ways to act and speak, and seems to be concerned with controlling adult behavior in order to control children's behavior; when one is slavishly following prescribed curricula, there is little time for curiosity about the meaning behind children's behavior or questions with which children are struggling ... These concepts of questioning, reflecting and community membership provide us with goals of honoring diversity, learning to listen to each other, listening to ourselves and respecting all our community members. These broad goals can give meaning and direction to our practice. (p. 148)

Duncan (2009) described how she took photographs of the different activities in the toddler room while on her knees, viewing everything from a 2-year-old's perspective. These insights caused her to rethink the environment, lowering furniture heights, changing spaces, and improving management issues, resulting in the toddlers being able to participate more fully in classroom activities because they could see and reach materials better. Toddler caregivers could use this strategy to improve their ability to take a toddler's perspective on the environment. Such actions can clearly improve the situation for both the children and the caregivers.

Caregivers need to understand the possibilities that toddlers pose as learners and as participants in their own learning rather than assuming that what a toddler learned was the result of adult management. Leavitt (1994) described the plight of caregivers who have little access to professional development or education. In many ways, the caregivers are marginalized by society as much as the children in their classrooms. The field has a long way to go to improve infant and toddler group care everywhere, especially in unregulated settings, and substantially for the adults providing the care. Leavitt's plea to caregivers is "that they recognize the importance of intersubjectivity, emotionality, particularity, and entering the world of the other as they engage in their caregiving task" (p. 93). Responsively engaging with toddlers, by entering into their world and treating them as real persons, would make a measurable difference in many low-quality settings.

Research needs

This study emphasizes the need for more study of the very young children in group settings (Zaslow, Tout, Halle, Whittaker, & Lavelle, 2010) as well as their teachers. Brownlee and Berthelsen (2009) noted that "very little research describing child care teachers' beliefs about knowing and learning exist[s]" (p. 95). "New ways of thinking are needed that acknowledge young children's agency and competencies which are not based on judgments of children's age-defined capabilities. Adults also need to be willing to truly engage in the learning process with the child" (Berthelsen, 2009, p. 7). This call for a review of how contemporary societies and cultures view very young children and the existing quality levels of childrearing settings has been echoed by other researchers in the field (Degotardi, 2010; Goouch & Powell, 2012; Hallam et al., 2009).

Because these settings tend to be of mediocre quality at best (Cost, Quality and Child Outcomes Study Team, 1995; Hyson & Tomlinson, 2014), experts must consider how to improve the quality of education for infants and toddlers through the study of diverse settings that provide high-quality child care across populations and cultures. Berthelsen (2009) stated,

> We know very little about how these young children *live* their lives in their group care settings; how they experience encounters with peers and teachers; what they learn; and under what conditions they learn. We also know little about how educators working with these young citizens perceive their goals; what their aspirations are in their work; and how they view and relate to the children. (p. xiii)

Thus, research on both the children and the teachers is needed. This lack of research was corroborated by Hallam et al. (2009) as they recommended a bottom-up approach to understanding the lived experiences of toddlers in classroom settings. That is, experts need to examine what individual children experience as part of the overall assessment of classroom quality. The need for multiple ways of knowing how young children grow, develop, learn, communicate, and participate allows for a variety of research studies.

In addition, the need to learn what the most effective and productive professional development strategies are for any particular group of caregivers is compelling. For some caregivers, learning what other teachers do can be a strong strategy for changing their own teaching style (Goouch & Powell, 2012). Providing caregivers with opportunities to talk to others working in the field appears to be a simple way to start professional development in an effort to improve child care quality (Goouch & Powell, 2012). Leavitt (1994) herself called for additional research into caregivers' beliefs and values as well as how these affect the quality of the classroom experience. Work in several states defining teacher competencies in early childhood classrooms may also lead to clear professional development needs for toddler teachers and assistants, with accompanying research studies to validate these strategies. After all, the teacher does make the difference (Göncü et al., 2009).

ORCID

Jill Uhlenberg http://orcid.org/0000-0003-1380-5505

References

Berthelsen, D. (2009). Participatory learning: Issues for research and practice. In D. Berthelsen, J. Brownlee, & E. Johansson (Eds.), *Participatory learning in the early years: Research and pedagogy* (pp. 1–11). New York, NY: Routledge.

Brownlee, J., & Berthelsen, D. (2009). Beliefs about toddlers' learning in child care programs in Australia. In D. Berthelsen, J. Brownlee, & E. Johansson (Eds.), *Participatory learning in the early years: Research and pedagogy* (pp. 93–108). New York, NY: Routledge.

Center on the Developing Child at Harvard University. (2011). *Building the brain's "air traffic control" system: How early experiences shape the development of executive function* (Working Paper No. 11). Retrieved from http://developingchild.harvard.edu/resources/building-the-brains-air-traffic-control-system-how-early-experiences-shape-the-development-of-executive-function/

Child Care Aware. (2014). *Child care in America: 2014 state fact sheets.* Retrieved from http://usa.childcareaware.org/sites/default/files/19000000_state_fact_sheets_2014_v04.pdf

Cost, Quality and Child Outcomes Study Team. (1995). *Cost, quality and child outcomes in child care centers.* (2nd ed.). Denver: University of Colorado at Denver, Economics Department.

Creswell, J. W. (2013). *Qualitative inquiry and research design.* Thousand Oaks, CA: Sage.

Degotardi, S. (2010). High-quality interactions with infants: Relationships with early-childhood practitioners' interpretations and qualification levels in play and routine contexts. *International Journal of Early Years Education, 18*(1), 27–41. doi:10.1080/09669761003661253

Dewey, J. (1902). *The child and the curriculum.* Chicago, IL: University of Chicago Press.

Duncan, J. (2009). If you think they can do it—then they can: Two-year-olds in Aotearoa New Zealand kindergartens and changing professional practices. In D. Berthelsen, J. Brownlee, & E. Johansson (Eds.), *Participatory learning in the early years: Research and pedagogy* (pp. 164–184). New York, NY: Routledge.

Elliot, E. (2009). Dialogue, listening and discernment in professional practice with parents and their children in an infant program: A Canadian perspective. In D. Berthelsen, J. Brownlee, & E. Johansson (Eds.), *Participatory learning in the early years: Research and pedagogy* (pp. 145–163). New York, NY: Routledge.

Göncü, A., Main, C., & Abel, B. (2009). Fairness in participation in preschool. In D. Berthelsen, J. Brownlee, & E. Johansson (Eds.), *Participatory learning in the early years: Research and pedagogy* (pp. 185–202). New York, NY: Routledge.

Goouch, K., & Powell, S. (2012). Orchestrating professional development for baby room practitioners: Raising the stakes in new dialogic encounters. *Journal of Early Childhood Research, 11*(1), 78–92. doi:10.1177/1476718X12448374

Hall, E. L., & Rudkin, J. K. (2011). *Seen and heard: Children's rights in early childhood education.* New York, NY: Teachers College Press.

Hallam, R., Fouts, H., Bargreen, K., & Caudle, L. (2009). Quality from a toddler's perspective: A bottom-up examination of classroom experiences. *Early Childhood Research and Practice, 11*(2). Retrieved from http://ecrp.uiuc.edu/v11n2/hallam.html

Hyson, M., & Tomlinson, H. B. (2014). *The early years matter: Education, care, and the well-being of children, birth to 8.* New York, NY: Teachers College Press.

Johansson, E., & Emilson, A. (2010). Toddlers' life in Swedish preschool. *International Journal of Early Childhood, 42*(2), 165–179. doi:10.1007/s13158-010-0017-3

Leavitt, R. (1994). *Power and emotion in infant-toddler day care.* New York, NY: Teachers College Press.

Liberator. (2014). In *World English Dictionary.* Retrieved from http://dictionary.reference.com/browse/Liberator

Mauzy, D. (2014). *New workforce data.* Retrieved from the National Association for the Education of Young Children website: http://www.naeyc.org/files/naeyc/Denise%20Mauzy%20Workforce%20Data%20Panel%20Final.pdf

McMullen, M. B., & Dixon, S. (2009). In support of a relationship-based approach to practice with infants and toddlers in the United States. In D. Berthelsen, J. Brownlee, & E. Johansson (Eds.), *Participatory learning in the early years: Research and pedagogy* (pp. 109–128). New York, NY: Routledge.

McMullen, M. B., & Lash, M. (2012). Babies on campus: Service to infants and families among competing priorities in university child care programs. *Early Childhood Research and Practice, 14*(2). Retrieved from http://ecrp.uiuc.edu/v14n2/mcmullen.html

National Association for the Education of Young Children. (2009). *Standards for professional preparation.* Retrieved from http://www.naeyc.org/positionstatements/ppp

Penn, H. (2009). International perspectives on participatory learning: Young children's perspectives across rich and poor countries. In D. Berthelsen, J. Brownlee, & E. Johansson (Eds.), *Participatory learning in the early years: Research and pedagogy* (pp. 12–25). New York, NY: Routledge.

Piaget, J. (1954). *The construction of reality in the child* (M. Cook, Trans.). New York, NY: Basic Books.

Raikes, H., & Edwards, C. P. (2009). *Extending the dance in infant and toddler caregiving: Enhancing attachment and relationships*. Baltimore, MD: Brookes.

Recchia, S. L., Lee, S. Y., & Shin, M. (2015). Preparing early childhood professionals for relationship-based work with infants. *Journal of Early Childhood Teacher Education, 36*(2), 100–123. doi:10.1080/10901027.2015.1030523

Sheridan, S. M., Edwards, C. P., Marvin, C. A., & Knoche, L. L. (2009). Professional development in early childhood programs: Process issues and research needs. *Early Education & Development, 20*(3), 377–401. doi:10.1080/10409280802582795

U.S. Administration for Children and Families, Office of Planning, Research and Evaluation. (2015). *Toddlers in Early Head Start: A portrait of 2-year-olds, their families, and the programs serving them: Vol. I. Age 2 report* (OPRE Report No. 2015-10). Retrieved from http://www.researchconnections.org/childcare/resources/29252/pdf

Zaslow, M., Tout, K., Halle, T., Whittaker, J. V., & Lavelle, B. (2010). *Toward identification of effective professional development for early childhood educators: Literature review*. Washington, DC: U.S. Department of Education.

Teacher–Child Interactions in Early Head Start Classrooms: Associations With Teacher Characteristics

Sherri Castle, Amy C. Williamson, Emisha Young, Jessica Stubblefield, Deborah Laurin, and Nicole Pearce

ABSTRACT

Research Findings: The current study examined characteristics of 71 Early Head Start lead teachers in relation to classroom interactions with infants and toddlers. Measured teacher characteristics included education, years of experience, beliefs about child rearing, depressive symptoms, and the temperamental characteristics of positivity and frustration. Teacher–child interactions were measured using the Classroom Assessment Scoring System, Toddler Version (La Paro, Hamre, & Pianta, 2012). Results indicated that field of degree was directly associated with the majority of dimensions of teacher–child interactions. Examination of teachers' years of experience and intrapersonal characteristics revealed a number of significant interactions, indicating that teacher experience and appropriate beliefs may serve as protective factors in the presence of psychosocial risk factors. *Practice or Policy*: Overall, our findings suggest that both early childhood education degrees and years of experience are directly or indirectly associated with multiple dimensions of teacher–child interactions, confirming that these patterns established for preschool teachers hold for teachers of infants and toddlers. These results also suggest that years of experience and progressive beliefs about children may be especially important for teachers who are depressed or who have low levels of positivity and high levels of frustration. Implications for future research, as well as preservice and in-service professional development, are discussed.

Infants and toddlers who experience rich, supportive interactions with teachers tend to demonstrate higher levels of emotional, behavioral, and cognitive development than do children in less supportive classrooms (Bandel, Aikens, Vogel, Boller, & Murphy, 2014; La Paro, Williamson, & Hatfield, 2014; Mortensen & Barnett, 2015; Ruzek, Burchinal, Farkas, & Duncan, 2014). This may be particularly true for children attending Early Head Start (EHS) programs who enter early childhood programs already at risk for developmental difficulties because of the contextual consequences of living in poverty (Bandel et al., 2014; McCartney, Dearing, Taylor, & Bub, 2007; Watamura, Phillips, Morrissey, McCartney, & Bub, 2011). In 2013, the Office of Head Start reported that more than 150,000 children attend EHS programs on an annual basis in a targeted effort to improve developmental outcomes for very young children experiencing poverty. To effectively reach this goal, early childhood educators in these programs must be able to provide consistent, quality interactions with the infants and toddlers in their classrooms. A number of studies have examined teacher–child interactions in preschool classrooms (see Hamre, 2014, for a review), but to date less empirical attention has been given to interactions in classrooms serving infants and toddlers. Despite the significant contribution of the National Institute of Child Health and Human Development child care study (National Institute of Child Health and Human Development Early Child Care Research Network [NICHD ECCRN], 1998) to experts' understanding of interactions caregivers have with infants and toddlers, more research in this area is needed to better understand correlates of high-quality interactions in infant/toddler classrooms.

Quality teacher–child interactions for this age group are often operationalized as interactions that are emotionally and behaviorally supportive to build trust in the caregiver–child relationship and/or cognitively supportive to facilitate problem solving and language development (La Paro, Hamre, & Pianta, 2012). Optimal development for infants and toddlers takes place within the context of relationships with significant caregivers who act as a secure base and are able to scaffold the child through developmental milestones with reciprocal, trust-based, and consistently sensitive interactions (Mortensen & Barnett, 2015; Rosenblum, Dayton, & Muzik, 2009). Thus, characteristics associated with the ability of infant and toddler teachers to establish these kinds of relationships with the children in their care are an important area for investigation in understanding infants' and toddlers' experiences in EHS programs.

Education level and experience have been linked to quality teacher–child interactions in infant and toddler classrooms (Bandel et al., 2014; Thomason & La Paro, 2013). However, recent calls from the field suggest the need to extend the focus to include other kinds of teacher characteristics, such as psychosocial characteristics, as important contributors to the nature of interactions within early childhood classrooms (Li-Grining et al., 2010; Raver, Blair, & Li-Grining, 2012). Emerging research has identified levels of psychosocial risk factors such as adverse childhood experiences (Esaki & Larkin, 2013; Whitaker et al., 2014) and depressive symptoms (Whitaker, Becker, Herman, & Gooze, 2013) among Head Start and EHS teachers that are more prevalent than among similar populations not working in early education. Such risk factors could impact the support teachers are able to provide to children through their daily interactions. Given the intimacy and importance of interactions between infants and toddlers and their caregivers, further exploration of teachers' psychosocial risk factors is warranted.

Teacher characteristics and classroom interactions

The theoretical model that guides this exploration of teacher characteristics and classroom interactions is Bronfenbrenner's (2001) bioecological model of human development. This model suggests that human development is fueled in part by the interrelationships among characteristics of people, the contexts they are situated in, and the processes that take place within those contexts. Bronfenbrenner referred to these interrelationships as the process–person–context–time model, and he labeled the processes within this model "proximal processes." According to this model, proximal processes are interactions between the developing person and other people in his or her environment that occur with regularity and increasing complexity. Proximal processes are the "primary engines of development" (p. 6965) and are the mechanisms through which adult characteristics, such as psychosocial characteristics, impact child development. Within this study, proximal processes are conceptualized as teacher–child interactions.

Bronfenbrenner (2001) suggested that the energy that drives proximal processes comes from characteristics of the person/people participating in them. Specifically, Bronfenbrenner named temperamental characteristics (w he referred to as "force" characteristics) as well as individuals' skills and experiences (referred to as "resource" characteristics) as theoretically important variables in relation to human interactions (Bronfenbrenner & Morris, 1998). Thus, a bioecological lens necessitates a hypothesis that teacher–child interactions are in part associated with characteristics of the teacher. Accordingly, this study examines teachers' depressive symptoms, child rearing beliefs, and temperamental characteristics of positivity, frustration, and effortful control, along with their training and experience in early childhood education (ECE), as intrapersonal characteristics that may contribute to classroom interactions in EHS classrooms.

Teacher psychosocial characteristics

Evidence suggests that teacher–child interactions are shaped in part by the psychosocial characteristics of teachers that are explored in this study. Links between teachers' depressive symptoms and their classroom interactions are sparse but consistent. Current research consistently demonstrates that teachers who experience higher levels of depressive symptoms have less positive relationships and interactions with children in their classrooms (Hamre & Pianta, 2004; Hamre, Pianta, Downer, & Mashburn, 2008; Jeon, Buettner, & Snyder, 2014; Whitaker, Dearth-Wesley, & Gooze, 2015). For example, Hamre and Pianta (2004) found that teachers with self-reported higher levels of depressive symptoms were not as sensitive and were more withdrawn in the care they provided young children.

To date, research on teacher depression has been almost solely conducted with teachers of children ages 3 and older. Minimal research exists on depressive symptoms among infant and toddler caregivers. Given the poor outcomes infants and toddlers experience when they have depressed primary caregivers, such as mothers with postpartum depression (e.g., Bornstein, Mash, Arterberry, & Manian, 2012), an examination of depressive symptoms among teachers who work with infants and toddlers is overdue. In a recent statewide health and wellness study of Head Start staff in Pennsylvania (which included EHS teachers), Whitaker et al. (2013) found that 25% of Head Start teachers were clinically depressed, which is much higher than the national average. In addition, more than 50% of those teachers who met the cutoff for clinical depression reported not ever having received a diagnosis or treatment for depression.

Teachers' beliefs have also been found to be associated with teaching behavior. Teachers' beliefs are determined by their values, knowledge, and experiences and can often guide their teaching practices (Brownlee, Berthelson, & Segaran, 2009; NICHD ECCRN, 1998; Rimm-Kaufman, Storm, Sawyer, Pianta, & La Paro, 2006). Teacher beliefs with demonstrated links to classroom behaviors include beliefs about discipline practices, curriculum/teaching practices, and beliefs about children (Rimm-Kaufman et al., 2006; Susman-Stillman, Pleuss, & Englund, 2013; Wen, Elicker, & McMullen, 2011). In a study of caregiver beliefs, Susman-Stillman et al. (2013) demonstrated that teachers' beliefs about whether responding to a baby's cries causes spoiling significantly predicted their responsiveness in caregiving interactions. In addition, Stipek and Byler (1997) found that child-centered teacher beliefs were positively associated with a supportive and constructive climate for fostering social and emotional development.

Teacher temperament has received little attention among researchers as a variable associated with classroom interactions. *Temperament* is defined as individual differences in reactivity and self-regulation that are moderated by interactions between heredity and environment (Rothbart & Derryberry, 1981), and models of adult temperament are often focused on factors related to positive emotionality, negative emotionality, and effortful control (e.g., Rothbart & Ahadi, 1994). Although there has been little to no examination of the link between teacher temperament and classroom practices, parents' temperamental characteristics have been positively linked to the manner in which adults interact with children (Goldstein, Diener, & Mangelsdorf, 1996; NICHHD ECCRN, 2000b) and with other established correlates of adult–child interactions, such as parent stress (Oddi, Murdock, Vadnais, Bridgett, & Gartstein, 2013). For example, the NICHD ECCRN (2000b) demonstrated that fathers with more positivity were more sensitive during caregiving activities with their infants and toddlers ages 6–36 months. In addition, parental negative affectivity has been positively associated with parental intrusive behavior and negatively associated with parental sensitivity for parents of toddlers (Goldstein et al., 1996; NICHD ECCRN, 2000b). Similarly, parental effortful control has been positively associated with sensitive and involved parenting (see Crandall, Deater-Deckard, & Riley, 2015, for a review).

Teachers' field of degree and time in the field

Teacher education is a commonly studied predictor of teacher–child interactions in early childhood programs, and research has linked both education level and type of degree with quality interactions in preschool classrooms (Bowman, Donovan, & Burns, 2001; Helburn, 1995; Hestenes et al., 2015; see Whitebook, 2003, for a review). Specifically, teachers who have earned a bachelor's degree typically provide higher quality care to children than do teachers without degrees (Burchinal, Cryer, Clifford, & Howes, 2002). In addition, some research has indicated that teachers who have college-level training focused on ECE tend to engage in higher quality teaching practices than do teachers with training in other fields, although this finding is not consistent (Early et al., 2007). It is important to note that although many of the samples establishing the link for preschool quality and teacher education included infant and toddler classrooms, separate analyses were not conducted to examine specific relationships restricted to infant/toddler classrooms. However, there is also emerging evidence that this link exists in infant and toddler classrooms as well (e.g., Bandel et al., 2014; Thomason & La Paro, 2013).

Teachers' longevity in the field is another variable that has been empirically linked to classroom interactions. Findings from the NICHD ECCRN (2000a) demonstrated that teachers' years of experience predicted observed caregiving interactions such that teachers with more years of experience demonstrated more positive caregiving (as measured by the Observational Record of the Caregiving Environment) for children 6–36 months of age. In addition, recent research findings from the EHS Family and Child Experiences Study (Baby FACES) survey showed significant positive correlations between teachers' years of experience teaching infants and toddlers and their emotional and behavioral support in EHS 2-year-old classrooms but not 3-year-old classrooms (Bandel et al., 2014). Thus, evidence supports links between teachers' education, years of experience, and classroom interactions, but further investigation is needed to clarify these associations.

There is also some evidence to suggest that teachers' education level and years of experience may moderate the relationship between their psychosocial characteristics and interactions with young children. For example, Hamre and Pianta (2004) observed that harsh, controlling behaviors were more likely to occur in classrooms of depressed teachers when those teachers had lower levels of education. Moreover, training specific to ECE is also a demonstrated moderator of teachers' depression and teaching behaviors such that when teachers had more ECE training, their depressive symptoms had a lessened association with classroom interactions (Gerber, Whitebook, & Weinstein, 2007).

Relative to the moderating effects of education and experience on the links between teacher beliefs and teaching practices, Wen et al. (2011) found that both training and experience moderated the relationship between beliefs and classroom practices. Teachers who had additional training and experience implementing their beliefs (in this case, child-initiated vs. teacher-directed learning) were more successful at interacting in their classrooms in ways that were consistent with their stated beliefs. Evidence on education and experience as a moderator between teachers' temperamental characteristics of positivity or frustration and their classroom interactions is currently lacking. However, given the links between temperament and adult–child interactions as well as the evidence demonstrating that education and experience moderate the ways in which other teacher psychosocial factors are related to teacher–child interactions, further exploration of this is warranted.

Purpose of the study

The purpose of this study is to explore the complex relations among teachers' characteristics and the interactions they engage in with children. This study brings together several characteristics of teachers that have at least preliminary theoretical or empirical evidence linking them to classroom practices. Although these associations are supported in literature on preschool classrooms, we expand this work by focusing on teachers of infants and toddlers. Because this line of inquiry is still quite new, we first provide a description of the characteristics of the EHS teachers participating in this study. Following this, we explore how teachers' intrapersonal characteristics are associated with the quality of teacher–child interactions. Finally, we examine how more established correlates of quality interactions, such as teacher education and years of experience, may moderate associations between teachers' psychosocial characteristics and their classroom interactions with infants and toddlers in EHS classrooms.

Method

Procedure

Data were collected across two academic years in conjunction with a local evaluation study of a large EHS program. Observations of teacher–child interactions were collected for all agency classrooms in the fall semester. Teachers who agreed to participate in the research study completed a questionnaire to provide information regarding their demographic characteristics as well as their temperamental characteristics, depressive symptoms, and beliefs about children.

Participants

Sixty EHS classrooms located in one south-central state participated in the study and were observed in the fall of both academic years. All EHS programs were managed by the same agency and were housed in 10 sites. The classrooms consisted of 42 toddler rooms (24–36 months) and 18 mixed-age rooms (6 weeks to 23 months). A total of 95 surveys were completed by lead teachers (out of 120 possible); surveys included demographic and background information. For teachers ($n = 24$) who had observation and questionnaire data for 2 years, we retained the latter year, resulting in a final sample of 71. The majority (97%) of participants were female, and all worked full time in their current positions. Nearly half (48%) were age 32 years or younger. The majority (75%) of teachers had at least 5 years of experience working with young children, and 92% of teachers had completed their bachelor's degrees. Approximately half of the teachers (47%) were Caucasian, 34% were African American, 11% were Native American, 3% were Asian, and the remainder were multiracial or another race.

Measures

Teacher depressive symptoms

To measure caregivers' feelings of depression we used two measures. The first-year questionnaire included a three-question depression screener (RAND, 1998) that asked teachers to rate how often they had felt "sad," "empty," or "depressed" within the past 2 years, 12 months, and/or the previous month. Teachers answered "yes" or "no" to those three questions. The positive predictive value for this measure is 55% (Wells, 1999). In the second year of the study, the questionnaire was updated to include the Center for Epidemiologic Studies–Depression scale (Radloff, 1977). This scale includes 20 items to assess depressive symptoms experienced in the past week. Participants rate statements, such as "I had trouble keeping my mind on what I was doing," according to how often the symptom was experienced in the past week by choosing from four options ranging from *rarely or none* to *most or all of the time*. Each item is assigned 0–3 points based on the participant's response, then summed to calculate an overall score of 0–60 for depressive symptoms. Higher scores indicate more symptoms, with a clinical cutoff of 16 points or more deemed an indicator of likely depression. The Center for Epidemiologic Studies–Depression scale has good internal consistency ($\alpha = .85$; Radloff, 1977) and is one of the most widely used depressive symptom scales in developmental research. Both measures were dichotomized to a binary indicator with 1 representing a positive screen for depression. The percentage of teachers who scored above the cutoff was similar for both measures.

Teacher temperament

Teacher temperament was measured using subsections from the Adult Temperament Questionnaire (Evans & Rothbart, 2007). Subscales that were used included Activation Control, Attentional Control, Inhibitory Control, Frustration, and Positive Affect. Respondents answered statements using a 7-point Likert scale; ratings ranged from 1 = *extremely untrue of you* to 7 = *extremely true of you*. Sample items for the Activation Control scale ($\alpha = .92$) are "I am often late for appointments" (reverse coded) and "I can make myself work on difficult tasks even when I don't feel like trying." Other examples of items include "It's often hard for me to alternate between two different tasks" (Attentional Control scale; α = .87) and "It is easy for me to hold back laughter in a situation when laughter wouldn't be appropriate" (Inhibitory Control scale; α = .91). For descriptive analyses, an effortful control scale was created per the authors' recommendations by computing the mean of Activation Control, Attentional Control, and Inhibitory Control.

Teacher beliefs

Teacher beliefs were measured using the Parent Modernity Scale (Schaefer & Edgerton, 1985). The Parent Modernity Scale captures a teacher's traditional or progressive beliefs about child rearing. Items were measured on a 5-point Likert-type scale from 1 (*strongly disagree*) to 5 (*strongly agree*). Items were adapted to be relevant to teachers and classroom settings. Teachers were asked to indicate how much they agreed with statements like "The most important thing to teach children is absolute obedience to parents" (reverse coded) and "Children should be allowed to disagree with their parents if they feel their own ideas are better." Items were reverse coded as needed to result in a scale score for which higher values represent more progressive beliefs about children (α = .88).

Teacher demographic information

The demographic section of the questionnaire contained questions regarding gender, age, race, marital status, income, and educational background. The scale also gathered information regarding the teacher's training, number of years in the early childhood field, and length of employment at the current agency. Because of sample size constraints, area of degree was recoded as a dichotomous variable, with 1 indicating that the teacher's degree was in ECE and 0 indicating that the degree was in another field.

Teacher–child interactions

Teacher–child interactions were measured using the Classroom Assessment Scoring System (CLASS), Toddler Version (La Paro et al., 2012). The CLASS-Toddler is structured into two domains: Emotional and Behavioral Support (EBS) and Engaged Support for Learning (ESL). The EBS domain includes five dimensions: Positive Climate, Negative Climate, Teacher Sensitivity, Regard for Child Perspective, and Behavior Guidance. These dimensions focus on the emotional connection between teachers and children. They consider teachers' responsiveness to children, teachers' awareness of children's developmental and individual needs, the degree to which classroom activities and interactions reflect the interests of the children and encourage child autonomy, and the use of effective methods to prevent and redirect problem behavior. The ESL domain is assessed through the dimensions of Facilitation of Learning and Development, Quality of Feedback, and Language Modeling. These dimensions consider teachers' ability to facilitate classroom routines, materials, and activities to support children's learning and developmental opportunities; their ability to provide feedback and scaffolding to children to deepen their learning; and their use of language facilitation techniques to encourage children's language development.

Coding for the CLASS-Toddler is completed using a cycle of 20 min observing and 10 min coding for four observation cycles. Each dimension is rated on a scale from 1 (*low*) to 7 (*high*) based on the frequency, intensity, and duration of interactional behaviors observed across the 20-min segment. Dimension scores are then averaged across the cycles to yield a classroom score for each dimension. The CLASS-Toddler is used widely in research and classroom evaluation assessments and has good internal consistency, with reliability estimates of .88–.89 (Bandel et al., 2014; La Paro et al., 2014; Thomason & La Paro, 2009). Observers for this study all completed the online reliability testing and achieved reliability per the recommendations of the CLASS-Toddler authors (80% agreement within 1 point).

The classrooms in this study all had at least two teachers present throughout the observation. Following the protocol specified by the authors of the CLASS-Toddler, observers attended to interactions occurring throughout the room—with either or both teachers, as well as among children—and incorporated all of this information into their scoring of each cycle. In cases when two teachers were engaged with different groups of children, the observers utilized guidance from the CLASS manual and weighted the interactional quality of each teacher according to the proportion of children in the classroom who were engaged in the interaction to determine the score for that cycle.

Analytic plan

Our primary aims were, first, to describe the beliefs and psychosocial characteristics of EHS teachers and, second, to examine how these characteristics were associated with observed classroom practices as measured by the CLASS-Toddler. Preliminary analyses and descriptive statistics were conducted in SPSS (Version 22). To test for relations between teacher characteristics and classroom practices, we estimated structural equation models using Mplus 7.11 (Muthén & Muthén, 1998–2012).

Results

Description of teacher characteristics

Nearly all (92%) of the teachers in this sample had completed a bachelor's degree. Of these teachers, 31% had received their degree in ECE; 26% in psychology, human development, or social work; 26% in education (areas other than ECE); and 17% in other fields. The amount of experience teaching young children ranged from less than 1 year up to 39 years ($M = 10$ years, $SD = 9.5$).

Regarding teachers' psychosocial characteristics, 16% of teachers screened positive for depression. On average, teachers in this sample were temperamentally predisposed to moderately high levels of positivity, moderately low levels of frustration, and moderate levels of effortful control. Overall, teachers reported moderately progressive beliefs with respect to children's development and the role of adults in supporting that development. Table 1 provides means, standard deviations, and ranges for these and other study variables.

To examine associations among the teacher characteristics, we conducted a series of descriptive analyses. Zero-order correlations indicated that teachers' progressive beliefs were significantly associated with their temperamental positivity ($r = .31$, $p < .01$) but not with frustration or effortful control. In addition, teachers' years of experience teaching young children was also positively related to progressive beliefs ($r = .30$, $p < .05$) and approached significance for positivity ($r = .23$, $p = .07$).

Independent-samples t tests indicated that teachers with depressive symptoms were likely to report higher levels of temperamental positivity ($t = 2.23$, $p < .05$) and effortful control ($t = 1.78$, $p = .08$) and lower levels of frustration ($t = -2.15$, $p < .05$). Teacher depressive symptomology was

Table 1. Descriptive data.

Variable	M	SD	Min	Max
Years of experience	10.01	9.51	1	39
Beliefs	3.56	0.63	2.31	4.75
Positivity	5.10	0.95	2.80	7.00
Frustration	3.32	1.02	1.17	6.00
Effortful control	4.78	0.89	2.78	7.00
CLASS-Toddler				
Positive Climate	5.81	0.99	3.25	7.00
Negative Climate	1.29	0.38	1.00	2.50
Teacher Sensitivity	5.58	0.93	2.50	7.00
Regard for Child Perspective	5.28	0.85	3.00	7.00
Behavior Guidance	5.21	0.95	3.00	6.75
Facilitation of Learning and Development	4.20	1.16	1.50	6.75
Quality of Feedback	3.66	1.27	1.50	6.00
Language Modeling	4.01	1.27	1.25	6.50

Note. CLASS = Classroom Assessment Scoring System.

unrelated to number of years teaching and field of degree. Field of degree was not significantly associated with teachers' beliefs about children, temperamental positivity, effortful control, frustration, or number of years of experience teaching young children.

Teacher–child interactions

Observed teacher–child interactions in this sample were on average moderately high on Positive Climate, Teacher Sensitivity, Regard for Child Perspective, and Behavior Guidance (see Table 1). Overall, teacher–child interactions rated low on Negative Climate, so much so that the range was restricted and the standard deviation was quite small. Teacher–child interactions in the dimensions of Facilitation of Learning and Development, Quality of Feedback, and Language Modeling were rated on average in the moderate range. Independent-samples *t* tests indicated that teachers' field of degree was significantly associated with observed teacher–child interactions (see Table 2 for means), however years of experience in the field was unrelated to observed interactions.

To explore associations of teacher characteristics with teacher–child interactions, we estimated a series of structural equation models. Classroom data were nested within 10 EHS centers. Inspection of the intraclass correlation indicated that only a small proportion of the variance was accounted for at the site level (intraclass correlation values). Because multilevel modeling techniques may result in underestimation of group-level variance and standard errors when the number of groups is small (Maas & Hox, 2005), we did not use multilevel modeling. However, we utilized the type = complex function in Mplus to account for dependency in the data.

Confirmatory factor analysis indicated that these data fit the previously identified two-factor model well (root mean square error of approximation [RMSEA] = .047, comparative fit index [CFI] = .97; La Paro et al., 2012), and thus all models examining associations with teacher–child interactions used the factors Emotional and Behavioral Support (EBS) and Engaged Support for Learning (ESL). Another confirmatory factor analysis model was estimated to confirm the utility of loading the five adult temperament subscales onto one latent factor. The one-factor temperament model demonstrated adequate fit and was used in subsequent analyses (RMSEA = .051, CFI = .95).

Teacher psychosocial characteristics and interactions with children

To test our primary hypotheses examining associations between teacher–child interactions and teachers' psychosocial characteristics, we next estimated identical models for EBS and ESL (models could not be combined because of sample size). These models included all measured teacher psychosocial characteristics—temperament, beliefs about children, and depressive symptoms. All models controlled for teachers' area of degree and years of experience teaching young children.

The first model examined EBS as the outcome variable and indicated that the model fit the data relatively well (CFI = .963, RMSEA = .058). Associations with temperament, beliefs about young children, and depressive symptoms were nonsignificant. Teachers' field of degree was a significant predictor, indicating that teachers who held degrees in ECE tended to have classrooms with higher

Table 2. Observed teacher–child interactions by teachers' field of degree.

Dimension	ECE Degree M	ECE Degree SD	Other Degree M	Other Degree SD
Positive Climate	6.17	0.62	5.51	1.07
Negative Climate	1.21	0.23	1.38	0.46
Teacher Sensitivity	5.77	0.83	5.38	0.98
Regard for Child Perspective	5.56	0.57	5.05	0.87
Behavior Guidance	5.42	0.86	5.01	1.00
Facilitation of Learning and Development	4.39	1.13	4.02	1.12
Quality of Feedback	3.79	1.20	3.36	1.19
Language Modeling	4.25	0.90	3.68	1.30

Note. ECE = early childhood education.

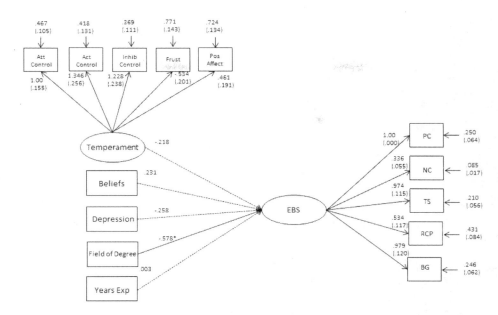

Figure 1. Structural model predicting EBS from teacher characteristics. Att Control = Attentional Control; Act Control = Activation Control; Inhib Control = Inhibitory Control; Frust = Frustration; Pos Affect = Positive Affect; Exp = Experience; EBS = Emotional and Behavioral Support; PC = Positive Climate; NC = Negative Climate; TS = Teacher Sensitivity; RCP = Regard for Child Perspective; BG = Behavior Guidance. *$p < .05$.

levels of EBS ($p = .02$). Teachers' years of experience in the field was not significantly associated with observed levels of EBS (see Figure 1).

The second model was estimated to examine associations between observed ESL and the same teacher psychosocial characteristics included in Model 1. The second model also fit the data satisfactorily (CFI = .888, RMSEA = .08). ESL was not significantly associated with temperament, beliefs about young children, or depressive symptoms. Results indicated a significant effect of field of degree, with teachers who had degrees in ECE teaching in classrooms with higher levels of ESL ($p < .05$), but years of experience was unrelated to ESL (see Figure 2).

Teachers' field of degree and experience as moderators

As a follow-up to our primary research question, we estimated additional models to examine whether teachers' field of degree or years of experience moderated the association between the teacher psychosocial characteristics and teacher–child interaction quality. To achieve the most parsimonious models, while allowing for model identification, we estimated these models separately for each teacher characteristic–moderator pair (i.e., six models: Temperament × Field of Degree, Temperament × Years of Experience, Depression × Field of Degree, etc.). The first two models examined teacher temperament as the independent variable. The fit was acceptable for the models with temperament moderated by field of degree (CFI = .90, RMSEA = .06) and years of experience (CFI = .89, RMSEA = .06). Results indicated that field of degree significantly moderated the association between teacher temperament and observed EBS, such that more positive teacher temperament was associated with higher levels of EBS for teachers who had a degree in ECE but not for teachers with another field of degree. Years of experience did not significantly moderate the association between teacher temperament and EBS or ESL.

Next models were estimated to examine possible interactions between field of degree or years of experience and depressive symptoms. Model fit was acceptable for both (CFI = .99, RMSEA = .07). Results indicated that field of degree did not significantly moderate the association between depressive symptoms and EBS or ESL. Years of experience was found to be a significant moderator

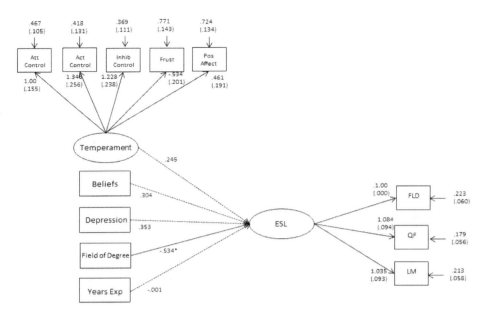

Figure 2. Structural model predicting ESL from teacher characteristics. Att Control = Attentional Control; Act Control = Activation Control; Inhib Control = Inhibitory Control; Frust = Frustration; Pos Affect = Positive Affect; Exp = Experience; ESL = Engaged Support for Learning; FLD = Facilitation of Learning and Development; QF = Quality of Feedback; LM = Language Modeling. *$p < .05$.

of the association between both EBS ($p = .01$) and ESL ($p < .01$). See Figure 3 for these results. Probing of the interaction indicated a significant association between teachers' depressive symptomology and both EBS and ESL for teachers with less time in the ECE field but not for teachers with more years of experience in the field.

Identical models were estimated for teachers' beliefs about young children as the independent variable. Results indicated no evidence for moderation of this association by either field of degree or years of experience.

Discussion

This study provides an examination of the ways in which various teacher characteristics are related to teachers' interactions with children. Our study adds information in areas with prior mixed results and extends preliminary work reported recently (Whitaker et al., 2015) by examining a broader set of teacher characteristics and by focusing on teacher–child interactions in settings with infants and toddlers.

The data reported in this study included teachers and classrooms that were somewhat atypical of infant/toddler settings. Specifically, the quality of teacher–child interactions observed was notably higher than other published data using the CLASS-Toddler. For example, the average dimension scores of this sample ranged from 3.59 ($SD = 1.23$) for Quality of Feedback to 6.68 ($SD = 0.95$) for Negative Climate (reverse coded). In comparison, classrooms observed in the Baby FACES study ranged from a mean score of 2.9 ($SD = 0.15$) for Language Modeling in classrooms of 3-year-old children to 5.6 ($SD = 0.12$) for Positive Climate in classrooms of 2-year-old children (Bandel et al., 2014). The high quality of teacher–child interactions observed provided an opportunity to explore teacher characteristics that might be associated with providing such positive classroom practices.

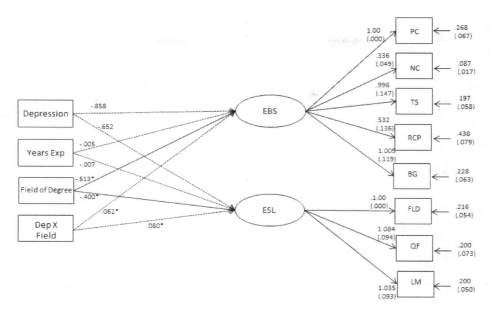

Figure 3. Structural model examining the interaction between depressive symptoms and years of experience. Exp = experience; Dep = depression; EBS = Emotional and Behavioral Support; ESL = Engaged Support for Learning; PC = Positive Climate; NC = Negative Climate; TS = Teacher Sensitivity; RCP = Regard for Child Perspective; BG = Behavior Guidance; FLD = Facilitation of Learning and Development; QF = Quality of Feedback; LM = Language Modeling. *$p < .05$.

Teacher characteristics and classroom interactions

Contrary to expectation, we did not find any main effects of teachers' beliefs about children, temperament, or depressive symptoms on observed teacher–child interactions. Instead, these models indicated a consistent effect of the field in which the teacher had earned his or her bachelor's degree.

Our sample is unusual in that it demonstrated education levels far exceeding the typical level of training for infant/toddler teachers. The National Survey of Early Care and Education Project Team (2013) recently reported that among center-based teachers and caregivers of children birth to 3 years old, only 19% had completed a bachelor's degree and the majority (64%) had completed only high school or some college. In contrast, the data used in this study included mostly teachers with bachelor's degrees. Although unusual, this data set gave us the opportunity to explore the fields in which teachers received their bachelor's degrees and associations with observed classroom processes.

Our findings indicated that field of degree was significantly associated with teacher–child interactions in both EBS and ESL domains. Specifically, teachers with degrees in ECE provided higher levels of emotional and instructional support than did those with degrees from other fields. These results are consistent with a body of literature indicating that both level of education and field of study are associated with high-quality care (see Whitebook, 2003, for a review). However, these findings differ from those in a recent report from the Baby FACES study that did not find a significant difference in teacher–child interactions for teachers with ECE degrees compared to those with other types of degrees (Bandel et al., 2014). One possible explanation for the null findings for field of degree in the Baby FACES study is a lack of power due to sample size. Only 32% of teachers in the Baby FACES sample held a bachelor's degree (Vogel et al., 2015), resulting in only a small subsample among which comparisons for field of degree could be made. As more teachers with college degrees join the infant/toddler ECE workforce, it will be important to continue to explore the role of field of degree in shaping classroom practice and quality.

We found no direct association between number of years of experience working with children and observed teacher–child interactions. As discussed previously, teachers' tenure in the field has demonstrated inconsistent associations with classroom practices (e.g., Burchinal et al., 2002; NICHD ECCRN, 2000a). Further demonstrating the inconsistency of results in this area, the recent report from the Baby FACES study also found a significant association between years teaching infants and toddlers and EBS for classrooms of 2-year-old children but not for 3-year-olds. In addition, teachers' years of experience was not associated with ESL for either age group (Bandel et al., 2014). Our findings add additional data points for the role of structural characteristics such as teacher education and experience, but even more than this provide additional evidence for the need to look beyond these characteristics.

Field of degree and time in field as moderators

Although these data did not support the significance of any main effects for teachers' psychosocial characteristics, findings in the literature suggest that these characteristics are associated with teaching practices for at least some teachers. To explore these patterns of association further, we considered the possibility that teachers' intrapersonal characteristics may be more or less salient to teaching practices according to teachers' field of degree or time in the field. Findings from these analyses provide limited support for these interactional effects.

Specifically, results indicated that for teachers with a degree in ECE, but not for those with degrees in other fields, an adaptive temperament (high levels of positivity and effortful control and low levels of frustration) was associated with higher quality interactions supporting children's engaged learning and cognitive development. In addition to a direct effect of field of degree, perhaps teachers who have adaptive temperamental characteristics are able to yield additional benefit from their ECE training, allowing them to better use high-quality practices for supporting toddlers' cognitive development. That is, adaptive temperamental characteristics may allow teachers to better cope with the demands of teaching infants and toddlers who have limited language and social skills and thus require a different level of care than do older children. Teachers who are temperamentally predisposed to remaining calm and positive despite these demands may be able to access and implement skills and knowledge gained in ECE degree programs, thus making them especially strong at providing high-quality teacher–child interactions.

In addition, the association between teachers' depressive symptomology and interactions with children was moderated by their time in the field. Specifically, teachers who screened positive for depression provided lower quality EBS and ESL, but this effect was only significant for teachers with fewer years in the ECE field. These findings suggest that when teachers exhibit depressive symptoms, they may be able to draw on their years of experience teaching young children, allowing them to provide high-quality emotional and instructional interactions despite the depressive symptoms. Teachers who are new to the field and experiencing depressive symptoms may find themselves overwhelmed by the demands of working with infants/toddlers and unable to provide high-quality interactions. Perhaps teachers who experience depressive symptoms but have been in the field longer have developed coping mechanisms for working with young children, allowing them to engage with infants and toddlers in high-quality interactions in a way that is on par with teachers who do not have depressive symptoms.

It is important to note that although the current sample had a lower incidence of depressive symptoms than another recent examination of EHS and Head Start teachers (Whitaker et al., 2013), the incidence level in the current sample was still greater than in national surveys of the U.S. population (Pratt & Brody, 2008). Depressive symptoms are more common among women, individuals living in poverty, and individuals with less than a bachelor's degree (Pratt & Brody, 2008). Because the current sample included individuals with higher levels of education and income than are typical among ECE teachers, it is likely that this study reports depression rates that are lower than those of the overall population of EHS and Head Start teachers. Thus, these findings regarding the role of depression in shaping teacher–child interactions are particularly important and warrant further research.

In contrast to findings for depressive symptoms, neither field of degree nor years of experience was found to moderate the association between teachers' beliefs about child rearing and their interactions with children. These null findings in this area are surprising given the relatively strong support in the literature for the role of beliefs in teacher practices (e.g., Rimm-Kaufman et al., 2006; Stipek & Byler, 1997). There are many possible reasons for this, including types of beliefs measured and the possibility that these beliefs are not as salient of a variable in teaching behaviors for infant and toddler teachers as they are for teachers of older children.

Limitations and future directions

This study includes several limitations that should be considered. First, it is important to note that this study was correlational in nature, and no determination of causality can be made. Second, all of the teacher characteristics in this data set were self-reported by the teachers. Self-report data have well-established limitations but remain an integral piece of developmental science. Future studies should build on these findings by including additional measures of teacher characteristics, possibly including direct task-based assessment of various temperamental traits or additional data gathered by observers. In addition, this study had less than optimal statistical power for many of the analyses. In addition to a relatively small sample size, limited variability in some dimensions of observed classroom practices may have limited our ability to detect effects, thus increasing the possibility for Type II error. Furthermore, the ranges and means reflected in the CLASS scores were quite different from the averages reported in the literature, both among community settings and in EHS programs (Bandel et al., 2014; La Paro et al., 2014). These unusually high CLASS scores, along with the highly qualified teachers included in this sample, should be considered carefully and may limit generalizability to more typical child care settings. Additional studies with larger, more diverse samples are needed to replicate these findings and further explore the role of teacher characteristics in teacher–child interactions.

Overall, the findings from this study highlight the benefits of obtaining specialized training in ECE to provide teachers with the knowledge and skills needed to provide optimal care for infants and toddlers. The EHS agency in which this research was conducted is unusual in its focus on placing degreed teachers in infant/toddler classrooms, and this model may not be sustainable for some EHS agencies or community child care settings. However, increasing the ECE-focused training for these groups to the extent possible may be an important intermediate step to improve the practices of infant/toddler teachers. Subsequently, if and when the nation moves toward more adequate funding for child care, these findings, if replicated, can lead to recommendations for the requirement of a specialized degree for teachers of even the youngest children.

This study joins an emerging literature highlighting the complexity of associations between teachers' characteristics and the quality of classroom practices they provide. It also provides preliminary information about characteristics of infant/toddler teachers not typically measured, such as temperament and depression. Finally, findings from this study suggest that the complex relationships among teacher characteristics and teaching behaviors are as relevant in infant and toddler classrooms as they are in classrooms serving older children. Although the current study yielded consistent results suggesting the benefits of a specialized ECE degree, the mixed findings in the literature make it clear that education and time in field variables do not account for all of the observed variance in the quality of teacher–child interactions in early childhood classrooms. Accordingly, researchers must attend to teacher characteristics beyond the scope of the structural characteristics historically assessed in order to broaden their understanding of early childhood classroom quality.

References

Bandel, E., Aikens, N., Vogel, C. A., Boller, K., & Murphy, L. (2014). *Observed quality and psychometric properties of the CLASS-T in the Early Head Start Family and Child Experiences Survey* (OPRE Technical Brief No. 2014–23).

Washington, DC: U.S. Department of Health and Human Services, Administration for Children and Families, Office of Planning, Research and Evaluation.

Bornstein, M. H., Mash, C., Arterberry, M. E., & Manian, N. (2012). Object perception in 5-month-old infants of clinically depressed and nondepressed mothers. *Infant Behavior and Development, 35*, 150–157. doi:10.1016/j.infbeh.2011.07.008

Bowman, B. T., Donovan, M. S., & Burns, M. S. (Eds.). (2001). *Eager to learn: Educating our preschoolers*. Washington, DC: National Academies Press.

Bronfenbrenner, U. (2001). The bioecological theory of human development. In N. J. Smelser & P. B. Baltes (Eds.), *International encyclopedia of the social and behavioral sciences* (Vol. 10, pp. 6963–6970). New York, NY: Elsevier

Bronfenbrenner, U., & Morris, P. (1998). The ecology of developmental processes. In W. Damon & R. M. Lerner (Eds.), *Handbook of child psychology: Vol. 1. Theoretical models of human development* (5th ed., pp. 993–1028). New York, NY: Wiley.

Brownlee, J., Berthelsen, D., & Segaran, N. (2009). Childcare workers' and centre directors' beliefs about infant childcare quality and professional training. *Early Child Development and Care, 179*, 453–475. doi:10.1080/03004430701217688

Burchinal, M. R., Cryer, D., Clifford, R. M., & Howes, C. (2002). Caregiver training and classroom quality in child care centers. *Applied Developmental Science, 6*, 2–11. doi:10.1207/S1532480XADS0601_01

Crandall, A., Deater-Deckard, K. D., & Riley, A. W. (2015). Maternal emotion and cognitive control capacities and parenting: A conceptual framework. *Developmental Review, 36*, 105–126. doi:10.1016/j.dr.2015.01.004

Early, D. M., Maxwell, K. L., Burchinal, M., Alva, S., Bender, R. H., Bryant, D., & Zill, N. (2007). Teachers' education, classroom quality, and young children's academic skills: Results from seven studies of preschool programs. *Child Development, 78*, 558–580. doi:10.1111/j.1467-8624.2007.01014.x

Esaki, N., & Larkin, H. (2013). Prevalence of adverse childhood experiences (ACEs) among child service providers. *Families in Society, 94*, 31–37. doi:10.1606/1044-3894.4257

Evans, D. E., & Rothbart, M. K. (2007). Developing a model for adult temperament. *Journal of Research in Personality, 41*, 868–888. doi:10.1016/j.jrp.2006.11.002

Gerber, E. B., Whitebook, M., & Weinstein, R. S. (2007). At the heart of child care: Predictors of teacher sensitivity in center-based child care. *Early Childhood Research Quarterly, 22*, 327–346. doi:10.1016/j.ecresq.2006.12.003

Goldstein, L., Diener, M., & Mangelsdorf, S. (1996). Maternal characteristics and social support across the transition to motherhood: Associations with maternal behavior. *Journal of Family Psychology, 10*, 60–71. doi:10.1037/0893-3200.10.1.60

Hamre, B. K. (2014). Teachers' daily interactions with children: An essential ingredient in effective early childhood programs. *Child Development Perspectives, 8*(4), 223–230. doi:10.1111/cdep.12090

Hamre, B. K., & Pianta, R. C. (2004). Self-reported depression in nonfamilial caregivers: Prevalence and associations with caregiver behavior in child-care settings. *Early Childhood Research Quarterly, 19*, 297–318. doi:10.1016/j.ecresq.2004.04.006

Hamre, B. K., Pianta, R. C., Downer, J. T., & Mashburn, A. J. (2008). Teachers' perceptions of conflict with young students: Looking beyond problem behaviors. *Social Development, 17*(1), 115–136.

Helburn, S. W. (1995). *Cost, quality, and child outcomes in child care centers, technical report*. Denver: University of Colorado at Denver, Center for Research in Economic and Social Policy, Department of Economics.

Hestenes, L. L., Kintner-Duffy, V., Chen Wang, Y., La Paro, K. M., Mims, S. U., Crosby, D., & Cassidy, D. J. (2015). Comparisons among quality measures in child care settings: Understanding the use of multiple measures in North Carolina's QRIS and their links to social-emotional development in preschool children. *Early Childhood Research Quarterly, 30*, 199–214. doi:10.1016/j.ecresq.2014.06.003

Jeon, L., Buettner, C. K., & Snyder, A. R. (2014). Pathways from teacher depression and child-care quality to child behavioral problems. *Journal of Consulting and Clinical Psychology, 82*, 225–235. doi:10.1037/a0035720

La Paro, K. M., Hamre, B. K., & Pianta, R. C. (2012). *Classroom Assessment Scoring System manual, Toddler (CLASS-T)*. Baltimore, MD: Brookes.

La Paro, K. M., Williamson, A. C., & Hatfield, B. (2014). Assessing quality in toddler classrooms using the CLASS-Toddler and the ITERS-R. *Early Education & Development, 25*, 875–893. doi:10.1080/10409289.2014.883586

Li-Grining, C., Raver, C. C., Champion, K., Sardin, L., Metzger, M., & Jones, S. M. (2010). Understanding and improving classroom emotional climate and behavior management in the "real world": The role of Head Start teachers' psychosocial stressors. *Early Education & Development, 21*, 65–94. doi:10.1080/10409280902783509

Maas, C. J. M., & Hox, J. J. (2005). Sufficient sample sizes for multilevel modeling. *Methodology, 1*, 86–92. doi:10.1027/1614-1881.1.3.86

McCartney, K., Dearing, E., Taylor, B. A., & Bub, K. L. (2007). Quality child care supports the achievement of low-income children: Direct and indirect pathways through caregiving and the home environment. *Journal of Applied Developmental Psychology, 28*, 411–426. doi:10.1016/j.appdev.2007.06.010

Mortensen, J. A., & Barnett, M. A. (2015). Teacher-child interactions in infant/toddler child care and socioemotional development. *Early Education & Development, 26*, 209–229. doi:10.1080/10409289.2015.985878

Muthén, L. K., & Muthén, B. O. (1998–2012). *Mplus user's guide* (7th ed.). Los Angeles, CA: Authors.

National Institute of Child Health and Human Development Early Child Care Research Network. (1998). Early child care and self-control, compliance, and problem behavior at twenty-four and thirty-six months. *Child Development, 69*, 1145–1170.

National Institute of Child Health and Human Development Early Child Care Research Network. (2000a). Characteristics and quality of child care for toddlers and preschoolers. *Applied Developmental Science, 4*, 116–135. doi:10.1207/S1532480XADS0403_2

National Institute of Child Health and Human Development Early Child Care Research Network. (2000b). Factors associated with fathers' caregiving activities and sensitivity with young children. *Journal of Family Psychology, 14*, 200–219. doi:10.1037/0893-3200.14.2.200

National Survey of Early Care and Education Project Team. (2013). *Number and characteristics of early care and education (ECE) teachers and caregivers: Initial findings from the National Survey of Early Care and Education (NSECE)* (OPRE Report No. 2013–38). Washington, DC: U.S. Department of Health and Human Services, Administration for Children and Families, Office of Planning, Research and Evaluation.

Oddi, K. B., Murdock, K. W., Vadnais, S., Bridgett, D. J., & Gartstein, M. A. (2013). Maternal and infant temperament characteristics as contributors to parenting stress in the first year postpartum. *Infant and Child Development, 22*, 553–579. doi:10.1002/icd.v22.6

Pratt, L. A., & Brody, D. J. (2008). *Depression in the United States household population, 2005–2006* (NCHS Data Brief No. 7). Washington, DC: National Center for Health Statistics.

Radloff, L. S. (1977). The CES-D scale: A self-report depression scale for research in the general population. *Applied Psychological Measurement, 1*, 385–401. doi:10.1177/014662167700100306

RAND. (1998). *Depression screener.* Retrieved from http://www.rand.org/content/dam/rand/www/external/health/surveys_tools/depression/screener_scoring.pdf

Raver, C. C., Blair, C., & Li-Grining, C. (2012). Extending models of emotion self-regulation to classroom settings: Implications for professional development. In C. Howes, B. K. Hamre, & R. C. Pianta (Eds.), *Effective early childhood professional development: Improving teacher practice and child outcomes* (pp. 113–130). Baltimore, MD: Brookes.

Rimm-Kaufman, S. E., Storm, M. D., Sawyer, B. E., Pianta, R. C., & La Paro, K. M. (2006). The teacher belief Q-sort: A measure of teachers' priorities in relation to disciplinary practices, teaching practices, and beliefs about children. *Journal of School Psychology, 44*, 141–165. doi:10.1016/j.jsp.2006.01.003

Rosenblum, K. L., Dayton, C. J., & Muzik, M. (2009). Infant social and emotional development. In C. H. Zeanah (Ed.), *Handbook of infant mental health* (pp. 80–103). New York, NY: Guilford Press.

Rothbart, M. K., & Ahadi, S. A. (1994). Temperament and the development of personality. *Journal of Abnormal Psychology, 103*, 55–66. doi:10.1037/0021-843X103.1.55

Rothbart, M. K., & Derryberry, D. (1981). Development of individual differences in temperament. In M. E. Lamb & A. Brown (Eds.), *Advances in developmental psychology* (Vol. 1, pp. 37–86). Hillsdale, NJ: Lawrence Erlbaum.

Ruzek, E., Burchinal, M., Farkas, G., & Duncan, G. J. (2014). The quality of toddler child care and cognitive skills at 24 months: Propensity score analysis results from the ECLS-B. *Early Childhood Research Quarterly, 29*, 12–21. doi:10.1016/j.ecresq.2013.09.002

Schaefer, E. S., & Edgerton, M. (1985). Parent and child correlates of parental modernity. In I. E. Sigel (Ed.), *Parental belief systems: The psychological consequences for children* (pp. 287–318). Hillsdale, NJ: Erlbaum.

Stipek, D. J., & Byler, P. (1997). Early childhood education teachers: Do they practice what they preach? *Early Childhood Research Quarterly, 12*, 305–325. doi:10.1016/S0885-2006(97)90005-3

Susman-Stillman, A., Pleuss, J., & Englund, M. M. (2013). Attitudes and beliefs of family- and center-based child care providers predict differences in caregiving behavior over time. *Early Childhood Research Quarterly, 28*, 905–917. doi:10.1016/j.ecresq.2013.04.003

Thomason, A. C., & La Paro, K. M. (2009). Measuring the quality of teacher-child interactions in toddler child care. *Early Education & Development, 20*, 285–304. doi:10.1080/10409280902773351

Thomason, A. C., & La Paro, K. M. (2013). Teachers' commitment to the field and effective teacher-child interactions in early childhood classrooms. *Early Childhood Education Journal, 41*, 227–234. doi:10.1007/s10643-012-0539-4

Vogel, C. A., Caronongan, P., Xue, Y., Thomas, J., Bandel, E., Aikens, N., ... Murphy, L. (2015). *Toddlers in Early Head Start: A portrait of 3-year-olds, their families, and the programs serving them* (OPRE Report No. 2015–28). Washington, DC: U.S. Department of Health and Human Services, Administration for Children and Families, Office of Planning, Research and Evaluation.

Watamura, S. E., Phillips, D. A., Morrissey, T. W., McCartney, K., & Bub, K. (2011). Double jeopardy: Poorer social-emotional outcomes for children in the NICHD SECCYD experiencing home and child-care environments that confer risk. *Child Development, 82*, 48–65. doi:10.1111/cdev.2011.82.issue-1

Wells, K. B. (1999). The design of Partners in Care: Evaluating the cost-effectiveness of improving care for depression in primary care. *Social Psychiatry and Psychiatric Epidemiology, 34*, 20–29. doi:10.1007/s001270050107

Wen, X., Elicker, J. G., & McMullen, M. B. (2011). Early childhood teachers' curriculum beliefs: Are they consistent with observed classroom practices? *Early Education & Development, 22*, 945–969. doi:10.1080/10409289.2010.507495

Whitaker, R. C., Becker, B. D., Herman, A. N., & Gooze, R. A. (2013). The physical and mental health of Head Start staff: The Pennsylvania Head Start staff wellness survey, 2012. *Preventing Chronic Disease, 10.* doi:10.5888/pcd10.130171

Whitaker, R. C., Dearth-Wesley, T., & Gooze, R. A. (2015). Workplace stress and the quality of teacher-children relationships in Head Start. *Early Childhood Research Quarterly, 30,* 57–69. doi:10.1016/j.ecresq.2014.08.008

Whitaker, R. C., Dearth-Wesley, T., Gooze, R. A., Becker, B. D., Gallagher, K. C., & McEwen, B. S. (2014). Adverse childhood experiences, dispositional mindfulness, and adult health. *Preventive Medicine, 67,* 147–153. doi:10.1016/j.ypmed.2014.07.029

Whitebook, M. (2003). *Early education quality: Higher teacher qualifications for better learning environments—A review of the literature.* Berkeley, CA: Center for the Study of Child Care Employment.

Attachment Predicts College Students' Knowledge, Attitudes, and Skills for Working With Infants, Toddlers, and Families

Claire D. Vallotton, Julia Torquati, Jean Ispa, Rachel Chazan-Cohen, Jennifer Henk, Maria Fusaro, Carla A. Peterson, Lori A. Roggman, Ann M. Stacks, Gina Cook, and Holly Brophy-Herb

ABSTRACT

Research Findings: Adults' attitudes about attachment relationships are central to how they perceive and respond to children. However, little is known about how attachment styles are related to teachers' attitudes toward and interactions with infants and toddlers. From a survey of 207 students taking early childhood (EC) courses at 4 U.S. universities, we report relations among students' attachment styles and their (a) career goals, (b) attitudes about caring for and educating infants and young children, and (c) interaction skills for responding in developmentally supportive ways. Overall, attachment security was positively associated with career goals focused on working with younger children, knowledge about infant/toddler development, attitudes that acknowledge the importance of adult support in children's development, and developmentally supportive interaction skills. Students who scored high on attachment fearfulness minimized the importance of adults in children's lives, minimized the importance of the early years for later learning, and endorsed strict and controlling forms of child guidance. *Practice or Policy*: A conceptual mediation model linking a path from attachment to caregiving skill through knowledge and attitudes is articulated. We propose a person-centered pedagogy for infant/toddler professional preparation that provides opportunities for reflection on one's own attachment and its effects on work with young children.

Researchers are truly in the infancy of understanding the motivations of individuals who enter the early care and education workforce, the characteristics of those best suited to being teachers in early care and education settings, or how to optimize training and educational experiences to best prepare individuals for this important role. Early childhood (EC) and elementary teachers' implicit attitudes are associated with pedagogy and classroom practices (e.g., Cassidy & Lawrence, 2000; Charlesworth et al., 1993; Pajares, 1992). Here we understand teacher attitudes to include beliefs and values that "house the evaluative, comparative, and judgmental functions of beliefs and replace predisposition with an imperative to action" (Pajares, 1992, p. 314). Brownlee and colleagues have described the belief systems of toddler teachers[1] and their association with Squires's (2004) key affective, cognitive, and executive functions of teaching (Berthelsen & Brownlee, 2005, 2007; Brownlee & Berthelsen,

---

[1]We choose to use the term *teacher* here for infant and toddler professionals working in the classroom, and we use the term as inclusive of the terms *educator*, *caregiver*, and *child care provider*.

2006, 2009; Brownlee, Berthelsen, & Boulton-Lewis, 2004; McMullen & Dixon, 2006). Other research has connected infant teachers' mind-mindedness, or the attribution of mental states and processes to children's behavior, to observed teaching practices, specifically to increased sensitivity and stimulation levels (Degotardi & Davis, 2008; Degotardi & Sweller, 2012; Susman-Stillman, Pleuss, & Englund, 2013). These limited associations between attitudes and teacher practices have not been fully examined for teachers of infants and toddlers, particularly for future teachers. Furthermore, given that the teacher role is fundamentally relationship based in EC (Margetts, 2005), teachers' own attachment styles may influence their attitudes and classroom practices as well as the quality of their relationships with children. Because teacher–child relationships are a crucial determinant of quality in infant and toddler care (Raikes & Edwards, 2009), teachers' attachment styles and attitudes may have particular relevance for pedagogy and practice.

Following this line of thinking, some researchers have used attachment theory as a framework to investigate teacher characteristics that promote the social and emotional well-being of the children in their care (e.g., Ahnert, Pinquart, & Lamb, 2006; Belsky & Rovine, 1988). This work has focused on teacher sensitivity and child attachment rather than on teachers' attachment styles. Berlin (2012) reviewed research on the role of sensitive, supportive care in promoting child well-being and recommended that hiring interviews for infant/toddler teachers include questions about applicants' attachment-related values and states of mind and that attachment-based training be instituted to help teachers understand how their own attachment security influences their work with children. However, to date there is no empirical evidence linking current or future teachers' attachment security to their attitudes, beliefs, or behaviors related to educating and caring for infants and toddlers. We address this gap by investigating relations among university students' attachment styles (for both EC majors and those in classes with childhood development content); their expectations regarding future professional roles; and their knowledge, attitudes, and skills related to working with infants and toddlers.

Attachment, attitudes, and behaviors

To explore how EC teachers' attachment styles may relate to their attitudes and behaviors regarding infants and toddlers, we drew on literature describing adult attachment styles. Adult attachment has been conceptualized as a caregiving behavioral system regulated by internal working models of self and others that organize thoughts and feelings about relationships (Ainsworth, 1979; Bowlby, 1969; George & Solomon, 1999; Main, Kaplan, & Cassidy, 1985; Sroufe & Waters, 1977). Four primary styles have been identified: (a) secure or autonomous, (b) insecure-entangled or preoccupied, (c) insecure-avoidant or dismissing, and (d) disoriented-disorganized or fearful. These internal working models guide attitudes and beliefs about relationships, including parents' appraisals of and responses to children's behavior (e.g., Bretherton, 1990; Crowell & Feldman, 1991; Steele, Steele, & Fonagy, 1996).

Attachment security benefits parents in many ways. Secure mothers are able to appraise a child's behavior amid relevant contextual cues; regulate their own emotional responses to the child's behavior; and respond in a way that meets the child's needs with sensitivity, warmth, and affection (Crowell & Feldman, 1991; De Wolff & van Ijzendoorn, 1997; DeOliveira, Moran, & Pederson, 2005) without being overly intrusive, negative, detached, rejecting, or controlling (Adam, Gunnar, & Tanaka, 2004; Ainsworth, Blehar, Waters, & Wall, 1978; Bretherton, 1990; Main & Goldwyn, 1984; Mills-Koonce et al., 2011; Roskam, Meunier, & Stievenart, 2011; Whipple, Bernier, & Mageau, 2011). Secure parents can be present in the moment with children and respond to them relatively unencumbered by ghosts from past attachment relationships (Fraiberg, 1980). In turn, their children tend to be more secure, socially competent, and autonomous compared to children with insecure parents (e.g., Grossman, Fremmer-Bombik, Rudolph, & Grossman, 1988; Pearson, Cohn, Cowan, & Pape Cowan, 1994; Stevenson-Hinde & Shouldice, 1995; van Ijzendoorn, 1995).

In contrast, insecure individuals adopt strategies for coping with unmet security needs (Main, Goldwyn, & Hesse, 2002). Dismissing individuals deactivate the attachment system by minimizing the importance of attachment needs for themselves and others and are less nurturing and more controlling than secure parents (George & Solomon, 1999). Preoccupied individuals hyperactivate the attachment system, resulting in overprotective and intrusive behaviors (George & Solomon, 1999). As parents, they can be angry and intrusive (Adam et al., 2004). Fearful individuals are more prone to feeling fear and anxiety during interactions with their infants and to withdrawing emotionally from children as a coping strategy. Moreover, fearful adults can exhibit confusing and contradictory caregiving behaviors, such as approaching the infant but then turning away from the infant's cues for closeness, or intrusive behaviors that reflect misalignments in affective communication (Lyons-Ruth & Spielman, 2004). Parents with insecure attachment styles report more parenting stress, more negative parental attitudes, and lower parenting self-efficacy (Kohlhoff & Barnett, 2013; Trillingsgaard, Elklit, Shevlin, & Maimburg, 2011).

Although adult attachment consistently predicts parenting behaviors, especially during the infant and toddler period, much less is known about how attachment styles of EC professionals may influence their thoughts and feelings toward, and interactions with, young children. However, research with young adults is instructive for considering how attachment affects professionals. For example, women with insecure attachment styles less accurately identify infant emotions, make more negative attributions about a distressed infant, report more irritation in response to infant crying, and are less likely to respond with empathy than secure women (Leerkes & Siepak, 2006; Riem, Bakermans-Kranenburg, van Ijzendoorn, Out, & Rombouts, 2012). Insecure college students hold more negative models of parenting and parent–child relationships, expect to be easily aggravated by children, endorse stricter disciplinary practices, and are less confident in their ability to relate to children (Rholes, Simpson, Blakely, Lanigan, & Allen, 1997).

Attachment and preparation of EC professionals

The attachment-related patterns and associations described in the previous section may be similar for EC teachers and for students preparing to enter that field. Although parents are children's primary attachment figures, children spend a substantial amount of time with their EC teachers, who can also contribute to their security needs (Kuhl, 2011; Meltzoff, Kuhl, Movellan, & Sejnowski, 2009; Pianta, 1992; Siegel, 1999; Sroufe, Egeland, Carlson, & Collins, 2005). Child care is a context that elicits attachment-related challenges such as transitions from one setting, teacher, or major activity to another (McMullen & Dixon, 2006) as well as the need to share teachers' attentions with other children. For instance, one study found that 91% of children who spent more than 12 months with a high-ability teacher were securely attached compared to only 50% of those who had been with their teachers 5 to 8 months (Raikes, 1993). Group size was also linked with attachment in a study of Israeli children: 72% of children in classrooms with a 1:3 or better adult:child ratio were securely attached compared to only 57% of children in classrooms with worse ratios (Berlin, 2012).

It follows that it is worthwhile to apply attachment theory to research on the childrearing-related feelings and ideas of current and future EC professionals. Teachers' attachment styles may influence their attitudes and behaviors toward young children in ways similar to those of parents (Edwards & Raikes, 2002; Honig, 2002). In fact, the attachment theory framework has already led to useful insights beyond the parent–child relationship. First, there is evidence that professionals' attachment plays a role in other child- and family-related practices: In home visiting, providers' attachment security predicts better program implementation, higher home visitor self-efficacy, and greater family engagement and trust (Burrell et al., 2009; McFarlane et al., 2010). Second, there is evidence that attachment style is associated with EC career intentions. Horppu and Ikonen-Varila (2004) found that secure EC education students were more likely than dismissing students to report that working with younger (as opposed to older) children was their first career choice.

Third, there is evidence that children benefit when their teachers have secure working models of relationships. Stability of care and teacher sensitivity are associated with children's secure attachment relationships with nonparental caregivers (Ahnert et al., 2006; De Schipper, Tavecchio, & van

Ijzendoorn, 2008; Elicker, Fortner-Wood, & Noppe, 1999; Raikes, 1993). Fourth, children who have secure relationships with their teachers demonstrate greater social competence, including prosocial behavior, and less hostile aggression and withdrawal (Howes, Matheson, & Hamilton, 1994; Howes, Rodning, Galluzzo, & Myers, 1988). For these reasons, knowledge about teachers' attachment styles in relation to their attitudes about and interactions with young children could inform preparation programs for infant/toddler professionals and in-service training. Yet there is only sparse knowledge about the role of undergraduate students' own attachment styles in forming their career expectations, their ideas about the nature of children, and their thoughts about best practices in child care.

America's universities train many EC professionals (Honig & Hirallal, 1998; Hyson, Horm, & Winton, 2012). In higher education settings, students' attachment styles likely influence their (a) decisions to enter the early care and education field, as they do for elementary and secondary teachers (Riley, 2009; Wright & Sherman, 1963); (b) attitudes and approaches toward coursework and practicum experiences that include relationships with children and families; and (c) ability to acquire knowledge and skills about, and change attitudes toward, children and families (Ambrose, Bridges, DiPietro, Lovett, & Normán, 2010). Yet there is limited research on these associations and no comprehensive models for addressing the effects of these psychosocial factors on students' learning and career paths related to early care and education. Horm, Hyson, and Winton (2013) proposed a model of education and career development for EC professionals that focuses primarily on essential content in students' program of study rather than on the underlying psychosocial characteristics that may influence choice of major and subsequent learning. However, they pointed out the need for further research specifically on the education of infant/toddler teachers in order to create a model for effective education and training of these future professionals, and the need to consider learner characteristics in such models.

The current study and introduction to the research questions

A group of child development scholars across multiple universities have collaborated to address the gap in research that undermines the development of a comprehensive model of effective education for future infant/toddler teachers.[2] The group first used a rigorous vetting process to articulate a set of competencies based on empirical evidence and professional standards (i.e., Zero-to-Three Core competencies; competencies of the Council for Exceptional Children's Division for Early Childhood). Group members each nominated up to five competencies with justification and evidence statements, and content analysis was conducted to integrate and align the competencies. Nine competency dimensions, which each included specific knowledge, attitudes, and skills that EC teachers need to work effectively with infants, toddlers, and their families, were articulated and then reviewed and critiqued by the group members. Next we began to develop measures to assess these competencies and the factors that may influence them. As a starting point, the group concentrated on three competency dimensions that are at the center of the current study: understanding and supporting relationships, understanding and supporting learning, and guidance of infant/toddler behavior. There is substantial evidence and professional guidelines underpinning these competences. For example, evidence for the importance of understanding and supporting relationships comes from attachment research described previously (Kuhl, 2011; Meltzoff et al., 2009; Pianta, 1992; Siegel, 1999; Sroufe et al., 2005). Furthermore, child development knowledge based on developmental science is critical to preparing teachers to support children's learning and development (Copple & Bredekamp, 2009; Horm et al., 2013; Pianta, Hitz, & West, 2010). Evidence that these competencies are necessary for developmentally supportive practices with young children is based on associations between adults' knowledge, attitudes, and behaviors within each dimension and children's positive development (e.g., Hamre, Hatfield, Pianta, & Jamil, 2014).

---

[2]This group is called the Collaborative for Understanding the Pedagogy of Infant/Toddler Development.

Though the robust body of research on attachment provides the grounding for informed hypotheses regarding its effects on EC professionals, we understand little about whether attachment affects EC teachers', or preservice teachers', attitudes or practices. We hypothesize, however, that EC education students' attachment impacts their tendencies to endorse supportive caregiving practices that demonstrate warmth and sensitivity, avoid over- or undercontrolling the child's behavior, and identify appropriate developmental expectations for children. Furthermore, attachment insecurity may limit students' abilities to gain knowledge and skills for working with young children, particularly if they are unaware of its effects on their learning and behavior. Understanding how adult attachment influences EC-related attitudes and skills may help university instructors better understand their students and help students better understand their own attitudes and responses toward children. The current study examines associations between adult attachment styles and the knowledge, attitudes, and skills that college students in child development courses have related to the development, care, and education of infants and toddlers. Specifically, we ask the following questions:

(1) How is attachment style associated with the career goals of students in child development courses?
(2) How is attachment style associated with child development students' knowledge and attitudes about infants, toddlers, and young children?
(3) Do attitudes mediate effects of attachment and knowledge on child development students' skills for working with infants and toddlers in developmentally supportive ways?

Method

Participants

The participants were 207 college students enrolled in child/human development and early education courses at four U.S. universities. The majority were juniors or seniors (68%), were female (92.7%), were between 18 and 23 years old (89.4%), and had been born in the United States (95.4%). The majority identified as White (68%), with 11% Black or African American, 12% Asian or Pacific Islander, 2% Native American, and 7% other; 8% of respondents identified as Hispanic/Latino. Respondents were not asked about income, but they did report on how they were paying for their education by indicating all non–mutually exclusive categories: 67% received support from family, 34% worked, 49% had scholarships or grants, 47% had loans, and 8% participated in work study indicating income eligibility.

Procedures

Students received an e-mail (in Spring 2014) inviting them to participate in a study of their attitudes, knowledge, and skills related to infant and toddler care and education. Students willing to participate clicked on a hyperlink to open a consent form, then another to open the survey on the Qualtrics website. The survey took about 45 min to complete and consisted of five sections: (a) background information, including demographics (age, race/ethnicity, country of origin, financial support for school), courses taken, and career aspirations (major, career goals after college); (b) attachment style; (c) knowledge of child development; (d) attitudes regarding early child development, care, and education aligned with the three competency dimensions; and (e) a set of 12 vignettes designed to assess students' likelihood of choosing developmentally supportive responses to realistic situations in infant/toddler care and education.

Measures

Table 1 presents psychometric properties of the measures of attachment styles, knowledge, and attitudes, including the number of items in each measure, descriptive and psychometric information

Table 1. Descriptive and psychometric information about each scale.

Construct	No. of items	α	M (SD)	Sample item	Source(s)
Attachment style					
Secure	8	.84	3.78 (0.65)	"I trust other people and I like it when other people can rely on me."	Attachment Styles Questionnaire (Van Oudenhoven et al., 2003)
Fearful	4	.88	2.70 (0.95)	"I am wary to get engaged in close relationships because I'm afraid to get hurt."	
Dismissive	5	.59	3.32 (0.58)	"I feel comfortable without having close relationships with other people."	
Preoccupied	7	.82	2.93 (0.76)	"I often wonder whether people like me."	
Knowledge of infant/toddler development					
Knowledge of individual differences	5	.52	76% (24%)	"Some normal babies do not enjoy being cuddled."	Seventeen items from the Knowledge of Infant Development Inventory (MacPhee, 1981); one new item on biting parallel to the hitting item
Developmentally appropriate expectations	10	.63	70% (21%)	"A baby is about 7 months old before he/she can reach for and grab things."	
Knowledge of effective discipline	3	.60	85% (26%)	"A good way to train children not to hit is to hit them."	
Attitudes about understanding and supporting relationships					
Support for children's bonds with caregivers	3	.65	3.25 (0.76)	"It is important for infants and toddlers to move up into a new room with new teachers and children when they achieve certain milestones, such as walking."	Beliefs About Infant Toddler Education and Care scale (BAITEC; Anderson & McMullen, 2013)
Support for the parent–child relationship	7	.83	3.96 (0.63)	"It is important that parents feel welcome to observe or come into the classroom at any time of the day."	One item from BAITEC; six new items developed for this study
Attitudes about understanding and supporting learning					
Optimistic view of early development					
Belief that development is self-righting	3	.41	3.40 (0.56)	"I believe that most children develop in a healthy way, at their own pace."	Trust in Organismic Development Scale (Landry et al., 2008b)
Belief that teachers must closely monitor development (reversed)	4	.68	3.71 (0.65)	"I think it's important to carefully supervise each child's development to make sure that it is normal."	
Belief that teachers have little influence on development (reversed)	6	.58	1.89 (0.54)	"The way children turn out often has little to do with how their child care teachers treated them."	Parental Opinion Survey (POS; Luster et al., 1989), reworded for teachers
Belief that early learning matters	5	.71	4.23 (0.60)	"Reading to a child before the child is 2 years old probably has little effect on the child." (reverse-scored)	Four items from the POS; one new item
Child-led supports for learning					
Endorsement of active, child-directed learning	5	.73	3.76 (0.59)	"Children learn best through active, self-initiated exploration."	Three items from the Parental Modernity Scale (Schaefer & Edgerton, 1985); two items from the Teaching Beliefs Scale (TBS; Stipek & Byler, 1997)
Endorsement of teacher-directed learning (reversed)	8	.67	3.10 (0.50)	"Teachers should not permit a child to leave an activity/task before finishing it."	Six items adapted from the TBS; two new items

(Continued)

Table 1. (Continued).

Construct	No. of items	α	M (SD)	Sample item	Source(s)
Belief that children should be treated as individuals	3	.71	3.19 (1.07)	"It is okay to let children opt out of an activity if they are not interested."	New items developed for this study
Attitudes about guidance of infant/toddler behavior					
Concern about spoiling	7	.91	2.30 (0.88)	"A child care teacher can spoil a baby by giving him/her a great deal of attention."	POS
Endorsement of strictness	4	.72	2.14 (0.69)	"Children who are held to strict rules grow up to be the best adults."	POS
Endorsement of spanking	4	.79	2.36 (0.91)	"Spanking teaches children right from wrong."	Adult-Adolescent Parenting Inventory (Bavolek & Keene, 2001)
Belief that all children should be treated the same	3	.81	3.19 (1.07)	"In order to be fair, child care teachers must treat all children alike."	New items developed for this study

pertaining to the current sample, sample items, and sources. Table 2 provides examples of the vignettes used to assess students' skills for responding to infants and toddlers in developmentally supportive ways. The measurement of each concept is described next.

Career goals

We asked students about their majors, career goals, and the populations with whom they wanted to work. For career goals, we listed 23 different human services careers that were common goals for those in child development courses (e.g., child care provider, elementary teacher, social worker, medical doctor, clinical psychologist). We let students choose all that applied and write in other career options. To identify those with a career goal involving work with young children, we selected those who identified the following careers: child care center director, child care provider, child life specialist, child psychologist, early child educator, early interventionist, home visitor, and preschool center director. We also asked respondents to rate the degree to which they wanted to work with children of various age groups (pregnant women, infants <1 year, toddlers 1–3 years, preschoolers 3–5 years, kindergartners, first through third graders, and fourth graders or older) with and without disabilities on a scale of 1 (*no desire to work with this population*) to 5 (*strong desire to work with this population*).

Table 2. Sample narrative vignettes and response options.

Dante is 8 months old and the youngest in your group of infants. He often cries throughout the day. Today, when you put him in his crib for nap time, he cries and cries.
  *You sit by Dante's crib and pat him, saying softly, "It can be hard to go to sleep alone. I'm right here." Then you sing a song you think he likes, hoping it will calm him.
  You leave Dante alone in his crib and let him cry it out so that he will learn how to soothe himself.
  You pick Dante up out of his crib, give him an extra bottle, and rock him until he falls asleep, then put him back into his crib.
You are an educator in a class of eight infants between 3 and 16 months. You are sitting near the pretend play area, watching Jasmine (13 months) and Elaine (11 months) play near each other in the corner with the kitchen toys. Jasmine is using a spoon and lifting it to a doll's mouth, and Elaine is filling a muffin tin with plastic fruit from a big bowl. Jasmine sticks her spoon into Elaine's tin and makes a stirring motion. Elaine watches her, then goes back to playing with the plastic fruit.
  *You scoot closer to the girls, and say, "Jasmine, do you think your baby might want a piece of fruit? Elaine, can you help Jasmine get some fruit ready for her baby?"
  You watch to make sure that both girls are still playing nicely with each other but do not see a need to say or do anything.
  You scoot closer to the girls and say, "Jasmine, can you move over a little, so that Elaine has more room to play?" Then you hand another doll to Elaine and say, "Here, you can feed your baby, too."

Note. Developmentally supportive responses are indicated with asterisks.

Attachment styles

Four attachment styles (secure, dismissive, preoccupied, and fearful) were assessed via the Attachment Styles Questionnaire (Van Oudenhoven, Hofstra, & Bakker, 2003), which measures general attachment rather than attachment to a specific person.

Competencies for working with infants, toddlers, and families

Participants completed measures of knowledge, attitudes, and practices/skills related to infant and toddler development and care. We used existing measures of knowledge and attitudes if possible and adapted or created items as necessary (described here). Measures were factor analyzed, and the resulting scales and factors are described here; attitude measures are organized by the competency they assessed. We developed the measure of practices/skills specifically for this study.

Knowledge of infant/toddler development. A total of 17 items from the Knowledge of Infant Development Inventory (KIDI; MacPhee, 1981) were used; an additional new item was designed for this study. This new item related to biting and was parallel to the hitting item. Students indicated whether they (a) agreed, (b) disagreed, or (c) were not sure about the accuracy of the 18 statements about caregiving practices and developmental processes and milestones during the first 2 years of life. Responses were then scored as either correct (1 point) or incorrect or unsure (0 points). Exploratory factor analysis of the current data resulted in a conceptually consistent three-factor solution. We labeled the factors Knowledge of Individual Differences, Developmentally Appropriate Expectations, and Knowledge of Effective Discipline. Subscales were then created using items that loaded most highly onto each of these three. A composite score was created by averaging the percentage of items correct, such that a higher score indicates more accurate knowledge of infant/toddler development.

Attitudes about infant/toddler development and care. A total of 56 Likert items tapped students' attitudes related to the three competencies that are the foci of this study (understanding and supporting relationships, understanding and supporting learning, and guidance of infant/toddler behavior). Students indicated their level of agreement with each statement (1 = *strongly disagree* to 5 = *strongly agree*). Many statements were reworded from existing instruments developed for parents so as to be appropriate for childless individuals as well as for parents.

A series of exploratory factor analyses followed by tests of inter-item reliability identified 13 conceptually coherent factors, each of which fell into one of the three competency dimensions we set out to assess. First we examined factors within sets of items that came from the same scale (e.g., all items from the Parental Modernity Scale), then we examined factors within our preconceptualized dimensions (e.g., all items related to support for autonomy). Next we analyzed all 56 items together. This analysis of all items produced factors more similar to the preconceptualized dimensions than to the factors within the preexisting scales; thus, we used factors that were derived from subsets of conceptually similar items that originated across measures. Using the sets of items that loaded most highly onto each factor (with each item belonging to only one set), we analyzed each set for reliability using Cronbach's alpha. We eliminated only items that loaded onto their own factor or without which the alphas were made higher. Each set of items, generated from the factors, was then made into a composite by averaging the scores, reversed as needed, so that a higher score indicates a higher endorsement of the specific attitude or belief. We describe each factor next, organized by competency.

Competency 1: Understanding and supporting relationships. Two factors tapped students' attitudes concerning the importance of infants' and toddlers' relationships with teachers and parents. The first factor, Support for Children's Bonds with Caregivers, drew its three items from the Beliefs About Infant Toddler Education and Care scale (BAITEC; Anderson & McMullen, 2013). It assessed attitudes about infants' and toddlers' needs for care from a small number of consistent adults. The second factor, Support for the Parent–Child Relationship, consisted of six newly created items plus one item from the BAITEC. These items assessed awareness of everyday teacher practices that can support the parent–child relationship.

Competency 2: Understanding and supporting learning. Seven factors emerged from items concerning infant/toddler learning, which can be organized into two overarching concepts: an optimistic view of early development and child-led supports for learning.

Optimistic view of early development. Items in the four factors within this conceptual domain were derived from two scales, the Trust in Organismic Development Scale (Landry, Smith, Swank, & Guttentag, 2008a) and the Parental Opinion Survey (POS; Luster & Rhoades, 1989). The first two factors were derived from the Trust in Organismic Development Scale items. The first of these, Belief That Development is Self-Righting, assessed the expectation that one need not worry much about normal, healthy child development because it tends to unfold naturally and at the child's individual pace. Conversely, the second factor, Belief That Teachers Must Closely Monitor Development, assessed the belief that healthy development depends on close adult supervision. Though these two beliefs were negatively correlated, they were not two ends of the same belief continuum but separate beliefs that could be held simultaneously. The items from the POS also formed two factors with opposing directionality. The first, Belief That Teachers Have Little Influence on Development, measured beliefs that teachers have little ultimate impact on the development of children in their care. The second factor, Belief That Early Learning Matters, tapped beliefs that infants and toddlers are engaged in important learning that will influence later development.

Composite scores for each of these four factors were created by averaging the items within them. The scores for Belief That Teachers Must Closely Monitor Development and Belief That Teachers Have Little Influence on Development were both reversed. Together the composite scores for these four factors created a conceptually and empirically coherent domain ($\alpha = .62$). Thus, for our final analyses, we created one variable representing this domain by averaging the z scores of the four factors.[3]

Child-led supports for learning. Items in the three factors related to this domain were largely from the Teaching Beliefs Scale (Stipek & Byler, 1997) and the Parental Modernity Scale (Schaefer & Edgerton, 1985), along with three newly created items focused on treating children as individuals. The factor Endorsement of Active, Child-Directed Learning assessed the valuing of child autonomy in play and exploration. Conversely, the factor Endorsement of Teacher-Directed Learning included statements expressing belief in the importance of high teacher control. The Belief That Children Should Be Treated as Individuals factor consisted of three new items stating that allowances should be made for individual differences.

Together these factors produced one conceptually and empirically coherent set of attitudes related to child-led supports for learning. We created composite scores for each of the factors by averaging associated items. The Endorsement of Teacher-Directed Learning composite score was reversed. Together these three composite scores created a conceptually coherent domain ($\alpha = .57$); thus, for our final analysis, we created one variable to represent the composite of these beliefs by averaging the z scores of the three factors.

Competency 3: Guidance of infant/toddler behavior. Four factors related to infant/toddler guidance were identified. The 18 items making up the four factors were largely from the POS and the Adult-Adolescent Parenting Inventory (Bavolek & Keene, 2001), along with newly created items related to treating children equally despite individual differences. Four factors emerged from these items: Three were explicitly related to discipline (Concern About Spoiling, Endorsement of Strictness,

---

[3]Although the individual factors had stronger alphas than the composites, it was necessary to develop fewer variables for our final regression models testing attachment, knowledge, and attitudes as simultaneous predictors of skills. Because of the covariance between the related composite scores, they would have competed with each other if entered separately in a regression framework, and the great number of variables would have limited our degrees of freedom.

and Endorsement of Spanking), and the final one was Belief That All Children Should be Treated the Same. The factor Concern About Spoiling included all seven statements from the spoiling subscale of the POS (Luster & Rhoades, 1989) and assessed beliefs that infants and toddlers will be spoiled if caregivers are highly responsive and physically affectionate. The four items from the POS discipline and control subscale produced our Endorsement of Strictness factor. High scores on these items indicated a valuing of obedience and firm discipline, even with babies. The Endorsement of Spanking factor assessed the belief that spanking is an effective form of discipline and was formed by four items from the Adult-Adolescent Parenting Inventory (Bavolek & Keene, 2001). Finally, the factor Belief That All Children Should be Treated the Same consisted of three new items assessing the belief that caregivers should treat all children alike regardless of their individual differences. Together the composite scores for these four factors formed one conceptually coherent dimension on beliefs about guidance ($\alpha = .63$); thus, we created a composite score by averaging the z scores.

Skills for responding in developmentally supportive ways. To assess infant/toddler education skills, we created 12 vignettes to elicit responses in six dimensions commonly observed in measures of interaction quality: sensitive responding to children's needs, support for autonomy, structure and limit setting, verbal communication, developmental stimulation, and fostering positive peer interactions (see Table 2 for examples). We used a multiple-choice format in which one response was more developmentally supportive whereas alternatives reflected low warmth/sensitivity, over/undercontrol by the teacher, or inappropriately high or low developmental expectations.[4] Stems and response options were piloted among a group of 15 infant/toddler and early education scholars and modified until at least 70% of these expert respondents chose the option designed as developmentally supportive. On average 82% of student respondents chose the developmentally supportive option (range = 70%–92%) for the vignettes in their final versions. Students' total interaction skill scores were calculated as the percentage of developmentally supportive responses selected ($M = 57.7\%$, $SD = 17.7\%$).

Analyses and results

Preliminary analyses

Of the 207 participants who completed the survey, 199 provided data for all measures. To reduce missing data, when creating the composite scores for attachment, knowledge, attitudes, and skills, we averaged the existing items answered by each respondent, as long as no more than one item was missing for that composite. In all subsequent analyses, if data were missing for an individual respondent, that respondent was eliminated from that specific analysis.

The participants came from four different universities and were pooled into a single sample. We used analysis of variance to explore possible differences between participants from different universities that could have potentially influenced our analyses. There were no differences between universities in participants' attachments, career goals related to working with young children, or several of the attitude dimensions. However, there were differences in the numbers of courses taken, percentage of KIDI items correct, four of the broad attitude dimensions, and the percentage of vignette responses that were developmentally supportive. Thus, we controlled for university in our final regression analyses using dummy variables for three of the four universities. The possible

---

[4]Defining developmentally appropriate practice in an ecologically valid way is necessarily a complex endeavor. Some controversy exists, for example, over whether such definitions can accommodate sociocultural context and children's unique developmental needs (see Raines & Johnston, 2003). We thank an anonymous reviewer for calling our attention to this controversy. We acknowledge that *appropriateness* in practice necessitates responsiveness to a particular child in a particular context. The concern for responsivity to cultural and individual factors is not unique to this study but is relevant to any effort to measure or define high-quality teaching practices.

Analytic approach

All analyses were conducted in SPSS. First we describe mean levels and associations between students' coursework and career goals, knowledge of infant/toddler development, attitudes toward infant/toddler care and education, and caregiving skills. Next we examine associations among students' attachment styles and their knowledge, attitudes, skills, and career goals, including differences between those who did and did not intend to work with young children. Finally, we use a series of regression models to examine the mediating role of attitudes in the associations between attachment styles and caregiving skills and between knowledge and skills. We examined these relations both for the whole sample of student respondents (reflecting the breadth of students who may be in entry-level courses that include child development and family content) and for the subgroup of respondents who planned to have careers involving work with young children (reflecting the students likely to be in upper division or major-only courses focused on young children).

Career goals

A total of 82 respondents (40%) indicated that they intended to pursue careers working with young children in positions such as child care center director (9.2% of 207), child care provider (14%), child life specialist (8.2%), child therapist (2.4%), EC educator (22.2%), early interventionist (6.3%), and preschool center director (4.3%). See Table 3 for the degree to which respondents wanted to work with children of various ages with and without disabilities.

Table 3. Descriptive statistics and correlations with attachment for populations of professional interest.

Population of professional interest	M (SD)	% Rating 4 or 5	Security	Fearfulness	Dismissiveness	Preoccupation
Pregnant women	2.58 (1.19)	19.9%	−.072	−.018	.016	.044
Parents of typically developing children	3.26 (1.16)	42.4%	.088	−.076	−.063	.056
Parents of children with special needs	3.16 (1.24)	43.6%	.180	−.260*	.118	−.167
Infants (<1 year) who are typically developing	3.19 (1.36)	47.1%	−.027	−.024	.044	.038
Infants (<1 year) with special needs	3.05 (1.37)	43.7%	.172	−.201†	.015	−.214†
Toddlers (1–3 years) who are typically developing	3.50 (1.25)	57.3%	.195†	−.150	.035	−.069
Toddlers (1–3 years) with special needs	3.26 (1.30)	46.8%	.286**	−.264*	.112	−.231*
Preschoolers (3–5 years) who are typically developing	3.57 (1.22)	58.6%	.151	−.129	−.117	−.078
Preschoolers (3–5 years) with special needs	3.39 (1.30)	52.2%	.100	−.201†	−.031	−.178
Kindergartners who are typically developing	3.61 (1.26)	60.8%	.197†	−.119	−.250*	−.073
Kindergartners with special needs	3.36 (1.33)	51.4%	.233*	−.267*	−.032	−.242*
First through third graders who are typically developing	3.39 (1.34)	53.2%	.171	−.143	−.060	.006
First through third graders with special needs	3.18 (1.34)	45.3%	.178	−.200†	−.019	−.152
Fourth graders or older who are typically developing	3.07 (1.33)	45.9%	.121	−.151	.028	.034
Fourth graders or older who have special needs	2.95 (1.31)	40.0%	.161	−.241*	.067	−.123

Students' average desire to work with each population, from No Desire (1) to Strong Desire (5) (n = 202). Correlations with attachment for students whose career goals involved young children (n = 82).

†$p < .10$. *$p < .05$. **$p < .01$.

Associations between attachment and students' education and career goals

To investigate effects of students' attachment on education and career goals, we tested associations of the attachment subscales with courses taken; whether students' career goals involved work with young children; and, for those who wanted to work in EC, the specific populations with whom they most wanted to work. We suspected that those with more secure attachments would be more willing to work with populations that might be perceived as requiring closer teacher–child relationships or a higher degree of emotional availability, such as toddlers and/or children with special needs.

Courses taken

The average number of child-related courses taken across all participants was 1.85 (SD = 1.49), with a range of 0 to 6. The average number of more general human development or education classes was 2.31 (SD = 1.91), ranging from 0 to 9. Attachment fearfulness was negatively correlated with the number of courses taken related to children (r = −.19, p < .01) and with human development or education courses (r = −.22, p < .01).

Career goals

Students whose career goals focused on EC had significantly higher attachment security (M_{EC} = 3.89 vs. M_{other} = 3.70; t = 2.07, p = .04) and lower attachment fearfulness (M_{EC} = 2.52 vs. M_{other} = 2.82; t = −2.25, p = .03) compared to students who did not have career goals involving young children.

Populations of interest

On average, among those who had EC career goals, students had less desire to work with children who have special needs than with those who are typically developing. Furthermore, paired-samples t tests indicated a lower average desire to work with children with special needs compared to those who are typically developing for children in most age groups: toddlers (t = 2.49, p = .02), preschoolers (t = 2.38, p = .02), and kindergartners (t = 2.16, p = .03). The difference for infants approached significance (t = 1.85, p = .07).

For students with EC career goals (n = 82), we correlated attachment scores with desire to work with each population. Attachment security was positively correlated with desire to work with toddlers and kindergartners, and children with special needs (see Table 3). Fearfulness and preoccupation were negatively correlated with desire to work with those with special needs.

Associations between attachment and knowledge of infant/toddler development

Among all participants, attachment security had a small positive correlation with the percentage of correct KIDI items (r = .15, p = .04) and particularly with knowledge of effective discipline (r = .24, p < .01); however, attachment was not related to knowledge for the group of students with EC career goals.

Associations between attachment and attitudes toward infant/toddler care and education

To examine the influence of students' attachment on attitudes related to infant/toddler development, care, and education, we examined correlations between each of the attachment subscales and each of the attitude scales for the whole sample and for those with EC career goals. As seen in Table 4, with a few notable exceptions, the patterns were very similar for both groups.

Attachment is associated with attitudes about relationships

For the whole sample, attachment security was related to endorsement of practices that support parent–child and child–caregiver relationships, whereas fearfulness was inversely associated with

Table 4. Correlations between attachment and knowledge, attitudes, and skills related to infant/toddler development, care, and education for all respondents and those whose career goal involved work with young children.

Competency dimension	Component knowledge, attitude, or skill	All participants (n = 204)					Those whose career goals involved work with young children (n = 82)				
		Security	Fearfulness	Dismissiveness	Preoccupation		Security	Fearfulness	Dismissiveness	Preoccupation	
Knowledge	Knowledge of individual differences	.108	-.065	-.078	.100		.138	-.125	-.024	.060	
	Developmentally appropriate expectations	.077	.037	-.041	.043		.007	.066	-.051	.105	
	Knowledge of effective discipline	.236**	-.084	.057	.021		.165	-.158	.001	.048	
Support relationships	Support teacher–child relationships	.157*	-.180*	-.158*	.035		.113	-.114	-.119	-.075	
	Support parent–child relationships	.351**	-.225**	-.014	-.049		.378**	-.341**	-.025	-.313**	
Understand learning	Development is self-righting	.297**	-.103	.085	.073		.336**	-.214†	-.036	-.069	
	Teachers must monitor development	.141*	-.004	-.041	.056		.173	.024	.074	-.132	
	Teachers have little influence	-.198**	.184**	.102	.002		-.236*	.129	.169	.074	
	Early learning matters	.324**	-.183**	.031	-.005		.351**	-.140	.039	-.103	
Support learning	Endorse child-led learning	.360**	-.190**	.031	.046		.350**	-.237*	-.090	-.105	
	Endorse teacher-directed learning	-.054	.242**	.212**	-.008		.084	.179	.170	-.101	
	Treat children as individuals	.280**	-.233**	-.091	.067		.241*	-.320**	-.220†	.014	
Guidance of infant/toddler behavior (strictness and control) skills	Treat children the same	.037	.046	.150*	-.038		.028	.014	.104	.004	
	Concern about spoiling	-.046	.123†	.105	-.021		-.005	.054	.141	-.137	
	Endorse strict discipline	-.124†	.256**	.152*	.115		-.123	.306**	.231*	.165	
	Endorse spanking	-.143*	.211**	.105	-.043		-.205†	.240*	.172	.174	
	Total interaction skills	.127†	-.166*	-.143*	-.003		.066	-.236*	-.139	-.233*	

†p < .10. *p < .05. **p < .01.

these endorsements. Dismissiveness was inversely associated with support for caregiver–child relationships but had no association with attitudes about parent–child relationships. As presented in Table 4, for the group with EC goals, attachment was unrelated to attitudes about practices that support the caregiver–child relationship, but security, fearfulness, and preoccupation were all associated in the expected directions with attitudes about supporting the parent–child relationship.

Attachment is associated with attitudes about learning
Attachment security was positively related to most attitudes thought to be supportive of children's development and learning. For example, security was positively correlated with more hopeful views of the nature of development and learning, including the attitudes that early learning matters for long-term development, that teachers can influence development, and that development is in general self-righting. Among the total sample, but not those with EC career goals, fearfulness was positively related to the belief that teachers have little influence on children's development and negatively related to the belief that early learning matters for later development. For both groups attachment security was related to attitudes about practices supportive of development. For the total sample, fearfulness and dismissiveness were associated with endorsement of teacher-directed learning.

Attachment is associated with attitudes about guidance of infant/toddler behavior
Attachment fearfulness was positively associated with attitudes endorsing greater strictness and control in infant/toddler guidance for both the total group and those with EC career goals; attachment security was inversely associated with these attitudes. In the total sample, dismissiveness was related to stronger attitudes in treating children the same despite individual differences; in the EC career group, dismissiveness was related to endorsing strict discipline.

Mechanisms of the influence of attachment and knowledge on interaction skills
To examine influences of students' attachment on skills for working with infants and toddlers, we treated students' choices of developmentally supportive responses in the vignettes as indicators of skills. Total interaction skill scores were correlated with students' knowledge of infant/toddler development (KIDI score) for the total sample ($r = .22$, $p < .01$) and those who planned to work with young children ($r = .35$, $p < .01$). As presented in Table 4, interaction skills scores were also associated with attachment. For both the overall and EC career samples, attachment fearfulness had the most robust association with interaction skills. Dismissiveness was inversely associated with interaction skills for the total sample, and preoccupation was inversely associated with interaction skills for those with EC career goals.

Attitudes as a mediator of attachment and interaction skills
Next we used linear regression to test whether attitudes mediated the associations between attachment fearfulness and interaction skills, controlling for knowledge of child development and university site. We used a composite score composed of the attitudes related to each competency dimension: understanding and supporting relationships, understanding and supporting learning, and guidance of infant/toddler behavior (see Table 4 for the alignment between specific attitudes and competency dimensions). First we used linear regression to establish the predictive relationships between attachment fearfulness and each of the attitude composites (see Table 5). Then we fit a series of regression models to test the effects of attachment on interaction skills, controlling for knowledge and university site, and systematically added the attitudes composites related to each competency to determine whether the effect of attachment fearfulness was diminished when each attitude was added (Table 6). We used the Sobel test of mediation significance to determine whether each attitude composite mediated effects of attachment fearfulness on interaction skills.

Table 5. Results of regression models (unstandardized betas, standard errors) for the effects of attachment fearfulness on attitude composite scores, controlling knowledge.

Model parameters	Model A: Support teacher–child relation	Model B: Support parent–child relation	Model C: Nature of learning: optimistic	Model D: Support for learning: child focused	Model E: Guidance: strictness and control
All participants ($n = 202$)					
Intercept (composite Zscore)	−0.06 (0.08)	−0.10 (0.09)	−0.09 (0.08)	−0.24** (0.08)	−0.18* (0.08)
University controls					
Attachment fearfulness (Zscore)	−0.15* (0.07)	−0.21** (0.07)	−0.15* (0.07)	−0.26*** (0.07)	0.24*** (0.07)
Knowledge (Zscore)	0.20** (0.07)	0.17* (0.07)	0.43*** (0.07)	0.34*** (0.07)	−0.29*** (0.07)
Model fit					
R^2	0.19	0.09	0.21	0.27	0.24
F	9.10**	3.75***	10.31***	14.35***	11.96***
Those whose career goals involve work with young children ($n = 82$)					
Intercept (composite Zscore)	0.25 (0.15)	0.20 (0.14)	0.00 (0.15)	0.08 (0.14)	−0.47** (0.14)
University controls					
Attachment fearfulness (Zscore)	−0.10 (0.11)	−0.33** (0.10)	−0.18 (0.11)	−0.34** (0.10)	0.13 (0.10)
Knowledge (Zscore)	0.38** (0.13)	0.09 (0.12)	0.43** (0.13)	0.44*** (0.11)	−0.33** (0.12)
Model fit					
R^2	0.26	0.18	0.20	0.34	0.38
F	4.88**	3.01*	3.49**	7.05***	8.39***

Note. The dependent variable and predictors are each in Zscore units so that betas represent effect sizes.
*$p < .05$. **$p < .01$. ***$p < .001$.

For the whole sample, there was evidence of mediation paths from attachment fearfulness through attitudes to students' interaction skills (see Figure 1); effects of students' fearfulness on interaction skills were mediated by attitudes related to supporting the parent–child relationship ($Z = 2.06$, $p < .05$) and showed a trend toward mediation through attitudes related to supporting the teacher–child relationship ($Z = 1.74$, $p = .08$). Attachment fearfulness was also mediated by attitudes related to child-focused supports for learning ($Z = 1.97$, $p < .05$) but only a trend of mediation through optimistic views of development ($Z = 1.81$, $p = .07$). Finally, the effect of fearfulness was mediated by attitudes regarding strictness and control in the guidance of infant/toddler behavior ($Z = 2.84$, $p < .01$).

For students with EC career goals, there was a direct effect of attachment fearfulness on interaction skills at the $p < .10$ level (see Table 6) but only one significant mediating path through attitudes toward supporting learning through child-focused strategies ($Z = 2.32$, $p < .05$). Attachment fearfulness predicted attitudes related to supporting parent–child relationships, but these attitudes did not mediate the association between attachment fearfulness and interaction skills.

Attitudes as a mediator of knowledge and skills

Next we tested whether the effect of students' knowledge of infant/toddler development (KIDI scores) on interaction skills was mediated by attitudes. For the whole sample (see Figure 2), attitudes related to an optimistic view of development ($Z = 2.97$, $p < .01$), child-focused supports for learning ($Z = 2.09$, $p < .05$), and strict and controlling guidance ($Z = 3.21$, $p < .001$) each mediated the association between knowledge and interaction skills; there was a trend toward mediation through supporting parent–child relationships ($Z = 1.84$, $p = .07$). For those with EC career goals, child-focused supports for learning ($Z = 2.49$, $p < .05$) and strict and controlling guidance ($Z = 1.99$, $p < .05$) mediated effects of knowledge on interaction skills.

Table 6. Results of regression models (unstandardized betas, standard errors) for the effects of attachment fearfulness, knowledge of development, and attitude composites on interaction skills.

	All participants (n = 204)				Those whose career goals involved work with young children (n = 82)			
Model parameters	Model A: Baseline	Model B: Relation	Model C: Learning	Model D: Guidance	Model E: Baseline	Model F: Relation	Model G: Learning	Model H: Guidance
Intercept	57.56**	58.14***	59.07***	56.40***	65.53***	64.64***	64.85***	62.46***
	(1.55)	(1.50)	(1.48)	(1.47)	(2.78)	(2.84)	(2.63)	(2.86)
University controls								
Attachment fearfulness	−2.81*	−1.52	−1.02	−1.22	−3.92†	−3.70†	−1.33	−3.04
	(1.22)	(1.22)	(1.19)	(1.19)	(1.98)	(2.10)	(2.02)	(1.91)
Knowledge	3.48**	2.14†	0.36	1.52	4.76*	3.29*	1.64	2.60
	(1.27)	(1.27)	(1.33)	(1.26)	(2.33)	(2.46)	(2.47)	(2.34)
Supporting teacher– child relationships		3.88*** (1.30)				3.97† (2.20)		
Supporting parent– child relationships		3.42** (1.21)				−0.48 (2.33)		
Nature of learning: optimistic			4.96** (1.46)				−1.04 (2.29)	
Supporting learning: child focused			3.27* (1.41)				8.09** (2.54)	
Guidance: strictness and control				−9.67*** (1.90)				−9.58** (3.34)
Model fit								
R^2	.11	.15	.22	.21	.24	.27	.35	.32
R^2 change from baseline model		.07***	.12***	.11**		.04	.11**	.08**
F	4.55**	5.85**	7.88***	8.58**	4.41**	3.67**	5.14***	5.43***
F change from baseline model		8.23***	14.60***	25.81***		1.63	5.53**	8.24**

Note. Predictors are each in Zscore units so that betas represent the effect of 1 *SD*.
†p < .10. *p < .05. **p < .01. ***p < .001.

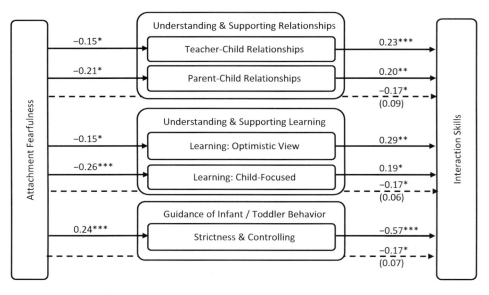

Figure 1. Mediation of the effect of attachment fearfulness on interaction skills through students' attitudes for all respondents (n = 199). Solid lines represent direct effects, whereas dashed lines represent mediation.

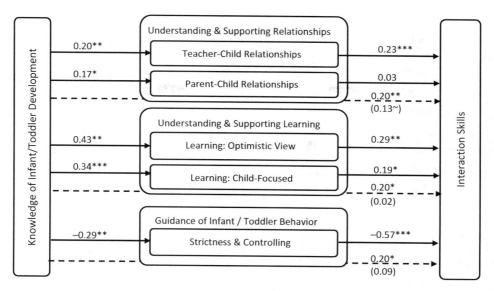

Figure 2. Mediation of the effect of knowledge on interaction skills through students' attitudes for all respondents (*n* = 199). Solid lines represent direct effects, whereas dashed lines represent mediation.

Discussion

The purpose of this study was to investigate associations among university EC students' attachment styles; their expectations regarding their future professional roles; and their knowledge, attitudes, and skills related to working with infants and toddlers. Our results demonstrate that EC students' attachment styles are related to their career interests and to their knowledge, attitudes, and skills relevant to infant/toddler development and care. Based on our results, we propose a conceptual model of a mediated relationship between students' adult attachment styles and caregiving skill via attitudes about children's early development and relationships. Together, but with some limitations, these results and the proposed model point to future research directions and implications for university teaching to prepare the future teachers of infants and young children.

Students who want to work with young children are more securely attached than others

Students whose career goals focused on working with young children reported a more secure attachment style than those wishing to work with others. This is consistent with the findings of Horppu and Ikonen-Varila (2004) that secure students were more likely than dismissing students to identify working with young children as their first career choice. It is also consistent with the findings of Riley (2009), which showed that although insecure attachment appeared to be a motivator for entering the teaching field in search of reparative experiences in relationships with children, those who wanted to work with younger students (in this case elementary compared to secondary students) were less anxious and less avoidant. In the current study, greater security and less fearfulness were positively related to the desire to work with younger children and those with disabilities. This addresses, in part, concerns within the field that educators with insecure attachments should not work with infants and toddlers (e.g., Berlin, 2012); in fact, there seems to be some self-selection at work, considering that greater attachment fearfulness was inversely associated with the number of child development courses taken and with the desire to work with younger children. According to theory, both fearfulness and avoidance stem from an internalization of early adverse experiences in the family. These early adverse experiences result in a disturbance in the capacity to form interpersonal attachments due to an internalized aversion to strong feelings (Bartholomew, 1990). Given that infants and young children are dependent on adults and express their needs with behaviors that can be interpreted as negative (i.e., clinginess, crying, tantrums), this self-selection effect is not surprising. Thus, it is possible that attachment has its first effects on students' knowledge, attitudes, and skills by influencing their career goals and related coursework.

Attachment security is associated with a positive orientation toward working with children who have special needs

Scores on attachment security were positively related to expressed interests in working with children who have special needs. Conversely, higher fearful or preoccupied attachment scores were associated with less interest in working with these children. This negative orientation toward working with children who have special needs may be related to fearful and preoccupied students' greater anxiety in general, which may be amplified when considering the challenges of working with a population about whom they likely have limited knowledge or whom they perceive to be more dependent on adults. According to Bartholomew (1990), fearful adults are averse to strong needs in self and others and thus deactivate and avoid negative feelings and intimate relationships. Perhaps the strong dependency needs of young children with special needs overwhelm adults with fearful attachment styles, leaving them to feel ineffective and helpless. The positive orientation toward working with children with special needs on the part of more secure students may be related to the higher social self-efficacy characteristic of individuals with a secure internal working model. This model may help students anticipate successfully meeting the needs of vulnerable children. It will be important to further investigate associations among attachment styles, knowledge, confidence, and social self-efficacy in order to inform the preparation of EC professionals who will work with vulnerable populations.

Attachment security is associated with more knowledge and more developmentally supportive attitudes

Security of attachment was positively associated with knowledge about infant/toddler development. Moreover, for the group with EC career goals, though attachment was not associated with attitudes about the caregiver–child relationship, it was related to attitudes about the parent–child relationship. Self-selection into EC emphasis areas may have limited attachment style variability among these students, or child development content in courses they have taken may have effectively addressed practices related to caregiver–child relationships, eliminating the effect of attachment security on these attitudes. Courses may not have sufficiently addressed parent–child relationships or professionals' roles in supporting these, however, leaving this attitude more vulnerable to the effects of students' own attachment styles.

Attachment security and fearfulness were consistently associated, in opposing directions, with attitudes about learning. Secure attachment is related to positive views of self and others and the ability to coherently reflect on the influences on one's own life (Bartholomew & Horowitz, 1991). It is not surprising, then, that those with secure attachments expressed more optimism about children's tendencies to make good choices and develop in positive ways. Also, they believed that as teachers, they will be responsible for influencing the lives of children in their care. Students who scored high on fearfulness tended to minimize the importance of adults in the lives of children and even the importance of the early years, which is consistent with their tendency to minimize the importance of intimate relationships. Fearfulness appears to have consistent negative associations with the attitudes and skills needed for working with infants, toddlers, and families, and its influence on skills—the ability to choose the most developmentally supportive response—appears to be largely mediated through attitudes.

Note that fearfulness and dismissiveness were associated with the endorsement of strict discipline and spanking, whereas more secure beliefs were inversely related to endorsement of these practices. These results are consistent with research showing that parents with insecure attachments score higher on the structure dimension of Baumrind's (1973) parenting styles, exerting more control, expecting more mature behavior from children, and showing less support for children's autonomy (Pearson et al., 1994). This may reflect differences in students' expectations for harsh or controlling interactions in close relationships. These findings extend Rholes and colleagues' (1997) report that insecure college students tend to endorse stricter disciplinary practices and those of Morris-Rothschild and Brassard (2006), who found that teachers with higher anxiety and avoidance approached classroom conflict management with less compromise and less integration of the needs of students and teachers into conflict resolution. Our findings suggest that this pattern is also evident among undergraduates with EC career interests. Whereas dismissing and fearful adult attachment styles both reflect the minimization of the importance of close relationships, a fearful attachment style represents a distortion in the balance between dependence and independence and a fear of losing boundaries (Bartholomew, 1990). According to George and Solomon (2008), adults have a biological drive to care for and protect children, called the *caregiving system*, which is activated by child distress. Adults with fearful attachment styles may experience anxiety and helplessness in response to children's distress, which dysregulates their caregiving system and results in harsher discipline strategies.

Conceptual model: attitudes mediate the effects of attachment and knowledge on interaction skills

We intended to conduct a theoretically driven examination of how students' attachment styles are related to their knowledge, attitudes, and skills for working with infants, toddlers, and their families within three of the competency dimensions deemed important for the infant/toddler workforce. Based on our results, and informed by attachment theory, we propose the conceptual model presented in Figure 3.

Our data are correlational and cross-sectional and thus cannot provide any causal conclusions. Therefore, we look to attachment theory to provide a conceptual explanation for how individuals' attachment style can influence knowledge, attitudes, and skills. This conceptual model also provides us with a roadmap for future investigation.

Attachment security and fearfulness both predicted, in opposite directions, students' career goals and related educational choices (i.e., courses taken). It is important to keep in mind that both securely and insecurely attached individuals place a high value on relationships, yet because individuals with an

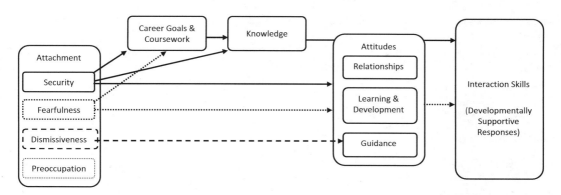

Figure 3. Proposed conceptual model. Solid lines represent effects of attachment security, dotted lines represent effects of attachment fearfulness, and dashed lines represent effects of attachment dismissiveness.

insecure attachment style are likely to have a history of inconsistently met security needs, they adopt strategies of either deactivating the attachment system to avoid emotional aspects of relationships to minimize anxiety or activating it in a hypervigilant way, which can result in consistently elevated anxiety. We propose that because secure and preoccupied individuals explicitly value attachment relationships, they are more oriented toward working with children, whereas dismissing and fearful individuals are less likely to choose a career working with young children; these choices represent consistency with attachment-based strategies of coping with relationship-related anxieties.

We propose an indirect influence of attachment on students' knowledge of infant/toddler development, as previous knowledge influences subsequent learning (Ambrose et al., 2010; Bauer, 2009). Internal working models operate as interpretive schemas, and it is much easier to learn information that confirms one's schemas than information that could disconfirm them (Atherton, 2013; Weston, Blagov, Harenski, Kilts, & Hamann, 2006). This may explain why dismissing individuals, who likely had their own bids for nurturance rebuffed, adopt a strategy of minimizing the importance of nurturance and child-centered approaches to caregiving (Bartholomew, 1990). When faced with a toddler who is upset, a dismissing individual may interpret crying or tantrums as behavior problems to control rather than as a sign that soothing and support in self-regulation are needed. Individuals with a fearful attachment style may have experienced having their own attachment needs rejected along with overwhelming negative affect from caregivers (Bartholomew, 1990). As a result, they may develop helpless caregiving representations and find themselves flooded with negative emotion and unable to respond to children in sensitive ways (George & Solomon, 2008; Solomon & George, 2011). Thus, we found that stricter, less developmentally supportive responses are preferred by insecure individuals. A secure individual is more likely to perceive a child's behavior as indicating his or her needs and have a script for comforting and helping him or her to regulate his or her behavior.

Our conceptual model also proposes that attachment directly influences attitudes about relationships, learning and development, and guidance. Individuals with fearful or dismissing internal working models are more likely to have negative models of others and the social world; thus, fearfulness and dismissiveness are associated with less developmentally supportive attitudes in these areas. For example, negative working models may include assumptions that children are hedonistic and will do whatever they can get away with to satisfy their own needs; thus, controlling guidance strategies are necessary. Conversely, individuals with secure beliefs may have working models characterized by assumptions that despite being immature and relatively self-centered, children have essentially prosocial orientations but need the guidance of supportive adults to develop social and self-regulatory skills. Examination of these hypotheses will await longitudinal studies that can examine moderating effects of attachment on actual openness to learning from coursework on child development and practices that support it.

Our model proposes that both attitudes and knowledge influence students' interaction skills, but knowledge may be partially mediated by attitudes. In this study, our findings suggest that security and fearfulness influence attitudes about relationships, learning and development, and guidance, whereas dismissiveness influences guidance specifically. Fearfulness appears to have the most consistent effect on both attitudes and interaction skills, and the effect on skills may be largely mediated by attitudes. Attitudes associated with internal working models may constrain or facilitate students' learning about children's development, learning, and family relationships as well as students' learning of interaction skills for working with children and families.

Limitations and future directions

We recognize that our study has limitations as well as strengths. For one, the study population represents, at present, only the 25% of the future infant/toddler workforce who will have a 4-year degree (National Survey of Early Care and Education Project Team, 2013). This more educated group of EC teachers is likely to have come from families facing less economic stress and home environments more conducive to secure attachment (Diener, Casady, & Wright, 2003).

This convenience sample was composed of students from four universities, and results should be interpreted with caution. Our proposed model of how attachment affects the knowledge, attitudes, and skills of the future infant/toddler workforce should be empirically tested with a larger and more diverse sample. This may help to resolve some of the low reliabilities of some of the factors found in the current sample and enable us to test site-level variations in factors. Furthermore, as we saw in our preliminary analyses, baseline levels of knowledge, attitudes, and skills are likely to vary in American subcultures, which will be reflected in university populations across U.S. regions. Thus, in addition to simply controlling for these differences, it would be useful to carefully address them from a sociocultural perspective and by using multilevel model techniques and to consider the implications of the results for higher education pedagogy.

Furthermore, a longitudinal design is needed to examine possible effects of adult attachment on changes in students' knowledge, attitudes, and skills, that is, learning produced via university coursework and other educational experiences. We expect that students' attachment styles will predict their choice of coursework, which will influence what they learn; then among those who choose courses related to infant/toddler development, their attachment styles could buffer or enhance their gains in knowledge, or change in attitudes, either of which could mediate the path from adult attachment to students' interaction skills with young children. Finally, we acknowledge that the use of vignettes with correct and incorrect responses constrained our ability to measure how well students would actually respond to children with particular developmental needs in particular social and cultural contexts. In future research, we need to move beyond self-reports to actual observations of infant and toddler teaching in real-world settings.

Furthermore, our multi-university group began this project with the acknowledgment that although all of the nine competencies we identified must inform EC practice and thus coursework, it was not feasible to construct a survey tapping student knowledge, attitudes, and skill in all competencies at once; thus, we chose to focus on three. One of the competencies we had identified was diversity and inclusion. The need to infuse respect for cultural diversity in EC professionals' understandings of the causes and outcomes associated with particular family and child care practices is great (Dahlberg, Moss, & Pence, 2013; Edwards & Raikes, 2002). It is important that future research include measures that permit the assessment of instructors' and students' knowledge, attitudes, and skills related to cultural and ability-related diversity. A number of important research questions could be posed. For example, perhaps secure attachment, because it is based on fundamental trust in others, is positively associated with openness to family diversity and a willingness to reflect on the appropriateness of specific child care practices for children of various cultural and family structure backgrounds. The same may be true concerning openness to individual differences, including differences in ability.

Pedagogical implications for preparing infant/toddler professionals

Our findings raise important questions for EC teacher education. Some argue, given the importance of teacher–child interactions, that attachment security is a critical disposition for infant/toddler teachers (Berlin, 2012). Although further research is needed, our findings suggest that adult attachment may also be important in the EC workforce and preservice teachers' education. Adults who remain insecure may "be less creative and flexible, and more defensive" (van Ijzendoorn, Juffer, & Duyvesteyn, 1995, p. 245), and faculty preparing future EC teachers may need to watch for indicators of difficulty in students' work with children and find ways to support better child–teacher interactions. Though Kilmann, Carranza, and Vendemia (2006) demonstrated that systematic intervention can significantly improve insecure college students' attachment-related beliefs and emotions, changing preservice teachers' attachment is often not a realistic goal; attachment representations, built over time, are relatively stable (Waters, Weinfield, & Hamilton, 2000). There is also a cultural issue to keep in mind as one considers intervention: it is not known whether there are cultural differences among college students in the strength of relations between adult attachment styles and the knowledge, attitudes, and skills students bring to work with children, especially infants and toddlers. It may be that in some cultural groups, attachment styles are less predictive than we found, perhaps because traditions allow less leeway for divergences in ways of caring for the youngest age groups.

A systematic approach to effectively incorporating knowledge of students' characteristics and dispositions into pedagogical considerations would require faculty members to undertake multiple steps, including (a) reliable assessment of attachment and other psychosocial factors; (b) adaptation of instruction to student characteristics; and (c) sensitive supervision designed to impart knowledge, develop skills and confidence, and enhance reflective functioning (RF). To date, no models that incorporate psychosocial factors that college students bring to EC training programs have been developed. However, in one study, attachment-focused, manualized intervention with insecure college students did significantly improve relationship beliefs, self-esteem, and regulation of anger compared to a no-intervention control group (Kilmann, Urbaniak, & Parnell, 2006). Although this intervention did not specifically target EC education students, it does indicate that attachment-related beliefs and emotions are amenable to change. The parenting literature also suggests that instead of targeting parents' working models directly, interventions can effectively target sensitive behaviors and RF (Slade, 2007; Suchman et al., 2010; van Ijzendoorn, 1995); perhaps this is also the case for preservice teachers. As van Ijzendoorn (1995) concluded from a meta-analysis of attachment interventions, increasing adults' sensitive behavior does not necessarily influence the teacher's attachment representations but could reinforce the importance of sensitivity. For example, the experience of noticing children's attachment-related cues and responding contingently can be rewarded via the impact on children's behavior and development, which in turn may enable teachers with insecure adult attachment to revise their beliefs about the importance of attachment relationships.

Targeting RF may be another effective way of supporting preservice teachers' abilities to notice infant cues and respond sensitively. RF is the ability to recognize thoughts, emotions, and intentions in oneself and others; link these mental states to behavior; and take another's perspective to understand his or her behavior (Fonagy, Steele, Steele, Moran, & Higgitt, 1991; Slade, 2005). Adults higher in RF are more likely to reflect on a child's internal experience (Slade, Grienenberger, Bernbach, Levy, & Locker, 2005) and respond sensitively to child behavior, fostering secure attachment (Kelly, Slade, & Grienenberger, 2005; Slade et al., 2005; Stacks et al., 2014). King and La Paro (2015) found that preschool teachers' use of mental state talk with children (an indicator of RF) was linked to indicators of classroom quality using the Classroom Assessment Scoring System (CLASS). Furthermore, parenting interventions targeting RF have improved parent sensitivity and child attachment (Suchman et al., 2010). RF training could be a central component in a model for educating infant/toddler professionals via higher education. Other disciplines utilize person-centered models in higher education that carefully consider students' backgrounds (Clouston & Whitcombe, 2005). These models include carefully crafting opportunities for cognitive dissonance that make students more aware of their own biases and reactions and provide opportunities to question their assumptions and attitudes (Neighbor, 1992). Such a model could be developed for future EC professionals, considering students' attachments and attitudes and utilizing cases or problems that produce cognitive dissonance as opportunities for RF training.

The National Center for Research on Early Childhood Education (NCRECE) systematically studies strategies that promote responsive teaching of young children, including the ability to respond in a supportive way to children's emotional, behavioral, and cognitive cues (Hamre et al., 2014). NCRECE research shows that future teachers need opportunities to observe and practice responsive teaching and receive ongoing coaching (Fixsen, Naoom, Blase, Friedman, & Wallace, 2005). Observing exemplar teacher videos has been associated with growth in emotionally supportive teacher behaviors (Pianta et al., 2014). University EC education faculty who teach infant/toddler courses may consider focusing on increasing knowledge and skills related specifically to developmentally supportive teacher–child interactions, including reading and responding to cues with sensitivity and warmth. Courses should include video examples and practice observing child cues and adult sensitive responses.

Another approach is offered by EC mental health consultation (Heller et al., 2012), which has been shown to improve teacher RF (Virmani, Masyn, Thompson, Conners-Burrow, & Mansell, 2013; Virmani & Ontai, 2010), teacher–child interactions, and child outcomes (Alkon, Ramler, & MacLennan, 2003; Heller et al., 2012; Perry, Allen, Brennan, & Bradley, 2010; Virmani et al., 2013). Early Childhood Education (ECE) faculty could build reflective supervision into student teaching by modeling a reflection; facilitating wondering about the meaning behind child behaviors; and asking about students' emotional reactions to case studies, vignettes, and video examples (Slade, 2007).

Conclusion

The attachment security of students studying child development is related to their knowledge, attitudes, and skills for working with infants, toddlers, and their families. Though higher education is unlikely to change students' attachment styles, experts must develop a student-centered pedagogical approach that is sensitive to students' relationship histories and that can help them understand the effects of those histories on their own attitudes about and responses to children—be they other people's children if they do enter the EC workforce, their own children if they are or become parents, or children they will encounter in other settings. Such a model could incorporate current understandings of attachment interventions that effectively support change in adults' attachment-related behaviors and ultimately support children's optimal development.

References

Adam, E. K., Gunnar, M. R., & Tanaka, A. (2004). Adult attachment, parent emotion, and observed parenting behavior: Mediator and moderator models. *Child Development, 75*, 110–122. doi:10.1111/j.1467-8624.2004.00657.x

Ahnert, L., Pinquart, M., & Lamb, M. E. (2006). Security of children's relationships with nonparental care providers: A meta-analysis. *Child Development, 77*, 664–679. doi:10.1111/j.1467-8624.2006.00896.x

Ainsworth, M. (1979). Infant-mother attachment. *American Psychologist, 34*, 932–937. doi:10.1037/0003-066X.34.10.932

Ainsworth, M. D. S., Blehar, M., Waters, E., & Wall, S. (1978). *Patterns of attachment: Observations in the Strange Situation and at home.* Hillsdale, NJ: Erlbaum.

Alkon, A., Ramler, M., & MacLennan, K. (2003). Evaluation of mental health consultation in child care centers. *Early Childhood Education Journal, 31*(2), 91–99. doi:10.1023/B:ECEJ.0000005307.00142.3c

Ambrose, S. A., Bridges, M. W., DiPietro, M., Lovett, M. C., & Normán, M. K. (2010). *How learning works: Seven research-based principles for smart teaching.* Hoboken, NJ: Wiley.

Anderson, T., & McMullen, M. (2013). *Beliefs About Infant Toddler Education and Care (BAITEC).* Unpublished document, Purdue University, West Lafayette, IN.

Atherton, J. S. (2013). *Cognitive dissonance and learning.* Retrieved from http://www.learningandteaching.info/learning/dissonance.htm

Bartholomew, K. (1990). Avoidance of intimacy: An attachment perspective. *Journal of Social and Personal Relationships, 7*(2), 147–178. doi:10.1177/0265407590072001

Bartholomew, K., & Horowitz, L. M. (1991). Attachment styles among young adults: A test of a four-category model. *Journal of Personality and Social Psychology, 61*, 226–244. doi:10.1037/0022-3514.61.2.226

Bauer, P. J. (2009). Neurodevelopmental changes in infancy and beyond: Implications for learning and memory. In O. A. Barbarin & B. H. Wasik (Eds.), *Handbook of child development and early education: Research to practice* (pp. 78–102). New York, NY: Guilford Press.

Baumrind, D. (1973). The development of instrumental competence through socialization. In A. D. Pick (Ed.), *Minnesota symposium on child psychology* (Vol. 7, pp. 3–46). Minneapolis: University of Minnesota Press.

Bavolek, S. J., & Keene, R. G. (2001). *Adult-Adolescent Parenting Inventory AAPI-2: Administration and development handbook.* Park City, UT: Family Development Resources.

Belsky, J., & Rovine, M. J. (1988). Nonmaternal care in the first year of life and the security of infant-parent attachment. *Child Development, 59*, 157–167. doi:10.2307/1130397

Berlin, L. J. (2012). Leveraging attachment research to re-vision infant/toddler care for poor families. In S. L. Odom, E. P. Pungello, & N. Gardner-Neblett (Eds.), *Infants, toddlers, and families in poverty: Research implications for early child care* (pp. 178–201). New York, NY: Guilford Press.

Berthelsen, D., & Brownlee, J. (2005). Respecting children's agency for learning and rights to participation in child care programs. *International Journal of Early Childhood, 37*(3), 49–60. doi:10.1007/BF03168345

Berthelsen, D., & Brownlee, J. (2007). Working with toddlers in child care: Practitioners' beliefs about their role. *Early Childhood Research Quarterly, 22*(3), 347–362. doi:10.1016/j.ecresq.2006.12.002

Bowlby, J. (1969). *Attachment and loss: Vol. 1. Attachment*. New York, NY: Basic Books.

Bretherton, I. (1990). Communication patterns, internal working models, and the intergenerational transmission of attachment relationships. *Infant Mental Health Journal, 11,* 237–252. doi:10.1002/1097-0355(199023)11:3<237::AID-IMHJ2280110306>3.0.CO;2-X

Brownlee, J., & Berthelsen, D. (2006). Personal epistemology and relational pedagogy in early childhood teacher education programs. *Early Years, 26*(1), 17–29. doi:10.1080/09575140500507785

Brownlee, J., & Berthelsen, D. (2009). Beliefs about toddlers' learning in child care programs in Australia. In D. Berthelsen, J. Brownlee, & E. Johansson (Eds.), *Participatory learning in the early years: Research and pedagogy* (pp. 93–108). Abingdon, England: Routledge.

Brownlee, J., Berthelsen, D., & Boulton-Lewis, G. (2004). Working with toddlers in child care: Personal epistemologies and practice. *European Early Childhood Education Research Journal, 12*(1), 55–70. doi:10.1080/13502930485209311

Burrell, L., McFarlane, E., Tandon, D., Fuddy, L., Duggan, A., & Leaf, P. (2009). Home visitor relationship security: Association with perceptions of work, satisfaction, and turnover. *Journal of Human Behavior in the Social Environment, 19,* 592–610. doi:10.1080/10911350902929005

Cassidy, D. J., & Lawrence, J. M. (2000). Teachers' beliefs: The "whys" behind the "how tos" in child care classrooms. *Journal of Research in Childhood Education, 14,* 193–204. doi:10.1080/02568540009594763

Charlesworth, R., Hart, C. H., Burts, D. C., Thomasson, R. H., Mosley, J., & Fleege, P. O. (1993). Measuring the developmental appropriateness of kindergarten teachers' beliefs and practices. *Early Childhood Research Quarterly, 8,* 255–276. doi:10.1016/S0885-2006(05)80067-5

Clouston, T. J., & Whitcombe, S. W. (2005). An emerging person centred model for problem-based learning. *Journal of Further and Higher Education, 29,* 265–275. doi:10.1080/03098770500166926

Copple, C., & Bredekamp, S. (Eds.). (2009). *Developmentally appropriate practice in early childhood programs serving children from birth through age 8* (3rd ed.). Washington, DC: National Association for the Education of Young Children.

Crowell, J. A., & Feldman, S. S. (1991). Mothers' working models of attachment relationships and mother and child behavior during separation and reunion. *Developmental Psychology, 27,* 597–605. doi:10.1037/0012-1649.27.4.597

Dahlberg, G., Moss, P., & Pence, A. (2013). *Beyond quality in early childhood education and care: Languages of evaluation* (3rd ed.). New York, NY: Routledge.

Degotardi, S., & Davis, B. (2008). Understanding infants: Characteristics of early childhood practitioners' interpretations of infants and their behaviours. *Early Years, 28,* 221–234. doi:10.1080/09575140802393686

Degotardi, S., & Sweller, N. (2012). Mind-mindedness in infant child-care: Associations with early childhood practitioner sensitivity and stimulation. *Early Childhood Research Quarterly, 27*(2), 253–265. doi:10.1016/j.ecresq.2011.09.002

DeOliveira, C. A., Moran, G., & Pederson, D. R. (2005). Understanding the link between maternal adult attachment classifications and thoughts and feelings about emotions. *Attachment & Human Development, 7,* 153–170. doi:10.1080/14616730500135032

De Schipper, J. C., Tavecchio, L. W. C., & van Ijzendoorn, M. H. (2008). Children's attachment relationships with day care caregivers: Associations with positive caregiving and the child's temperament. *Social Development, 17,* 454–470. doi:10.1111/j.1467-9507.2007.00448.x

De Wolff, M. S., & van Ijzendoorn, M. H. (1997). Sensitivity and attachment: A meta-analysis on parental antecedents of infant attachment. *Child Development, 68,* 571–591. doi:10.1111/j.1467-8624.1997.tb04218.x

Diener, M. L., Casady, M. A., & Wright, C. (2003). Attachment security among mothers and their young children living in poverty: Associations with maternal, child, and contextual characteristics. *Merrill-Palmer Quarterly, 49,* 154–182. doi:10.1353/mpq.2003.0007

Edwards, C. P., & Raikes, H. (2002). *Extending the dance: Relationship-based approaches to infant/toddler care and education*. Washington, DC: National Association for the Education of Young Children.

Elicker, J., Fortner-Wood, C., & Noppe, I. C. (1999). The context of infant attachment in family child care. *Journal of Applied Developmental Psychology, 20,* 319–336. doi:10.1016/S0193-3973(99)00019-2

Fixsen, D. L., Naoom, S. F., Blase, K. A., Friedman, R. M., & Wallace, F. (2005). *Implementation research: A synthesis of the literature* (FMHI Publication No. 231). Tampa: University of South Florida, Louis de la Parte Florida Mental Health Institute, National Implementation Research Network.

Fonagy, P., Steele, M., Steele, H., Moran, G. S., & Higgitt, A. C. (1991). The capacity for understanding mental states: The reflective self in parent and child and its significance for security of attachment. *Infant Mental Health Journal, 12*, 201–218. doi:10.1002/1097-0355(199123)12:3<201::AID-IMHJ2280120307>3.0.CO;2-7

Fraiberg, S. (1980). *Clinical studies in infant mental health*. New York, NY: Basic Books.

George, C., & Solomon, J. (1999). Attachment and caregiving: The caregiving behavioral system. In J. Cassidy & P. R. Shaver (Eds.), *Handbook of attachment: Theory, research, and clinical applications* (pp. 649–670). New York, NY: Guilford Press.

George, C., & Solomon, J. (2008). The caregiving behavioral system: A behavioral system approach to parenting. In J. Cassidy & P. R. Shayers (Eds.), *Handbook of attachment: Theory, research and clinical applications* (2nd ed., pp. 833–856). New York, NY: Guilford Press.

Grossman, K., Fremmer-Bombik, E., Rudolph, J., & Grossman, K. E. (1988). Maternal attachment representations as related to patterns of child-mother attachment and maternal sensitivity and acceptance of her infant. In R. A. Hinde & J. Stevenson-Hinde (Eds.), *Relationships within families* (pp. 241–260). Oxford, England: Oxford Science.

Hamre, B., Hatfield, B., Pianta, R., & Jamil, F. (2014). Evidence for general and domain-specific elements of teacher–child interactions: Associations with preschool children's development. *Child Development, 85*, 1257–1274. doi:10.1111/cdev.12184

Heller, S. S., Rice, J., Boothe, A., Sidell, M., Vaughn, K., Keyes, A., & Nagle, G. (2012). Social-emotional development, school readiness, teacher-child interactions, and classroom environment. *Early Education & Development, 23*, 919–944. doi:10.1080/10409289.2011.626387

Honig, A. S. (2002). *Secure relationships: Nurturing infant/toddler attachment in early care settings*. Washington, DC: National Association for the Education of Young Children.

Honig, A. S., & Hirallal, A. (1998). Which counts more for excellence in childcare staff—years in service, education level or ECE coursework? *Early Child Development and Care, 145*, 31–46. doi:10.1080/0300443981450103

Horm, D. M., Hyson, M., & Winton, P. J. (2013). Research on early childhood teacher education: Evidence from three domains and recommendations for moving forward. *Journal of Early Childhood Teacher Education, 34*, 95–112. doi:10.1080/10901027.2013.758541

Horppu, R., & Ikonen-Varila, M. (2004). Mental models of attachment as a part of kindergarten student teachers' practical knowledge about caregiving. *International Journal of Early Years Education, 12*, 231–243. doi:10.1080/0966976042000268708

Howes, C., Matheson, C. C., & Hamilton, C. E. (1994). Maternal, teacher, and child care history correlates of children's relationships with peers. *Child Development, 65*, 264–273. doi:10.2307/1131380

Howes, C., Rodning, C., Galluzzo, D. C., & Myers, L. (1988). Attachment and child care: Relationships with mother and caregiver. *Early Childhood Research Quarterly, 3*, 403–416. doi:10.1016/0885-2006(88)90037-3

Hyson, M., Horm, D., & Winton, P. (2012). Higher education for early childhood educators and outcomes for young children: Pathways toward greater effectiveness. In R. Pianta (Ed.), *Handbook of early childhood education* (pp. 553–583). New York, NY: Guilford Press.

Kelly, K., Slade, A., & Grienenberger, J. F. (2005). Maternal reflective functioning, mother–infant affective communication, and infant attachment: Exploring the link between mental states and observed caregiving behavior in the intergenerational transmission of attachment. *Attachment & Human Development, 7*, 299–311. doi:10.1080/14616730500245963

Kilmann, P. R., Carranza, L. V., & Vendemia, J. M. C. (2006). Recollections of parent characteristics and attachment patterns for college women of intact vs. non-intact families. *Journal of Adolescence, 29*(1), 89–102. doi:10.1016/j.adolescence.2005.01.004

Kilmann, P. R., Urbaniak, G. C., & Parnell, M. M. (2006). Effects of attachment-focused versus relationship skills-focused group interventions for college students with insecure attachment patterns. *Attachment & Human Development, 8*(1), 47–62. doi:10.1080/14616730600585219

King, E., & La Paro, K. (2015). Teachers' language in interactions: An exploratory examination of mental state talk in early childhood education classrooms. *Early Education & Development, 26*, 245–263. doi:10.1080/10409289.2015.989029

Kohlhoff, J., & Barnett, B. (2013). Parenting self-efficacy: Links with maternal depression, infant behaviour and adult attachment. *Early Human Development, 89*, 249–256. doi:10.1016/j.earlhumdev.2013.01.008

Kuhl, P. K. (2011, July 29). Who's talking? *Science, 333*, 529–530. doi:10.1126/science.1210277

Landry, R., Whipple, N., Mageau, G., Joussemet, M., Koestner, R., DiDio, L., ... Haga, S. M. (2008b). Trust in organismic development, autonomy support, and adaptation among mothers and their children. *Motivation and Emotion, 32*, 173–188. doi:10.1007/s11031-008-9092-2

Landry, S. H., Smith, K. E., Swank, P. R., & Guttentag, C. (2008a). A responsive parenting intervention: The optimal timing across early childhood for impacting maternal behaviors and child outcomes. *Developmental Psychology, 44*, 1335–1353. doi:10.1037/a0013030

Leerkes, E. M., & Siepak, K. J. (2006). Attachment linked predictors of women's emotional and cognitive responses to infant distress. *Attachment & Human Development, 8*, 11–32. doi:10.1080/14616730600594450

Luster, T., & Rhoades, K. (1989). The relation between child-rearing beliefs and the home environment in a sample of adolescent mothers. *Family Relations, 38,* 317–322. doi:10.2307/585059

Lyons-Ruth, K., & Spielman, E. (2004). Disorganized infant attachment strategies and helpless-fearful profiles of parenting: Integrating attachment research with clinical intervention. *Infant Mental Health Journal, 25,* 318–335. doi:10.1002/imhj.20008

MacPhee, D. (1981). *Manual for the Knowledge of Infant Development Inventory.* (Unpublished document). Chapel Hill, NC: University of North Carolina.

Main, M., & Goldwyn, R. (1984). Predicting rejection of her infant from mother's representation of her own experience: Implications for the abused-abusing intergenerational cycle. *Child Abuse & Neglect, 8,* 203–217. doi:10.1016/0145-2134(84)90009-7

Main, M., Goldwyn, R., & Hesse, E. (2002). *Adult attachment scoring and classification systems manual (Version 7.1).* Unpublished manuscript, University of California at Berkeley.

Main, M., Kaplan, N., & Cassidy, J. (1985). Security in infancy, childhood, and adulthood: A move to the level of representation. *Monographs of the Society for Research in Child Development, 50,* 66–104. doi:10.2307/3333827

Margetts, K. (2005). Responsive caregiving: Reducing the stress in infant toddler care. *International Journal of Early Childhood, 37*(2), 77–84. doi:10.1007/BF03165748

McFarlane, E., Burrell, L., Fuddy, L., Tandon, D., Derauf, D. C., Leaf, P., & Duggan, A. (2010). Association of home visitors' and mothers' attachment style with family engagement. *Journal of Community Psychology, 38,* 541–556. doi:10.1002/jcop.20380

McMullen, M., & Dixon, S. (2006). Building on common ground: Unifying the practices of infant toddler specialists through a mindful, relationship-based approach. *Young Children, 61*(4), 46–52.

Meltzoff, A. N., Kuhl, P. K., Movellan, J., & Sejnowski, T. J. (2009, July 17). Foundations for a new science of learning. *Science, 325,* 284–288. doi:10.1126/science.1175626

Mills-Koonce, W. R., Appleyard, K., Barnett, M., Deng, M., Putallaz, M., & Cox, M. (2011). Adult attachment style and stress as risk factors for early maternal sensitivity and negativity. *Infant Mental Health Journal, 32,* 277–285. doi:10.1002/imhj.20296

Morris-Rothschild, B. K., & Brassard, M. R. (2006). Teachers' conflict management styles: The role of attachment styles and classroom management efficacy. *Journal of School Psychology, 44,* 105–121. doi:10.1016/j.jsp.2006.01.004

National Survey of Early Care and Education Project Team. (2013). *Number and characteristics of early care and education (ECE) teachers and caregivers: Initial findings from the National Survey of Early Care and Education (NSECE)* (OPRE Report No. 2013-38). Washington, DC: U.S. Department of Health and Human Services, Office of Planning, Research and Evaluation.

Neighbor, R. (1992). *The inner apprentice.* Plymouth, England: Petroc Press.

Pajares, M. F. (1992). Teachers' beliefs and educational research: Cleaning up a messy construct. *Review of Educational Research, 62,* 307–332. doi:10.3102/00346543062003307

Pearson, J. L., Cohn, D. A., Cowan, P. A., & Pape Cowan, C. (1994). Earned- and continuous-security in adult attachment: Relation to depressive symptomatology and parenting style. *Development and Psychopathology, 6,* 359–373. doi:10.1017/S0954579400004636

Perry, D. F., Allen, M. D., Brennan, E. M., & Bradley, J. R. (2010). The evidence base for mental health consultation in early childhood settings: A research synthesis addressing children's behavioral outcomes. *Early Education & Development, 21,* 795–824. doi:10.1080/10409280903475444

Pianta, R. C. (1992). Conceptual and methodological issues in research on relationships between children and nonparental adults. In R. C. Pianta (Ed.), *Beyond the parent: The role of other adults in children's lives* (pp. 121–129). San Francisco, CA: Jossey-Bass.

Pianta, R. C., DeCoster, J., Cabell, S., Burchinal, M., Hamre, B. K., Downer, J., … Howes, C. (2014). Dose-response relations between preschool teachers' exposure to components of professional development and increases in quality of their interactions with children. *Early Childhood Research Quarterly, 29,* 499–508. doi:10.1016/j.ecresq.2014.06.001

Pianta, R. C., Hitz, R., & West, B. (2010). *Increasing the application of developmental sciences knowledge in educator preparation: Policy issues and recommendations.* Washington, DC: National Council for Accreditation of Teacher Education.

Raikes, H. (1993). Relationship duration in infant care: Time with a high-ability teacher and infant-teacher attachment. *Early Childhood Research Quarterly, 8,* 309–325. doi:10.1016/S0885-2006(05)80070-5

Raikes, H. H., & Edwards, C. P. (2009). *Extending the dance in infant and toddler caregiving: Enhancing attachment and relationships.* Baltimore, MD: Brookes.

Raines, S. C., & Johnston, J. M. (2003). Developmental appropriateness: New contexts and challenges. In J. P. Packer Isenberg & M. R. Jalongo (Eds.), *Major trends and issues in early childhood education: Challenges, controversies, and insights* (pp. 85–97). New York, NY: Teachers College Press.

Rholes, W. R., Simpson, J. A., Blakely, B. S., Lanigan, L., & Allen, E. A. (1997). Adult attachment styles, the desire to have children, and working models of parenthood. *Journal of Personality, 65,* 357–385. doi:10.1111/j.1467-6494.1997.tb00958.x

Riem, M. M. E., Bakermans-Kranenburg, M. J., van Ijzendoorn, M. H., Out, D., & Rombouts, S. A. R. B. (2012). Attachment in the brain: Adult attachment representations predict amygdala and behavioral responses to infant crying. *Attachment & Human Development*, 14, 533–551. doi:10.1080/14616734.2012.727252

Riley, P. (2009). An adult attachment perspective on the student–teacher relationship and classroom management difficulties. *Teaching and Teacher Education*, 25, 626–635. doi:10.1016/j.tate.2008.11.018

Roskam, I., Meunier, J.-C., & Stievenart, M. (2011). Parent attachment, childrearing behavior, and child attachment: Mediated effects predicting preschoolers' externalizing behavior. *Journal of Applied Developmental Psychology*, 32, 170–179. doi:10.1016/j.appdev.2011.03.003

Schaefer, E. S., & Edgerton, M. (1985). Parent and child correlates of parental modernity. In E. E. Sigel (Ed.), *Parent belief systems* (pp. 287–318). Hillsdale, NJ: Erlbaum.

Siegel, D. J. (1999). *The developing mind: How relationships and the brain interact to shape who we are*. New York, NY: Guilford Press.

Slade, A. (2005). Parental reflective functioning: An introduction. *Attachment & Human Development*, 7, 269–281. doi:10.1080/14616730500245906

Slade, A. (2007). Reflective parenting programs: Theory and development. *Psychoanalytic Inquiry*, 26(4), 640–657. doi:10.1080/07351690701310698

Slade, A., Grienenberger, J., Bernbach, E., Levy, D., & Locker, A. (2005). Maternal reflective functioning, attachment and the transmission gap: A preliminary study. *Attachment & Human Development*, 7, 283–298. doi:10.1080/14616730500245880

Solomon, J., & George, C. (2011). Disorganization of maternal caregiving across two generations. In J. Solomon & C. George (Eds.), *Disorganized attachment and caregiving* (pp. 22–51). New York, NY: Guilford Press.

Squires, G. (2004). A framework for teaching. *British Journal of Educational Studies*, 52(4), 342–358. doi:10.1111/j.1467-8527.2004.00272.x

Sroufe, L. A., Egeland, B., Carlson, E. A., & Collins, W. A. (2005). *The development of the person: The Minnesota study of risk and adaptation from birth to adulthood*. New York, NY: Guilford Press.

Sroufe, L. A., & Waters, E. (1977). Attachment as an organizational construct. *Child Development*, 48, 1184–1199. doi:10.2307/1128475

Stacks, A. M., Muzik, M., Wong, K., Beeghly, M., Huth-Bocks, A., Irwin, J. L., & Rosenblum, K. L. (2014). Maternal reflective functioning among mothers with childhood maltreatment histories: Links to sensitive parenting and infant attachment security. *Attachment & Human Development*, 16, 515–533. doi:10.1080/14616734.2014.935452

Steele, H., Steele, M., & Fonagy, P. (1996). Associations among attachment classifications of mothers, fathers, and their infants. *Child Development*, 67, 541–555. doi:10.2307/1131831

Stevenson-Hinde, J., & Shouldice, A. (1995). Maternal interactions and self-reports related to attachment classifications at 4.5 years. *Child Development*, 66, 583–596. doi:10.2307/1131936

Stipek, D., & Byler, P. (1997). Early childhood education teachers: Do they practice what they preach? *Early Childhood Research Quarterly*, 12, 305–325. doi:10.1016/S0885-2006(97)90005-3

Suchman, N. E., DeCoste, C., Castiglioni, N., McMahon, T. J., Rounsaville, B., & Mayes, L. (2010). The mothers and toddlers program, an attachment-based parenting intervention for substance using women: Post-treatment results from a randomized clinical pilot. *Attachment & Human Development*, 12(5), 483–504. doi:10.1080/14616734.2010.501983

Susman-Stillman, A., Pleuss, J., & Englund, M. M. (2013). Attitudes and beliefs of family- and center-based child care providers predict differences in caregiving behavior over time. *Early Childhood Research Quarterly*, 28, 905–917. doi:10.1016/j.ecresq.2013.04.003

Trillingsgaard, T., Elklit, A., Shevlin, M., & Maimburg, R. D. (2011). Adult attachment at the transition to motherhood: Predicting worry, health care utility and relationship functioning. *Journal of Reproductive and Infant Psychology*, 29, 354–363. doi:10.1080/02646838.2011.611937

van Ijzendoorn, M. H. (1995). Adult attachment representations, parental responsiveness, and infant attachment: A meta-analysis on the predictive validity of the adult attachment interview. *Psychological Bulletin*, 117, 387–403. doi:10.1037/0033-2909.117.3.387

van Ijzendoorn, M. H., Juffer, F., & Duyvesteyn, M. G. C. (1995). Breaking the intergenerational cycle of insecure attachment: A review of the effects of attachment-based interventions on maternal sensitivity and infant security. *Journal of Child Psychology and Psychiatry*, 36, 225–248. doi:10.1111/j.1469-7610.1995.tb01822.x

Van Oudenhoven, J. P., Hofstra, J., & Bakker, W. (2003). Ontwikkeling en evaluatie van de Hechtingstijlvragenlijst (HSL) [Development and evaluation of the Attachment Styles Questionnaire]. *Nederlands Tijdschrift Voor De Psychologie*, 58, 95–102.

Virmani, E. A., Masyn, K. E., Thompson, R. A., Conners-Burrow, N. A., & Mansell, L. W. (2013). Early childhood mental health consultation: Promoting change in the quality of teacher-child interactions. *Infant Mental Health Journal*, 34, 156–172. doi:10.1002/imhj.21358

Virmani, E. A., & Ontai, L. L. (2010). Supervision and training in child care: Does reflective supervision foster caregiver insightfulness? *Infant Mental Health Journal*, 31(1), 16–32. doi:10.1002/imhj.20240

Waters, E., Weinfield, N. S., & Hamilton, C. E. (2000). The stability of attachment security from infancy to adolescence and early adulthood: General discussion. *Child Development*, 71, 703–706. doi:10.1111/cdev.2000.71.issue-3

Weston, D., Blagov, P. S., Harenski, K., Kilts, C., & Hamann, S. (2006). Neural bases of motivated reasoning: An fMRI study of emotional constraints on partisan political judgment in the 2004 U.S. presidential election. *Journal of Cognitive Neuroscience, 18*, 1947–1958. doi:10.1162/jocn.2006.18.11.1947

Whipple, N., Bernier, A., & Mageau, G. A. (2011). A dimensional approach to maternal attachment state of mind: Relations to maternal sensitivity and maternal autonomy support. *Developmental Psychology, 47*, 396–403. doi:10.1037/a0021310

Wright, B., & Sherman, B. (1963). Who is the teacher? *Theory Into Practice, 2*(2), 67–72. doi:10.1080/00405846309541840

Index

accountability 3
accreditation 50, 52, 83, 109
Ackerman, D.J. 51
Activation Control 119–20
Activities 11
administrators 48, 50–1, 53, 57, 63, 66, 70–2, 76
Adult Interaction Scale 83–4
Adult Needs 11
Adult Temperament Questionnaire 119–20
Adult-Adolescent Parenting Inventory 139–40
adult-child ratios 6–7, 52, 83–6, 88, 90, 133
age factors 39, 41, 77–8, 80, 82; and master teacher roles 96, 98–9, 112; and student attachment attitudes 133, 135, 141, 147, 152; and teacher characteristics 120; and toddler social competence 84–6, 88–90
agency 106, 108, 112
aggression 80, 89, 134
Aguillard, A.E. 50, 68
American Academy of Pediatrics 13
analytic strategy 31–3
anchors 12
ANCOVAs 33, 38
anger 28, 31, 38, 40
anxiety 27, 33–5, 40, 60, 133, 147–50
Arnett, J. 7
assessors 12, 20
associate's degrees 3, 82, 85
attachment 3, 9, 18, 27, 39, 49, 60, 65, 68, 78–81, 89–90, 131–58
Attachment Styles Questionnaire 138
attachment theory 49–51, 78, 88–9, 132–3, 149
attention spans 104
Attentional Control 119–20
attitudes 131–58
autonomy 20, 98, 103, 110, 120, 132, 138–40, 149
avoidance 132, 147–50
axial coding 32

bachelor's degrees 2–3, 52, 84, 99, 117, 119, 121, 125–6
Bartholomew, K. 148
Bartlett's test 15
Basic Care 11
Baumrind, D. 149
Beliefs About Infant Toddler Education and Care (BAITEC) 138–9

Berlin, L.J. 132
Berthelsen, D. 98, 112
best practice 28, 47–8, 79, 111, 134
bioecological theory 1–3, 48, 116
boredom 102
bottom-up approaches 97, 112
Brassard, M.R. 149
Brief Infant-Toddler Social Emotional Assessment 84
Bronfenbrenner, U. 48, 57, 116
Brophy-Herb, H. 131–58
Brownlee, J. 112, 131
Byler, P. 117

career goals 135, 137, 140–9
Caregiver Interaction Scale (CIS) 7–8, 11–12, 14, 17, 20
caregiver-child interactions 1–2, 20, 77–95, 149
Carranza, L.V. 151
Cassidy, D.J. 51, 68, 89
Castle, S. 2–3, 115–30
Caughy, M.O. 52
Center for Epidemiological Studies 31, 119
Center for Law and Social Policy 47
Chazan-Cohen, R. 131–58
child care centers 1–3, 7–8, 11, 27–8, 30; and continuity of care 53; and master teacher roles 96, 98, 111; and maternal perspectives 36, 38, 42; and student attachment attitudes 137, 141; and toddler social competence 77–81, 88–90
child characteristics 28–9, 31, 33, 38–41, 81, 84–7, 89, 110
child development 6, 9, 20, 41, 54; and cognitive development 8, 10, 13, 15–16, 18, 21, 80, 115, 126; and continuity of care 59, 67–9; knowledge of 138; and master teacher roles 97, 105, 111; and perceptual and motor development 8; and social and emotional development 8; and student attachment attitudes 132, 134–5, 137, 139–42, 144–5, 147–8, 150, 152–3; and teacher characteristics 115–17, 120–1, 126; and toddler social competence 78–9, 88, 90–1
child-centered approach 99, 102, 108, 117, 150
child-directed learning 139
childbirth 42
Childcare Aware of America 47
Choi, J. 2, 50, 77–95

INDEX

Classroom Assessment Scoring System (CLASS) 2, 8, 20–1, 120–1, 124, 127, 152
Classroom Assessment Scoring System (CLASS) Infant 8
Classroom Assessment Scoring System (CLASS) PreK 8
Classroom Assessment Scoring System (CLASS) Toddler 2, 8, 120–1, 124
classroom culture 97, 99, 101–4, 106, 109–11
classroom interactions 2, 116–18, 125
co-lead structure 53, 58, 60–4, 69–70
cognitive dissonance 152
Cohen, J. 14
communities of families 28
concurrent validity 14–15, 17–18, 20
confirmatory factor analysis models 122
conflict management 9, 40, 61, 97, 103, 106, 149
conflict resolution 97
consistency 10, 12, 14, 60–1, 70, 78, 84, 88, 105, 115–20
construct validity 13, 17, 31
continuity of care (CoC) 2, 9, 17, 19, 99; benefits of 50, 67–8; and caregiver-child interactions 77–95; challenges of 50–1, 67–9; definitions 49; and positive caregiving 80–1; scale 94–5; and social competence 77–95; and stability 79–80; and toddler social competence 46–76
Cook, G. 131–58
Coping with Toddlers' Negative Emotions Scale 31
cortisol 28
Cost, Quality and Outcomes Study 84, 96
Council for Exceptional Children's Division for Early Childhood 134
coursework 98, 134, 141, 148–51
Cryer, D. 68, 80
cues 8–9, 80, 89, 132–3, 152–3
curriculum 2, 28, 83, 98, 101–2, 104–5, 107–11, 117

Dalli, C. 41
data collection 2, 7, 10, 12, 19–20; and continuity of care 48, 52, 58–9; databases 83; descriptive data 13–14; and master teacher roles 99–100, 109; and maternal perspectives 29; and student attachment attitudes 140; and teacher characteristics 119, 124, 127
De Schipper, J.C. 68
degree options 2, 117–18, 122–7
depressive symptoms 2, 28–9, 31, 33, 37–8, 40–2, 116–19, 121–7
Detachment 7, 11, 14, 17
Dewey, J. 105
difficulty of transition 31–41
directors 41–2, 53, 66, 82–3, 109, 137, 141
disabilities 9, 11, 16, 18, 82, 137, 141
discipline 84, 117, 133, 138–40, 142, 149
discontinuous care 50–1, 55, 59–60, 65, 68, 70
dismissiveness 136, 138, 141, 143–4, 149–50
dispositional resistance 51
distal processes 48
distress 28–9, 31–3, 37–8, 40–2, 50, 78, 80, 133, 149
divergent validity 14–15, 18
diversity 10, 18, 20, 27, 42, 98, 108–9, 111–12, 151

Dix, T. 28–9
Dixon, S. 111
documentation 12, 18, 20, 28, 57
Duncan, J. 98, 110–11
Dunlop, A. 70

early care and education (ECE) 2, 26–45, 116, 118, 120–1, 123, 125–7, 131, 134, 153
Early Child Care Research Network (ECCRN) 80, 88, 115, 117–18
early childhood (EC) 131–5, 141–2, 144–5, 147–53
Early Childhood Environment Rating Scales-Revised (ECERS-R) 11
Early Head Start (EHS) 1–3, 47, 79, 115–30
ease of transition 31–41
educational attainment 10, 83–5
Edwards, C.P. 41, 67, 110–11
effortful control 116–17, 120–2, 126
Elicker, J. 2, 50, 72, 77–95
Elliot, E. 111
emic/etic perspectives 101
Emilson, A. 97
Emotional and Behavioral Support (EBS) 120, 122–6
emotional functioning 28–30, 33, 38, 40–1, 84, 89, 104, 106, 108–9, 112, 115–18, 120, 122–3, 125–6, 132, 142, 150, 152–3
empathy 61, 133
empowerment 62–3, 67–8, 109
Encinger, A.J. 2, 26–45
Engaged Support for Learning (ESL) 120, 122–6
English language 11
Environment Rating Scale (ERS) 11–12, 14–15, 17–18, 20
Essa, E.L. 49–51
ethics 81, 91
ethnicities 10, 135
exosystems 48
experience 1–3, 5–7, 26–36, 38–42, 78; and continuity of care 46–76; lived experiences 97, 101–2, 109–10, 112; and master teacher roles 96, 98–9, 103–8; and student attachment attitudes 131, 134, 147, 149–52; and teacher characteristics 115–19, 121–7; and toddler social competence 80–3, 88–9
experts 13, 17, 63, 112, 115, 140, 153

factor analysis 1, 15–18, 20, 122, 138
Family Child Care Environment Rating Scale-Revised 7
family child care programs 3, 6–8, 10–12, 19, 49, 51–2, 79
Family and Child Experiences Study (Baby FACES) 118, 124–6
Family Day Care Rating Scale (FDCRS) 11
Family Partnerships, Cultural Responsiveness and Inclusive Care 6, 9, 11, 14–15, 18, 20
family-centeredness 39, 47–9, 51–2, 59, 62, 67–8, 70–1
fathers 41, 89, 117
fearfulness 28, 31, 37–41, 47, 132–3, 136, 138, 141–50
feedback 120, 122, 124
field of degree *see* degree options
findings 59–66

INDEX

force characteristics 116
frustration 35, 103, 116, 118–21, 123–4, 126
Fusaro, M. 131–58
future research 3, 18–21, 40–1, 51, 69–72; and master teacher roles 112; and student attachment attitudes 132, 134–5, 148–53; and teacher characteristics 116–18, 125–7; and toddler social competence 78–9, 81, 89–91

gearing up 64, 68–70
gender 81, 84, 86, 99, 120, 126, 133, 135
global quality 6–8, 11, 14, 17–18, 20–1
Goldsmith, H.H. 31
Goouch, K. 97
grounded theory 52
group size 6–7, 9, 13, 16–17, 19, 52, 66, 76, 83, 133
guidelines 12, 14, 28, 134
guilt 35, 39–40

Hall, E.L. 96
Hallam, R. 112
Halle, T. 3
Hamilton, C.E. 68, 80
Hamre, B.K. 117–18
Harshness 7, 11, 14, 17
Head Start 27, 47, 79, 115–30
hedonism 150
Hegde, A.V. 51, 68, 89
Henk, J. 131–58
hierarchical linear modeling (HLM) 86
High/Scope 47
history 60, 89, 101, 105–7, 109, 127, 150, 153
Horm, D.M. 1–4, 134
Horppu, R. 133, 147
Howes, C. 68, 80
Human Subjects Committee 57
hypervigilance 150
Hyson, M. 96, 98, 134

identity 9
Ikonen-Varila, M. 133, 147
inclusive settings 6, 9, 11, 13–15, 18–20
income 1, 10, 36–7, 41, 71, 84–7, 98, 120, 126, 135
increased knowledge 59, 67–8
individualization 41, 46, 49–50, 59, 68, 90
Infant Characteristics Questionnaire 84
Infant-Toddler Social Emotional Assessment 84
Infant/Toddler Environment Rating Scale 2
Infant/Toddler Environment Rating Scale-Revised (ITERS-R) 7, 11, 14, 20
Inhibitory Control 119–20
inserimento 27
interactive involvement 11, 30, 78–81, 84–91, 107–8
interdisciplinarity 3
internalization 80, 147–8
Interpersonal Reactivity Index 31
interrater reliability checks 12, 83, 138
interviews 12, 30, 57–8, 64, 75–6, 82, 99–101
intraclass correlation coefficients (ICCs) 86
intrapersonal characteristics 116, 118, 126
Ispa, J. 131–58

Israel 133
Italy 27–9, 41

Johansson, E. 97

Kaiser-Meyer-Olkin measure 15
key person caregiving 49
Kilmann, P.R. 151
Kim, H. 2, 46–76
kindergartens 19, 27, 46, 63
King, E. 152
kith and kin settings 8
Klausli, J.F. 52
Knoche, L.L. 110
Knowledge of Infant Development Inventory (KIDI) 138, 140, 142, 145
Kriener-Althen, K. 1, 5–25

La Paro, K. 152
Lally, J.R. 67
language 8, 11, 15, 18, 20, 116, 120, 122, 124, 126
Lash, M. 111
Laurin, D. 115–30
Lavelle, B. 3
leadership 58, 66, 109
learner characteristics 134
Learning Activities 11
Leavitt, R. 97–8, 100–5, 107–12
liberation 100–2, 108–9
licensing 48, 52, 83, 90
limit testing 109–10
limitations 41, 70–1, 90–1, 109, 127, 150–1
lived experiences 97, 101–2, 109–10, 112
looping model 49, 51, 53, 67, 69, 72, 77–8
low-income families 10, 41

McElwain, N.L. 2, 26–45
McMullen, M.B. 2, 46–76, 111
macrosystems 1, 48
majors 2, 132, 134–5, 137, 141
Mangione, P.L. 1–3, 5–25, 67
Marcella, J. 1, 5–25
Marvin, C.A. 110
master teachers 2, 96–114
master's degrees 52
Mata-Otero, A. 52
maternal perspectives 26–45
measures 5–25, 83, 119, 135–6, 138
mediation 80–1, 87–9, 102–4, 107–8, 110–11, 135, 141, 144–51
member checking 58
mentoring 110
mesosystems 2, 48
mess making 103–4, 107–8, 111
methods 10–12, 30–3, 52–8, 81–5, 98–101, 119–21, 135–40
microsystems 1, 48, 53, 57
Mihai, A. 2, 46–76
milestones 50, 77–8, 90, 116, 138
Ministry of Education, New Zealand 28
mixed age groupings *see* multiage groupings

161

INDEX

mixed methods 2–3, 26–45
Morris-Rothschild, B.K. 149
mothers 1, 26–45, 89, 132
multiage groupings 49, 53, 72, 77–8, 90, 119
multifaceted nature of care quality 5–25

National Association for the Education of Young Children (NAYEC) 27, 47, 52, 79
National Center for Research on Early Childhood Education (NCRECE) 152
National Child Care Staffing Study 84
National Head Start Association 47
National Household Education Survey 26
National Institute of Child Health and Human Development (NIHCD) 8, 80, 88, 115, 117–18
National Survey of Early Care and Education Project Team 125
neuroscience 46
New Zealand 28–9
noncontinuous care 77, 81–3, 85–91
nonparental care 26, 29, 33–6, 39, 78, 80, 89, 133
nonrelative homecare settings 1, 3
Norris, D.J. 1–4, 51
nutrition 10
NVivo 32

obedience 140
objectification 98, 100, 105, 107–9
Observational Record of the Caregiving Environment (ORCE) 8, 13, 20, 118
observations/observational skills 2, 6–7, 11–12, 48, 57; and continuity of care 59; and master teacher roles 98–101, 105, 109–10; and student attachment attitudes 151–3; and teacher characteristics 119–20, 122–3, 125; and toddler social competence 82–6, 91
optimism 136, 139, 145–8
Organization of Group Care 6, 9, 11, 14–15, 18
Ounce of Prevention Fund 47
outcomes 1, 3, 6–8, 17–18, 20–1; and and continuity of care 49–50, 52, 70; and master teacher roles 96, 111; and maternal perspectives 26; and student attachment attitudes 151, 153; and teacher characteristics 115, 117; and toddler social competence 78–9, 84, 86–7, 90–1
Owen, M.T. 52

Parent Modernity Scale 120, 138–9
Parent-Staff subscale 2
Parental Opinion Survey (POS) 139–40
parents 7, 9–12, 19, 26, 28–9; and and master teacher roles 97–8, 108–11; and continuity of care 46–76; parent questionnaires 31, 33; and student attachment attitudes 132–3, 138–9, 142, 144–5, 148–9, 152–3; and teacher characteristics 117, 120; and toddler social competence 84–6, 89, 91; and transition experiences 38, 40–2
participants 30, 53, 57, 81–2, 91, 98, 106, 109–10, 118–19, 135, 140, 142
participation 97–8, 102–3, 107–9, 111–12, 116
partnerships 2, 6, 9, 11, 13–15; and continuity of care 49, 59, 62–4, 67–71; and master teacher roles 105; and maternal perspectives 27–8, 34; and quality of care 18, 20
Pearce, N. 115–30
pedagogy 131–2, 151, 153
peers 8–9, 20, 39–40, 50, 58, 61, 65, 75, 80, 89–90, 112, 140
Permissiveness 7, 11
Personal Care Routines 11, 14–15, 18
Peterson, C.A. 131–58
phenomenology 52
photographs 28, 42, 111
Physical Environment 6, 9, 11, 14, 17–21
physiology 9
Pianta, R.C. 117–18
piloting 13, 17, 99–101, 110
planning 53, 57, 65, 85, 98–105, 108–10, 121
platykurtic kurtosis 14
pleasure 28, 31, 37–8, 40
Positive Affect 119–20
positive caregiving 80–1, 91
positivity 116–18, 121–2, 124, 126, 144, 148
postpartum depression 42
poverty 115, 126
Powell, S. 97
power sharing 97–104, 106–7, 109–11
predictive validity 18
preschools 5, 8, 46–9, 51–9, 63; and continuity of care 67–9, 75–6; and master teacher roles 99, 108; and student attachment attitudes 137, 141, 152; and teacher characteristics 115, 117–18; and toddler social competence 78–80; transition to 64–5, 70–1
primary caregiving 9, 13, 16–18, 27, 47–52; and continuity of care 57, 59, 61–2, 67, 69–71, 75; and teacher characteristics 117; and toddler social competence 78–80, 83, 91
problem behaviors 29, 50, 77–95, 120, 150
problem solving 116
procedure 12, 30, 57, 82–3, 99, 119, 135
process quality 6–8, 14, 18, 20–1
professional development 2–3, 7, 20–1, 41–2, 96; and master teacher roles 107, 110–12; professional experiences 46–76; professional organizations 47, 58, 79; professional preparation 131–58
Program for Infant Toddler Care (PITC) 1–2, 5–6, 8–15, 17–21, 47, 79
Program for Infant and Toddler Care Program Assessment Rating Scale (PITC PARS) 1–2, 5–6, 8–15, 17–21
Program Structure 11, 15, 18
Provisions for Exceptional Children 11
proximal processes 2, 48, 53, 116
psychology 41, 46, 121, 137
psychometrics 5, 7, 10, 17, 19–21, 29, 135–7
psychosocial factors 2, 116–18, 121–3, 126, 134, 152
public assistance programs 41
pull-and-dump approach 102–3

qualifications 20, 97, 127
qualitative methods 2, 29
Quality of Adult's Interactions With Children 6, 8, 11, 14–15, 17–18

INDEX

quality of care 1–2, 26, 38, 50–2, 57; and continuity of care 71; definitions 6–7; and master teacher roles 96–8, 110–12; measurement of 7–8; multifaceted nature of 5–25; and student attachment attitudes 132, 152; and teacher characteristics 115–18, 124–7; and toddler social competence 81, 83–4, 88–91
Quality Rating Improvement Systems (QRIS) 1–2, 7, 21, 48, 52, 82, 85–6
Qualtrics 135
quantitative methods 29–30, 33, 36–40

Race to the Top Early Learning Challenge 7
Raikes, H. 50, 67–8, 111
rapport 39
rating criteria/guidance 12, 17–18, 21, 52
Recchia, A.L. 51, 70
reciprocity 49, 105, 108, 116
recommendations 41–2, 51, 58–9, 66, 71–2, 79, 81, 111, 127, 132
reflective functioning (RF) 152–3
reflective practice 21, 42, 99–101, 103, 106, 109–11, 151
regression 59, 68–9
regulation 48, 52, 81, 112, 117
relationship-based practice 6, 52, 69, 77, 90–1, 111
reliability 12, 83
resistance 51, 104
resource characteristics 116
results 12–17, 85–8, 121–4, 140–7
reunions 29
revolving door model 60
Rholes, W.R. 149
Riley, P. 147
Rinaldi, C. 41
risk factors 116
Ritchie, S. 80
Roggman, L.A. 131–58
routines 6–7, 9–11, 13–20, 28, 42, 65, 84, 97–101, 104–9, 111, 120
Routines and Record Keeping 6, 10–11, 14–15, 17–19
Rudkin, J.K. 96
Ruprecht, K.M. 2–3, 50, 77–95

safety 10, 17, 19–20, 83
samples 10–11, 20, 38, 41, 50; and continuity of care 57, 71; and student attachment attitudes 137, 140–2, 144–5, 151; and teacher characteristics 118, 120, 122, 125–7; and toddler social competence 81–5, 90
Sandelowski, M. 52
scaffolding 102, 111, 116, 120
schedule flexibility 36, 42
security 8–9, 26, 28, 49–51, 57–8; and continuity of care 60–1, 68; and master teacher roles 108; and student attachment attitudes 132–6, 138, 141–4, 147–53; and teacher characteristics 116; and toddler social competence 78–81, 90
selective coding 32
sensitivity 7–9, 11, 13–16, 18, 29; and master teacher roles 97; and student attachment attitudes 132–3, 135, 140, 150, 152–3; and teacher characteristics 117, 120–3, 125; and toddler social competence 78

separation anxiety 27, 29, 33–4, 40–1
serve-and-return approach 97
settings 52
Sheridan, S.M. 110
sleep 10
Sobel tests 87, 144
social competence 2, 29, 77–95, 97, 112, 132, 134–5, 138–9, 144, 149, 151
Social Development 11
social relations 41, 48–51, 57, 59–71
socioeconomic status 7, 38, 48, 98, 109
sociology 46
space control 100–1, 108–9
Space and Furnishings 11, 14–15, 18
Spanish language 11
spanking 140, 149
special needs 9, 16, 18, 142, 148
Speirs, K.E. 2, 26–45
sphericity 15
spoiling 117, 139–40
Squires, G. 131
stability 9, 20, 26, 51, 59–60; and continuity of care 65, 67–8, 70–1; and student attachment attitudes 133, 151; and toddler social competence 78–80, 83, 88–9, 91
Stacks, A.M. 131–58
staffing patterns 70
standards 2, 10, 12–13, 19, 27, 47, 50, 52, 83, 134
Stephen, C. 70
Stipek, D.J. 117
strangers 27, 31
strengths-based perspective 11, 17
stress 9, 39, 60, 65, 67, 103, 133, 150
strictness 137, 139–40, 143–7, 150
structural quality 6–9, 14–15, 18–19, 21
Stubblefield, J. 115–30
students 131–58
subitems 11–12, 15, 18–19
subscales 2, 6, 8–20, 31, 84, 119, 122, 138, 140, 142
subsidies 10, 41–2
Support for Language Development and Interaction 14–15, 18
Support for the Parent-Child Relationship 138–9
support services 42
Susman-Stillman, A. 117
Swartz, R.A. 2–3, 26–45

tantrums 148, 150
teachers 6, 10–11, 17–21, 28, 34; beliefs 117–27, 131, 139–40; characteristics 115–30, 132; depressive symptoms of 119; master teachers 96–114; and maternal perspectives 41; and preparation programs 3; and student attachment attitudes 133, 137; teacher-child interactions 2, 7, 9, 115–30, 151–3; teacher-child ratios 9, 19, 39; teacher-directed learning 139; and toddler social competence 48, 51–3, 57–8, 61, 63–5, 68, 70–1, 76, 78–80, 83–4, 90–1
Teaching Beliefs Scale 139
temperament characteristics 28–9, 31, 33, 38–41, 81, 83–7, 89–90, 116–26

INDEX

tenure 125
theoretical foundations 1–3, 48–52, 78, 88–9, 116, 132–3, 149
time control 100–1, 108–9
Toddler Behavior Assessment Questionnaire 31
toddlers 1–17, 19–21, 26–31, 34, 38–42; and continuity of care 46–59, 61, 63–72, 75–6; and master teacher roles 96–112; and social competence 77–95; and student attachment attitudes 131–53; and teacher characteristics 115–21, 124–7
Tomlinson, H.B. 96, 98
Torquati, J. 131–58
Tout, K. 3
training 12, 20–1, 41, 79, 83–5, 117–18, 120, 127, 132, 134, 152
transcription 30, 32, 57–8, 100
transition experiences 26–45, 133
Trevarthen, C. 70
triangulation 58, 100
trust 9, 49–50, 58, 60–2, 65, 67, 106, 109–10, 116, 133, 151
Trust in Organismic Development Scale 139
turnover 47, 71, 98

Uhlenberg, J. 2, 96–114

United States (US) 1, 26–8, 42, 50–2, 57, 71, 96, 98, 126, 134–5, 151
university-affiliated programs 51–2, 63, 71, 98, 109, 151
user's guide 21

Vallotton, C.D. 2–3, 131–58
values 9, 48, 60, 67–8, 71, 98, 108–10, 112, 117, 131–2, 139–40, 149
Van Ijzendoorn, M.H. 152
Vendemia, J.M.C. 151

webcams 36
well-established continuity of care 46–76
Wen, X. 118
Whitaker, R.C. 3, 117
Williamson, A.C. 115–30
Winton, P.J. 134
withdrawal 80, 117, 133–4

Young, E. 115–30
Yun, N.R. 46–76

Zaslow, M. 3
Zero to Three 47, 79, 134